D1595693

WALTER FRYE
and the
CONTENANCE ANGLOISE

Da Capo Press Music Reprint Series

MUSIC EDITOR

BEA FRIEDLAND
Ph.D., City University of New York

WALTER FRYE

and the

CONTENANCE ANGLOISE

SYLVIA W. KENNEY

DA CAPO PRESS · NEW YORK · 1980

Library of Congress Cataloging in Publication Data

Kenney, Sylvia W
  Walter Frye and the contenance angloise.

  (Da Capo Press music reprint series)
  Reprint of the 1964 ed. published by Yale
University Press, New Haven, which was issued as
v. 3 of Yale studies in the history of music.
  Bibliography: p.
  Includes index.
  1. Frye, Walter, 15th cent. 2. Composers—
Biography. 3. Music—History and criticism—
Medieval, 400-1500. 4. Music, English—History
and criticism. I. Title. II. Series: Yale
studies in the history of music; v. 3.
  [ML410.F9654K5 1980] 784'.0942 79-24423
  ISBN 0-306-76011-8

Published by Da Capo Press, Inc.
A Subsidiary of Plenum Publishing Corporation
227 West 17th Street, New York, N.Y. 10011

YALE STUDIES IN THE HISTORY OF MUSIC, 3

William G. Waite, Editor

Madonna and Child with Six Angel Musicians.
Master of the Embroidered Foliage. Paris, Féral Collection.

WALTER FRYE and the

CONTENANCE ANGLOISE

SYLVIA W. KENNEY

New Haven and London, Yale University Press, 1964

Published with assistance from the Louis Stern Memorial Fund

In memory of

Lewis H. Kenney

Acknowledgments

THIS BOOK is an expansion of my doctoral dissertation under the supervision of Leo Schrade, to whom I owe especial thanks. To the many people who have assisted in the preparation of the book, I am most grateful. My parents have been a constant source of help and encouragement in matters of research as well as of stylistic questions and proofreading. The Very Reverend C. P. Hankey, Dean of Ely Cathedral, and his family were most kind, not only in helping me with questions about the history of the cathedral when I worked at Ely in 1959, but also subsequently in promptly supplying photographs. I am particularly indebted to the editors of the Yale University Press: Edward T. McClellan, Arts Editor, for his judgment in matters of style and artistic questions, and Elizabeth Swift, for her wise and meticulous copy-editing. Mrs. George Koglman, who typed the manuscript, is one of those rare helpers whose sense of when to correct and when not to is almost infallible. Anne L. Kish gave generously of her time for proofreading.

I owe debts of gratitude also to Bryn Mawr College for two grants given for research expenses and to The American Philosophical Society for a grant which enabled me to study in England during the summer of 1959. Permission has kindly been given by the editors to use material which had appeared in articles in *Revue belge de musicologie, Journal of the American Musicological Society, The Musical Quarterly,* and *Music and History.* Thanks are due to A. W. Kerr for permission to use the jacket photograph of the Ely Cathedral Octagon.

Sylvia W. Kenney

Bryn Mawr
July 1964

Contents

List of Illustrations

List of Abbreviations

A. *Manuscripts*

Ash 191	Oxford, Bodleian Library, Ms. Ashmole 191
Ber	Berlin, Kupferstichkabinett, Ms. 78 C 28 (Hamilton 451)
BR 5557	Brussels, Bibliothèque Royale, Ms. 5557
Bux	Munich, Bayerische Staatsbibliothek, codex Cim 352^b (Mus. 3725; Buxheimer Orgelbuch)
Cord	Paris, Bibliothèque Nationale, chansonnier de Jean de Montchenu (H. Rothschild Coll.)
Esc	Escorial, Biblioteca del Escorial, Ms. IV a 24
F112 bis	Florence, Biblioteca Nazionale Centrale, Ms. Magliab. XIX, 112 bis
F176	Florence, Biblioteca Nazionale Centrale, Ms. Magliab. XIX, 176
FRic 1	Florence, Biblioteca Riccardiana, Ms. 2794
FRic 2	Florence, Biblioteca Riccardiana, Ms. 2356
Glog	Berlin, Staatsbibliothek, Mus. Ms. 40098 (Z. 98; Glogauer Liederbuch)
Lab	Washington, Library of Congress, M.2.1.L 25 Case (Laborde chansonnier)
M.C. 871	Monte Cassino, Archive e Biblioteca Abbaziale di Monte Cassino, Ms. 871
Mellon	New Haven, Yale University (Mellon chansonnier)
Niv	Paris, Bibliothèque G. Thibault (chansonnier Nivelle de la Chaussée)
P 4379	Paris, Bibliothèque Nationale, n.a., f. fr. 4379 The part of this manuscript which contains Frye's *Tout a par moy* has been shown by Plamenac to be a fragment of the Seville chansonnier, Colombina

	Ms. 5-I-43. (*Musical Quarterly*, 37 [1951], 501.) Therefore this Paris fragment has been referred to in the text of the article as "Seville."
Pe 431	Perugia, Biblioteca Communale di Perugia, Ms. 431 (g 20)
Pepys 1236	Cambridge, Magdalene College, Ms. Pepys 1236
Pix	Paris, Bibliothèque Nationale, f. fr. 15123 (Pixérécourt chansonnier)
Prag	Prague, Strahov D.G. IV. 47
Sched	Munich, Bayerische Staatsbibliothek, codex 810 (Cim 351ª; Mus. 3232; Schedel Liederbuch)
Sev	Seville, Biblioteca Colombina, Ms. 5-I-43
Spec	Hadrec Králové (Czechoslovakia) Museum, codex Speciálník
TR 90	Trent, Castello del Buon Consiglio, codex 90
Wolf	Wolfenbüttel, Herzog August Bibliothek, Ms. Extravag. 287
Ver 757	Verona, Biblioteca Capitolare, Ms. 757

B. *Periodicals*

AM	*Acta Musicologica*
AMF	*Archiv für Musikforschung*
AMW	*Archiv für Musikwissenschaft*
BAMS	*Bulletin of the Americian Musicological Society*
JAMS	*Journal of the American Musicological Society*
JRBM	*Journal of Renaissance and Baroque Music*
KJ	*Kirchenmusikalisches Jahrbuch*
MD	*Musica Disciplina*
MfM	*Monatshefte für Musikgeschichte*
ML	*Music and Letters*
MQ	*Musical Quarterly*
RB	*Revue belge de musicologie*
SIMG	*Sammelbände der Internationalen Musikgesellschaft*

VMW	*Vierteljahrschrift für Musikwissenschaft*
ZMW	*Zeitschrift für Musikwissenschaft*

C. Books

AR	*Antiphonale Sacrosanctae Romanae Ecclesiae*
CS	Coussemaker, Charles Edmond Henri de, *Scriptorum de Musica medii aevi*
DTO	*Denkmäler der Tonkunst in Österreich*
GR	*Graduale Sacrosanctae Romanae Ecclesiae*
GS	Gerbert, Martin, *Scriptores ecclesiastici de musica sacra potissimum*
LU	*Liber usualis*
MGG	*Die Musik in Geschichte und Gegenwart*
PM	*Processionale Monasticum*

Introduction

THE FIFTEENTH CENTURY was an age of contradictions and contrasts. There were extreme contrasts—between piety and depravity, wealth and poverty, decadence and the spirit of discovery—and men wrote at length about both the "excellence of this age" and the "evils of the times." The specific conflicts and contradictions were at once manifestations and contributing causes of a larger phenomenon occurring during the century—the transition from a God-centered to a world-centered universe. In the fifteenth century, the mystical faith of the late Middle Ages and the humanism of the early Renaissance met on a footing that was singularly precarious and constantly shifting.

One curious contradiction of early Renaissance life is seen in the musical repertory of the fifteenth century. In an age which was becoming increasingly secular, there was suddenly a great flowering of sacred polyphony. Religious faith plainly survived the advent of humanism and was transformed by it, but the vigor of Renaissance sacred music attests something more than mere survival against odds. It was a medium in which composers showed a high degree of inventiveness and original creativity. Heinrich Besseler has proposed one explanation for the sudden rise to prominence of liturgical music after 1450 by associating it with the movement of the *Devotio Moderna* at Deventer, the spirit of Thomas a Kempis and the *Imitation of Christ,* and the lay pietism which, particularly in the Netherlands, arose as a reaction to the decadence of the secular courts and the church.[1] The difficulty with Besseler's suggestion has always been the absence of direct association between composers and the pietistic movement. The great composers of the fifteenth century—Dufay, Ockeghem, Dunstable,

1. Heinrich Besseler, *Die Musik des Mittelalters und der Renaissance* (Potsdam, 1931), p. 237.

and Busnois—wrote their Masses for the splendid courts of the kings of France and the dukes of Savoy, Burgundy, and Bedford, and not for the *Devotio Moderna*. Of all the gifted composers at that time, Obrecht was perhaps the only one who might conceivably have had much association with the circles around Deventer. But any such contact would hardly have proved fruitful for the development of sacred music, for the devout pietists were generally hostile to elaborate art, and thoroughly disapproved of counterpoint. Huizinga has pointed to the sharp division between the spheres of intellectual and moral life in the fifteenth century:

> On the one hand, the civilization of the court, the nobility and the rich middle classes: ambitious, proud and grasping, passionate and luxurious. On the other hand, the tranquil sphere of the "devotio moderna," of the *Imitation of Christ*, of Ruysbroeck, and of Saint Colette. One would like to place the peaceful and mystic art of the brothers Van Eyck in the second of these spheres, but it belongs rather to the other. Devout circles were hardly in touch with the great art that flourished at this time . . . They would probably have regarded the altarpiece of the Lamb as a mere work of pride, and actually did so regard the tower of Utrecht Cathedral.[2]

Thus, while the phenomenon of a flourishing religious faith in certain circles during the early Renaissance suggests a strong motive for the creation of sacred music and art, the link between cause and effect is missing.

While the mere appearance of sacred music in such abundance in the Age of Humanism is something of a contradiction, various technical aspects of Mass composition at that time also reflect the Renaissance synthesis of what seem irreconcilable opposites. The merger of sacred and secular elements in fifteenth-century Mass Ordinaries has a peculiarly Renaissance stamp, one which is altogether different from the Medieval synthesis. Incorporation of secular songs into Renaissance sacred music somehow seems far more blasphemous than the

2. J. Huizinga, *The Waning of the Middle Ages* (Garden City, N.Y., 1954), p. 260.

use of a sacred plainsong tenor in a secular motet of the thirteenth century. The difference between the religious spirits of the Middle Ages and the Renaissance is seldom better illustrated than by the complete reversal of sacred and secular functions between the thirteenth-century motet and the fifteenth-century Mass. The man of the thirteenth century, who was on fairly intimate terms with God, saw nothing sacrilegious about placing a fragment of chant at the base of a composition of which the texts were devoted to thoroughly earthy sentiments. His fifteenth-century descendants did not enjoy quite so comfortable and casual a relationship with God. Masses were commissioned in far greater numbers in the fifteenth century, Masses composed with the greatest musical sophistication. But there was so little interest in liturgical emphasis that it was always the Ordinary that was set, rather than the Proper, and it did not matter if the five movements of the Ordinary were unified by means of a fragment of chant that belonged elsewhere in the liturgy, or even by a secular tune.

The interest of musicians in Mass composition is understandable apart from the question of religious faith, for there was an artistic challenge involved. The creation of the first large multimovement form unified by a recurrent melody in all movements is a product of the mid-fifteenth century, and it is evidence of a keen and active musical imagination. Nevertheless one wonders what could have been the incentive to devote this lively imagination to sacred music, particularly in view of the remarkable durability of plainsong. There existed the chant repertory, which was not merely adequate to religious expression but exquisitely appropriate and responsive to all the subtle refinements of the Catholic ritual. The chant was copied century after century, and was performed in churches, as it is today. There must therefore have been a religious spirit which was strongly enough felt and powerful enough to be effective in demanding a new and contemporary style of musical expression, a style that conveyed the peculiarly humanistic character of religious faith.

"Style," as Carl Friedrich has said, "is a mysterious quality, true only if spontaneous, and spontaneous only if a projection of genuine feeling and true experience. Style convinces by its unique individuality. It cannot be 'proven.' " [3] The style of sacred music which appeared during the Renaissance is indeed convincing, so much so that Palestrina, one of its finest exponents, became a legendary figure, and his name, for four hundred years after him, has been considered synonymous with religious expression in music. Even in the twentieth century, the *Motu Proprio* of Pope Pius X advocated only Gregorian chant and Palestrina's music as suitable for divine worship.

The stylistic change which took place in western European music during the fifteenth century was a decisive one in many respects. For the first time since the creation of polyphony, France lost her hegemony in musical matters, and the impetus for growth and change originated elsewhere. Music historians have looked to both England and Italy for an explanation of this change. Until recently, Italy's musical history has been more thoroughly explored, undoubtedly because she was in many respects the leader of the Renaissance. In the sphere of music, however, Italy does not seem to have provided at that time a spiritual climate vigorous enough to prompt the creation of a new sacred style. The term "renaissance," or "rebirth," is more literally descriptive in Italy than anywhere else, for humanistic interest, particularly in literature, was in reviving the grandeur of classical antiquity. Petrarch, although he occasionally addressed himself to posterity, was above all concerned with reviving the beauty of the past. His lifelong interest was in restoring Rome to its ecclesiastical and civil supremacy, and his letters addressed to Cicero, Livy, Horace, Vergil, Homer, and other classical authors called upon the glory of the past to be fruitful again.[4] Boccaccio also stressed the revival of an older culture when he praised Petrarch for bringing back the laurel wreath after 1,000 years.[5] It was in Italy too, during the Renaissance, that musicians attempted to reinstate the diatonic, chromatic, and enharmonic genera of classical Greek music theory.

The northern countries, which did not inherit so directly the

3. *The Age of the Baroque* (New York, 1952), p. xiii.

4. Ernest Hatch Wilkins, *Life of Petrarch* (Chicago, 1961), pp. 51–52.

5. Letter to Jacopo Pizzinghe, ca. 1370. James Bruce Ross and Mary Martin McLaughlin, eds., *The Portable Renaissance Reader* (New York, 1959), pp. 124–26.

tradition of "the glory that was Greece and the grandeur that was Rome," turned their creative activity into more novel channels. They sought not only the new world of the western hemisphere, but new worlds in general. Italy's inventive spirit in painting and sculpture during the Renaissance is still unchallenged, but a recent revolution in literary criticism led by Anglo-American scholars focuses attention largely on the English poetry of the Renaissance. It has been claimed that the evolution of style was more rapid and more decisive in the northern countries and that England's pre-eminence in literature during most of the Renaissance equaled that of Italy in the fine arts.[6]

In music England was also a leader, for English composers wrote the first cyclic polyphonic Mass Ordinaries, and their style was frankly admired by Continental composers. While it is not the author's contention that sacred categories were the leading form in the stylistic transformation of Renaissance music, the fact that the new style embraced liturgical forms and produced such a major one as the cyclic Mass cannot be left out of account. The climate in fourteenth- and fifteenth-century England was conducive to the development of sacred music because religious services in Britain kept pace with the style of the times. The composition of sacred music in England was prompted by a religious spirit which, though perhaps no more deeply pious than that in Italy, France, and Germany, was somehow more down to earth. The cultivation of sacred polyphony in England had a closer connection with the grass roots than it had on the Continent, possibly because the English church was more realistic. The rich repertory of polyphonic carols which flourished in England from the fourteenth century until about 1550 is one of the clearest indices of the close link between popular worship and art music. There is no Continental form corresponding exactly to the quasi-liturgical and very lively musical form of the carol. The closest parallel is with the Italian lauda, which, however, showed little continuity between the thirteenth-century monophonic pieces and the polyphonic settings of the early sixteenth century. The

6. Wylie Sypher, *Four Stages of Renaissance Style* (Garden City, N.Y., 1955), p. 5.

fourteenth-century German Geisslerlieder are also similar, but neither the lauda nor the Geisslerlied played as important a role as the carol did in English musical life. The carol thus provides in England the link between cause and effect that was missing in Continental circles.

Another feature of English religious and musical life which shows a connection between lay piety and art music is the position of the cantor. While monastic communities in English cathedrals still sang plainsong, the composition of new sacred music received a decided impetus from the contact which the composer, or cantor, had with the laity. The duties of the fifteenth-century English cantor were specifically to provide music for the lay congregation with whom he had frequent direct contact. The music composed by the cantor still came from the bosom of the church, and he himself was supported by the church rather than by secular lords, but he was in touch with the secular world and well acquainted with the tastes of the diocese. His congregation probably knew such rousing polyphonic songs as "Tappster, Drinker, Fill Another Ale," and certainly they knew the carols. Probably even the minor clergy had a weakness for such songs. It is said that the Latin poems of the *Red Book of Ossory* were written by the Franciscan bishop Richard de Ladrede of Kilkenny between 1317 and 1360 for the minor clergy of his cathedral to replace the words in the bawdy secular songs they were wont to sing.[7] Thus, while plainsong continued to be the mainstay of the private monastic rites, the cantor in charge of music for the lay services composed for a more worldly audience, one which provided sufficient stimulus to create in a contemporary style.

The curious combination of naïveté and skill which characterizes English art as well as music during the late fourteenth and early fifteenth centuries may perhaps have resulted from the peculiar sort of rapport established between the English church and its congregation, a rapport which is symbolized both by the position of the cantor and by the carol repertory. The carols had a certain popular flavor which, in a sense, had been characteristic of all Medieval English music. Jacques

7. Frank Ll. Harrison, *Music in Medieval Britain* (London, 1958), p. 417; and Richard L. Greene, *The Early English Carols* (Oxford, 1935), p. cxviii.

Handschin, in comparing the English music of the thirteenth
and early fourteenth centuries with the French, described it
as "less reflective and studied, more bent on aesthetic per-
ceptibility." [8] Perhaps the strong appeal of English music for
the Continent during the middle years of the fifteenth century
arose from its popular character and immediate attractiveness.
Beyond that, however, the carols had a thoroughly distinctive
style; they were, in effect, "stylish."

The term "style" is a treacherous one, particularly when
used for analogies among the arts. Yet styles of different arts at
any given epoch seem to develop in similar directions. It has
been held, for example, that abstract art tends to flourish when
man feels alien to the natural world, whereas naturalistic technique emerges when man submits to nature and does not feel
the need to impose symbols.[9] In the period of the Renaissance,
one element common to almost all expressions of life and art
was an extraordinary refinement of style. On receiving the news
of the fall of Constantinople, the court of Burgundy organized
a crusade, and among the preparatory festivities was the famous Feast of the Pheasant at Lille in 1454. This was an elaborate affair, during which there appeared pastries so enormous
that they could house twenty musicians, who jumped out to
perform their bits at the proper moments. It was a party conceived on a scale of lavish refinement that has seldom been
equaled. The fact that the crusade was never carried out is
almost forgotten. All that remains vividly in man's memory
is the elegance and extravagance of the "farewell," the style of
it. There was fully as much concern among painters with a
different kind of refinement. The depraved creatures of Bosch
and Brueghel, no less than the sublime madonnas of Van Eyck
and Fra Angelico, display a technique of painting which ab-
jures the broad sweeping stroke in favor of rigorously con-
trolled line and unparalleled fidelity to detail. The more abstract representations of Medieval painting had given way to
a passion for realistic detail, even when the details also contained symbolic meanings. In music, too, one of the primary
elements of the stylistic change which took place in the mid-

8. "The Sumer Canon and its Background, II," *MD*, 5 (1951), 103.
9. Sypher, *Four Stages*, pp. 14–15.

fifteenth century was a great refinement of technique. By the last half of the century, composers had attained such a high degree of technical facility that they even began to impose artificial restrictions upon themselves in the form of curiously worked out canons at various pitches and time intervals.

An acute sense of simultaneous pitch relationships and a highly rational means of regulating them distinguish the music of the West from that of all Oriental civilizations, in which more sophisticated rhythmic and melodic concepts almost totally exclude serious concern for vertical harmony. Vertical harmony has conventionally been discussed in terms of consonance and dissonance, and in the development of Western polyphony the balance between the two has constantly shifted. The style which began to evolve in 1450 and culminated in the late sixteenth century is one of the most rigorously consonant ones in the entire history of Western music. The soft sounds of the imperfect consonances (the third and sixth) were admitted to carefully prescribed use with the perfect consonances (the fifth and octave), and dissonance was severely curtailed. While sixteenth-century theorists gave precise and quite extensive rules for the care and handling of occasional dissonance, fifteenth-century musicians—theorists and composers alike—were far more casual about the matter, and there can hardly be said to be a consistent pattern of dissonance treatment before the end of the fifteenth century. Continental theorists of the late fifteenth century did give a moderate amount of attention to the problem of dissonance in what they called "diminished counterpoint," but English musicians seem to have been sublimely indifferent to the problem of the use of discord. The primary consideration, in any case, was the treatment of consonant intervals, and, seen in its historical perspective, this intense preoccupation with consonance illustrates a highly significant trend. The fifteenth century was approximately the mid-point in the ten centuries during which western Europe has developed polyphonic music. For the first five centuries preceding the fifteenth, music moved fairly steadily toward an increased use of consonance and the exclusion of dissonance. In the five centuries since then music has moved equally surely away from consonance and toward the reinstatement of dissonance as a positive aesthetic factor.

The fifteenth-century style, often referred to as the "Netherlandish style," found its earliest exponents among composers who lived and worked for some time in Franco-Netherlandish circles. Many of them were not Netherlandish at all, and many traveled widely, finding more lucrative positions elsewhere, especially in France and Italy. This traveling resulted in the creation of a genuinely international style. Thus there is some doubt about how "Netherlandish" in origin the style really was, since theorists and poets alike referred to foreign influences, especially from England. The purpose of this study is to examine the particularly English features that contributed to the formation of this style and to consider the fashion in which they were assimilated into the stream of Continental music. This has been done primarily through a study of one English composer, Walter Frye, whose works circulated widely on the Continent between 1450 and 1480 and whose career therefore seems to have been important in the transmission of the English musical idiom to France, Burgundy, and Italy.

For many years it was customary to regard the insular school of fifteenth-century English composers as quite distinct from that of their compatriots who traveled abroad. It had been assumed that the travelers were themselves influenced by foreign styles and that consequently their music no longer presented a pure, unsullied English strain. Recently, however, with the identification of many concordances between English and Continental manuscripts, Bukofzer, in his editon of Dunstable's works, has shown that the division of English composers into two schools cannot be maintained. The work of Walter Frye is a case in point, for he is far more widely represented in Continental manuscripts than in English ones, and yet his work stands squarely within English musical traditions. Frye is a thoroughly representative figure because his works extend over all three major categories of fifteenth-century composition: the Mass, the motet, and the secular song. He was a composer who carried on the tradition of the "contenance angloise," which had been introduced to European circles by John Dunstable and Lyonel Power in the first half of the century. Thus his works provide a standard by which one may measure the actual English contribution to the Golden Age of counterpoint.

Part I: The Historical Background

CHAPTER 1

The Role of English Musicians in Europe during the Fifteenth Century

THE STYLISTIC REVOLUTION which took place in the music of the fifteenth century was a drastic one. It completely transformed the three main categories of the century—the chanson, Mass, and motet. Broadly characterized, the change was from a soloistic art to one in which genuine counterpoint, or part-writing, prevailed. In the chanson medium, the style of accompanied solo-song gave way to a discant-tenor coupling, and eventually to a style in which all parts were identically conceived. The chanson is stylistically the leading form of the fifteenth century and the one in which the different stages of the whole musical evolution are most clearly discernible. Motet and Mass forms of the early fifteenth century were ill-defined, their styles diverse and lacking in any sort of identification with function. The motet had continued to draw upon fourteenth-century isorhythmic techniques in part, sometimes borrowed styles from secular forms like the ballade and caccia, and frequently retained the polytextuality which had characterized that form since its origin in the thirteenth century. But by the last half of the fifteenth century, the motet became an entirely vocal, contrapuntal composition, based on a *cantus firmus*, and usually having a single Latin liturgical text for all parts. The formal innovations of the fifteenth century are particularly significant in the sphere of Mass composition. During the first half of the century, individual movements of the Mass Ordinary had been composed in considerable numbers, frequently borrowing stylistically, like the motet, from secular forms. Occasionally two movements were paired together, particularly GLORIAS and CREDOS, by the use of the same *cantus firmus*. By 1475, however, the cyclic Mass, with a recurrent *cantus firmus* unifying all movements, was firmly established.

While a distinction along these lines can easily be drawn in a comparison of works written before 1440 with those after 1460, the intervening years present a rather puzzling picture because of the diverse elements which appear to have contributed to the formation of the Franco-Netherlandish style. This style, which began to appear about 1450 in the Netherlands, was rooted in both Continental and English traditions. At the present time, the Continental tradition has been more thoroughly explored, and the role of Guillaume Dufay, who was exposed very early to Italian music, has received a good deal of attention, while that of his contemporary, Gilles Binchois, whose affiliations were with the English, has received comparatively little until the recent work of Wolfgang Rehm.[1]

The study of English music has given rise to numerous interpretations, some of which are diametrically opposed. The only point on which there has been any kind of unanimity of opinion is that the death of John Dunstable in 1453 must have marked the end of English leadership in fifteenth-century music. Now even that must be questioned. Until recently, there was little known about any English composers working on the Continent after about 1450, and thus there has been comparatively little importance attached to England between 1450 and the work of Robert Fayrfax (1460–1521). Now the gap between Dunstable and Fayrfax is rapidly being filled in, with the publication of such repertories as *The Eton Choirbook*, the Carver manuscript, and the works of Frye and other English composers of a generation slightly younger than that of Dunstable. English musical activity most certainly continued unabated in England itself, and it received a decided impetus from the great collegiate as well as monastic foundations. How, and in what form, this English style was transmitted to the Continent remains to be studied.

The part played by Dunstable himself is fairly clear. He is

1. *Die Chansons von Gilles Binchois*, edited by Wolfgang Rehm (Mainz, 1957).

known to have worked on the Continent, for he served the Duke of Bedford in France at one time. Furthermore, the most important sources for his work are European, not English, manuscripts. Even up to the end of the sixteenth century, Dunstable was regarded by the theorists as one of the fathers of their style. First Tinctoris, in his *Liber de Arte Contrapuncti* of 1477, wrote that Ockeghem, Regis, Busnois, Caron, and Faugues all had the honor of studying with Dunstable, Dufay, and Binchois.[2] In 1537, Seybald Heyden wrote that Dunstable was the first to write in the new style and that he was followed by Dufay and Binchois in France and later by Ockeghem, Busnois, and Caron. As late as 1581, Vincenzo Galilei traced the Franco-Netherlandish style back one hundred fifty years to the work of Dunstable, Binchois, and Dufay. The most informative commentaries, however, are those of Dunstable's own contemporaries, or near contemporaries, particularly that of Johannes Tinctoris, who lived from 1435 until 1511. It was within Tinctoris' lifetime that all the diverse and conflicting tendencies of the early fifteenth century became reconciled, and there appeared a new and markedly characteristic style, which was to be maintained with no basic change for the next one hundred fifty years. In the *Proportionale,* written about 1467, Tinctoris speaks of this new art, of which the "fons et origo, apud Anglicos, quorum caput Dunstaple exstitit, fuisse perhibetur." [3] This passage is usually cited in reference to the work of Dunstable alone. Dunstable was the leader, to be sure, but it was to the entire English school that contemporaries most closely connected with the origins of the Franco-Netherlands style referred, and not just to the first and most gifted composer of that school. It was, then, not a question of individual genius alone, but of a whole tradition in English music which set it apart from Continental practice in several specific ways.

The exact nature of the English contribution has been only partially defined. Rudolf Ficker has long maintained that the polyphonic cyclic Mass was of English origin, and his thesis has been confirmed by the discovery of two complete Mass cycles by English composers before 1450, Lyonel Power's *Missa Alma*

2. *CS, 4,* 76ff.
3. *CS, 4,* 154ff.

redemptoris mater, and the *Missa Rex saeculorum,* which is variously attributed to Dunstable and Power.[4] Other scholars attribute to English influence various techniques such as placing the *cantus firmus* in the discant, the ornamentation of the *cantus firmus,* and the use of faburden or fauxbourdon. Charles Van den Borren, however, has pointed out that the general tenor of contemporary descriptions reflects very little interest in technicalities of this nature.[5] Tinctoris himself, who was given to quite explicit and detailed explanations on occasion, vouchsafed no such specific interpretation of why the new art was so indebted to the English. He merely referred to the "incomprehensible sweetness" of the new music and to the "sweetness suitable for the immortal gods."[6] Fifteenth-century commentaries for the most part are not couched in technical language, and the much-quoted passage from Martin Le Franc's *Le Champion des Dames,* in which he describes the new art practiced by Dufay and Binchois, is typical:

> Car ilz ont nouvelle pratique
> De faire frisque concordance
> En haulte et en basse musique,
> En fainte, en pause, et en muance,
> Et ons prins de la contenance
> Angloise et ensuy Dunstable
> Pour quoy merveilleuse plaisance
> Rend leur chant joyeux et notable.[7]

Certainly the use of the same tenor *cantus firmus* in all the movements of a Mass is not a procedure likely to evoke such expressions as "joyeux et notable" on the part of a poet. Neither would he be affected in such a fashion because the *cantus firmus* was placed in the discant or ornamented in the manner of a chanson. The descriptions of both Tinctoris and Le Franc im-

4. See Oliver Strunk, review of *Documenta Polyphoniae Liturgicae,* Ser. I, 1 & 2, in *JAMS,* 2 (1949), 108. The *Missa Rex saeculorum* is included by Bukofzer in his edition of the complete works of Dunstable.

5. "Considérations générales sur la conjonction de la polyphonie italienne et de la polyphonie du Nord pendant la première moitié du XVe siècle," *Bulletin de l'Institut historique belge de Rome, 19* (1938), 184–85.

6. *CS, 4,* 154 (*Proportionale*) and *CS, 4,* 77 (*Liber de Arte Contrapuncti*).

7. Cited by Gustave Reese, *Music in the Renaissance* (New York, 1954), p. 13.

ply an entirely new sound, one which was immediately recognized as such by the listener and which differed markedly from the earlier style of the fifteenth century. Indefinable though it may be, the "contenance angloise" must have been the result of a fundamentally different approach to the art of composition to have had such a profound effect on Guillaume Dufay. By 1435, Dufay's reputation was well established, and he was accorded the highest respect throughout Europe. Some of his chansons are written in sheer imitation of the Italian caccia style. But the result of his contact with English music was not imitation. It was assimilation, and his own style consequently underwent a radical change. What knowledge Dufay may have had of the music of Dunstable or Lyonel Power, or of any of the other English composers of his time, is not known. There is no indication of any personal relationship, although it is possible that he met Dunstable at some time, and it is difficult to associate him directly with any of the other English composers in Europe during the middle years of the fifteenth century.

In spite of the unanimous testimony of theorists and poets with regard to the importance of English music, some scholars have regarded Italy, rather than England, as the source of the major innovations of the fifteenth century. There have been good reasons for abandoning the English school, for the activities of the English musicians on the Continent are generally obscure. Where and when Continental composers may have established contact with their English colleagues is problematic, except in the case of Binchois. Furthermore, while it is plain that the English descended upon northern France and the Netherlands in great numbers during the early fifteenth century, it is equally clear that a great many famous French and Flemish musicians, including Dufay, flocked to Italy at that time to profit by the lavish patronage of the wealthy dukes of Savoy, Medici, Este, and Malatesta. Many of them, like Dufay and Arnold de Lantins, found employment at the papal chapel. Actually, there were two periods of migration to Italy—one during the first third of the fifteenth century, and another during the last quarter—and both have been considered important in the development of musical style during the fifteenth century.

It is primarily Heinrich Besseler who attaches importance to the Italian sojourns of the earlier period. In 1928, Besseler wrote that the Burgundian chanson was derived from the Italian two-part compositions of the fourteenth century, and that discant coloring was to be related to Italy rather than to England.[8] Wolfgang Stephan similarly derived the discant-tenor style of the Burgundian chanson from the Italian ballata.[9] With the publication of *Bourdon und Fauxbourdon* in 1950, Besseler reiterated his theory of Italian influence, and carried it further by a detailed study of Dufay's works during the 1430s. He acknowledged Dufay's debt to the English in the realm of pure sound. He referred to the harmonic richness achieved by the constant use of thirds and sixths, together with a "conductus-like" style in which all voices move simultaneously.[10] But Besseler did not consider these characteristics fundamental to the new style, and he continued to see the decisive impulse for change as coming from Italy. These theories of Besseler and Stephan cannot easily be reconciled with the statements of fifteenth-century witnesses who testified to the importance of English musicians but did not mention Italian music as a source of artistic inspiration.

There is, perhaps, another aspect of the trips to Italy which has some bearing on the role played by English musicians. During the fifteenth century, English music seems to have been widely known not only in the Netherlands but also in Italy. The Italians, though not generally distinguished for creative activity themselves at that time, were nevertheless alert to the innovations of other countries, and Italy seems to have been the avant garde of the musical world as far as patronage and performance were concerned. An extraordinarily large number of manuscripts were compiled in Italy in the middle of the fifteenth century, and the repertory of these sources is international in character. A very large proportion of the compositions preserved in Italian manuscripts of this period consists of works by English composers.

In 1938 Van den Borren wrote that during the decade of the

8. "Von Dufay bis Josquin," *ZMW 11* (1928), 4–6.

9. *Die Burgundisch-niederländische Motette zur Zeit Ockeghems* (Kassel, 1937), p. 12.

10. *Bourdon und Fauxbourdon* (Leipzig, 1950), Thesis 20. See also pp. 15, 109.

1430s there must have been a great interchange and exchange of musicians along an axis running from London to Rome,[11] but when he later wrote his *Études sur le quinzième siècle musical* in 1941, he rejected the idea of an English school of importance in Italy on the grounds that the archives showed no traces of a sojourn there by English musicians.[12] He has suggested too that English music may have been taken to Italy by Netherlandish composers.[13] This may have been true in some cases, but there are many English compositions in Italian manuscripts which show concordances only with English sources, and Bukofzer, in his recent study of the Old Hall manuscript, points out that twelve concordances between Old Hall and manuscripts from Bologna, Modena, Aosta, Munich, and Trent show evidence of a direct relationship between Italian and English repertories.[14] Dunstable's works must have been particularly well liked in Italy, for the major sources of his works are Italian. It is significant too that the one theorist who spoke specifically about an English technique, that of faburden, was Guglielmus Monachus, who lived in Italy, and whose treatise is preserved in the hand of a northern Italian scribe of the later fifteenth century.[15] Thus, whether or not English musicians went to Italy themselves, their music and the theory that lay behind it were known there, and any transformation effected on Netherlandish composers who went to Italy could well have been due to their contact there with English music, rather than to the impact of Italian music.

How the English music got to Italy, it is hard to say. Political ties between England and Italy were not particularly close during the first half of the fifteenth century, for the heresy of John Wycliffe had already begun to loosen the hold of Rome on the English church. Nevertheless there was a strong papist element in England, and at the Council of Constance in 1417, Henry Beaufort, the emissary of Henry V, had forced the Emperor Sigismund to acquiesce in the election of the Pope Martin V. Pope Martin V was fundamentally antagonistic to the ecclesiastical liberties of England, and failed in most of his

11. "Considérations générales," p. 181.
12. *Etudes sur le XVᵉ siècle musical* (Antwerp, 1941), p. 25.
13. "Considérations générales," p. 183.
14. *Studies in Medieval and Renaissance Music* (New York, 1950), pp. 38–40.
15. Brian Trowell, "Faburden and Fauxbourdon," *MD, 13* (1959), 64.

attempts to bring England into subservience, but he had at all times the support of Henry Beaufort, Bishop of Winchester and Cardinal.

Beaufort was a powerful figure in English political life and held official positions almost continually from 1403 until 1447. When Henry V died in 1422, leaving no provision for the regency, it was Beaufort who led the opposition to the Duke of Gloucester and who held the reins of the government during the absence of both Gloucester and his brother, the Duke of Bedford. His ties with the Papacy remained strong throughout his career, and since he was a man of considerable influence it may well have been through his offices that English music was known in Rome. He is not known to have had any particular affinity for music, but among his staunch supporters in England was William de la Pole, Earl and Duke of Suffolk, whom Binchois served in France during the 'twenties. The peculiar nature of Beaufort's relations with Italy might, in fact, explain the presence of English music and the absence of English composers in Italian circles.[16] Whatever the means by which Italians acquired English music, Italy may perhaps be regarded as an important link between English musicians and the northern composers who journeyed there in the first half of the fifteenth century in search of worldly betterment.

The possibility of Italian influence during the last two decades of the century has attracted many more scholars. There are some elements of the later Netherlands music which seem to have no roots in the style of Ockeghem or Dufay. The use of short motives, sequences, and a tendency toward more square-cut melodic construction are generally foreign to Ockeghem's style, but appear in the works of Busnois, Obrecht, Isaac, Agricola, and Josquin. It has been thought that contact with the Italian frottola and other popular forms produced a new element of harmonic and formal clarity within the vaguely defined and rather nebulous style of the earlier Netherlands composers. Besseler is also of this opinion, for he explains the works of Obrecht, Tinctoris, Gaspar, and Agricola in terms of Italian influence, as a result of their sojourns in Italy.[17] Otto Gombosi,

16. K. B. McFarlane, "England: The Lancastrian Kings, 1399–1461," in *The Cambridge Medieval History, 8* (Cambridge, 1936), pp. 387–99.
17. *Die Musik des Mittelalters*, p. 241.

in his study of Obrecht, saw Italian influence after 1470 in the cultivation of smooth voice-handling, the setting off of sections by sharp divisions, and the deliberate use of imitation as a structural device.[18] Van den Borren, too, although less positive about it, thinks that Italian forms after 1480 may well have exerted a certain amount of influence on the Netherlands composers,[19] and Gustave Reese, in *Music in the Renaissance,* has inserted a chapter entitled "The Frottolists and their Contemporaries in Northern and Central Italy" between the discussion of Ockeghem and that of Josquin, in order to explain the new element that had crept into the Netherlands style as a result of the Italian journeys.

Against this interpretation is the fact that the frottola did not emerge as a musical form important enough to be regarded as an influential force before about 1480, whereas these "new" elements had begun to appear in the work of Obrecht before he went to Italy in 1474. The characteristics foreign to Ockeghem's style began to appear well before 1480, not only in the work of Obrecht but also in that of Barbireau, Hayne van Ghizeghem, Busnois, and Binchois, none of whom had any connection with Italy.

Thus the various attempts to explain this new style through Italian influence have been unsatisfactory on several counts. They leave out of consideration the major role of English musicians as well as that of the composers who never went to Italy, and they neglect the middle years of the century—the period between 1440 and 1470—which were the years when the most decisive turning point occurred. Even Besseler, after erecting a theory based on Dufay's isolated experiments of the 1430s, observes that it was only considerably later that this technique was really assimilated.[20] The new style emerged clearly only in about 1460 and only in the Netherlands, where English musicians had appeared in great enough numbers to have brought about a widespread familiarity with English musical practices. There had been many English musicians in the provinces of Hainaut,

18. *Jacob Obrecht: Eine stilkritische Studie* (Leipzig, 1925), pp. 15–16.

19. "De quelques publications récentes relative à la musique italienne du moyen âge et de la Renaissance," *Bulletin de la Classe des Beaux-arts de l'Académie royale de Belgique,* 22 (1940), 164–68.

20. *Bourdon und Fauxbourdon,* p. 165.

Artois, and Flanders during the early fifteenth century, and they
had been infiltrating the Low countries for some time. A steady
influx, not just of English music but of English composers
themselves, had resulted from commercial and political relationships since the fourteenth century between the countries border-
ing the channel.

England had long maintained close ties with Flanders,
Brabant, and Holland because of the textile industries. When
these territories came into the hands of the Dukes of Burgundy,
both English and Burgundians found it to their advantage to
join forces in opposing the French. Philip the Good (Duke of
Burgundy from 1419–67) established friendly relations with
Henry V at Malines as early as 1419, and in 1420 signed the
Treaty of Troyes, by which the Dauphin was deprived of his
rights to the French throne and France was delivered into the
hands of the English monarchy. In 1423, Philip arranged for the
marriage of his sister, Anne de Bourgogne, to the Duke of
Bedford.[21] The alliances that Philip made with the English
during the early years of his reign undoubtedly account for
much of the interaction between English and Burgundian
musicians during the 1420s and '30s. Binchois, for example,
after serving the Duke of Suffolk for a number of years, established himself at the Burgundian court in 1430 and remained
there, except for a few short absences, for the rest of his life.[22]

The fact that the English activities on the Continent were of
a military nature did little to dampen the musical enthusiasm
and aspirations of their equipages. "A la guerre, les sonneurs de
trompes ne sont pas seul present, les chantres, l'organiste font
partie de l'armée et entre deux batailles, des concerts
s'organisent dans les différents camps."[23] Anglo-Burgundian
relations were not unqualifiedly friendly, however. After the
death of Henry V, the Duke of Gloucester in 1424 led his troops
into Hainaut with the intention of acquiring part of this terri-
tory for England. Philippe de Luxembourg, however, testified
in a letter in 1428 that in spite of the losses sustained by the
Cathedral of Cambrai through the visitation of the Duke of

21. Henri Pirenne, *Histoire de Belgique* (Brussels, 1908) 2, 236.
22. Jeanne Marix, *Histoire de la musique et des musiciens de la Cour de
Bourgogne sous le règne de Philippe le Bon* (Strasbourg, 1939), p. 179.
23. Ibid., p. 23.

Gloucester, the solemn service was maintained in all its grandeur.[24] In all probability the service was even enhanced by the English musicians who accompanied Gloucester. Several of the choir books listed in the Burgundian inventories suggest English provenance, and one of them at least was acquired in 1435 from Hainaut.[25] Many of the musicians who came to the Netherlands with Gloucester or with the Duke of Suffolk must have remained there, for names such as Robert Morton, *chappellain anglois,* are found in the roster of the chapel of Philip the Good. It is also recorded that one Joh. van Soest (born 1448) repaired to Bruges in his youth in order to study music with two masters *uss engellant.*[26]

Philip's relationship with the English was never a really cordial one. His alliances with them were always made for the sake of political expedience, and his policy was essentially that of a vassal of the French king.[27] "Le duc," wrote Chastellain, "a déploré pendant toute sa vie qu'il ne lui fut pas permis de combattre du côté français à Azincourt, où tomba son oncle Antoine." [28] Philip chose to be a troublesome vassal, but nevertheless a vassal, and he did not look kindly upon binding commitments to England. The treaties which Philip made with the English, moreover, were limited to the early years of his reign, when he was bent on avenging his father's murder at Montereau. By the time this ambition was fulfilled in 1435, the English had outlived their usefulness for Philip.[29]

Relatively little attention has been paid by music historians to Philip's son Charles, or to the coincidence of Charles' deep love of music coupled with strong sympathies toward the

24. J. Houdoy, *Histoire artistique de la Cathédrale de Cambrai* (Paris, 1880), p. 58.

25. A large music book, starting with the words "Et in terra" and closing with "Ergo beata" was brought to the Duke of Burgundy from Hainaut by one Jehan Marlette. See Léopold Devillers, *Cartulaire des comtes de Hainaut* (Brussels, 1892), 5, 335–36 (cited in part by Marix, *Histoire de la musique,* pp. 19–20).

26. André Pirro, *Histoire de la musique de la fin du XIVe siècle à la fin du XVIe* (Paris, 1940), p. 115.

27. See Paul Bonenfant, *Philippe le Bon* (Brussels, 1944), chap. 3, "L'alliance anglaise," p. 31.

28. J. Huizinga, "L'Etat bourguignon, ses rapports avec la France et les origines d'une nationalité néerlandaise," *Le Moyen Age, 40* (1930–31), 184.

29. At the Treaty of Arras in 1435, Philip allied himself with Charles VII against the English.

English. Charles maintained close relationships with the English long after Philip had lost interest in them. The English policy of neutrality toward Burgundy, which had followed upon the Treaty of Arras in 1435, gave way during Charles' reign to a positive alliance.[30] Charles' rapport with the English was due to a profound difference in attitude from that of his father, for Charles did not consider himself a vassal of the French king. Bartier writes concerning Charles:

> Il savait qu'entre lui et Louis XI, la lutte serait implacable, et qu'il devait le détruire s'il voulait subsister. Tel était nécessairement le premier objectif qu'il devait s'assigner, le but suprème qu'il devait donner à sa politique.[31]

In his efforts to combat Louis XI, Charles allied himself with the English, first through a treaty of friendship with Edward IV in 1465, then by his own marriage to Edward's sister, Margaret of York. In 1468 he signed a treaty of intercourse between England and the Low Countries, to be valid for thirty years, and admitted Edward to the order of of the *Toison d'Or*.[32] Commines reports that Charles even spoke English fluently.[33] The rupture in Anglo-Burgundian relations occurred only two years before Charles' death, with the signing of a treaty between Edward and Louis XI in 1475.

Charles was far more of a musician than his father and took more personal interest in the musical activities of his English allies. He learned at an early age to play the harp, and there is some evidence that he studied music with Dufay, who had been named chaplain of the Duke of Burgundy in 1446 and was a canon of Cambrai.[34] There is ample testimony that Charles composed motets and chansons himself, even though no compositions survive with his name. A note found on one of the manuscripts of the library of Cambrai relates that:

> Charles, comte de Charolais, fils de Philippe de Bourgogne, fict un mottet et tout le chant, lequel fut chanté en sa présence après messe dite, en la vénérable église de Cambrai

30. Pirenne, *Histoire de Belgique*, p. 315.
31. John Bartier, *Charles le Téméraire* (Brussels, 1944), p. 49.
32. Pirenne, *Histoire de Belgique*, pp. 315–16.
33. Marcel Brion, *Charles le Téméraire* (Paris, 1947), p. 264, n. 10.
34. Charles Van den Borren, *Guillaume Dufay* (Brussels, 1926), pp. 57–58.

par le maître et les enfants, en l'an 1460, le 23e jour d'octobre.[35]

Unhappily, the quality of Charles' voice must have left something to be desired, for even so loyal a chronicler as Olivier de la Marche related that he "aimoit la musicque, combien qu'il eust mauvaise voix, mais toutesfois il avoit l'art, et fist le chant de plusieurs chanssons bien faictes et bien notées."[36] Philippe Wielant, too, contrasted Charles' vocal inadequacy with his talent for composition when he wrote that "Il prennoit aussy plaisir, passetemps en musicque, et estoit lui-mesme musicien et scavoit composer et chanter volontiers, combien qu'il n'avoit point bonne voix."[37] Molinet's praise was unqualified, however, and his remarks show less concern with Charles' own ability to perform than with his patronage and interest. Molinet compared Charles with Charlemagne, on the basis of his artistic and humanistic interests:

Aprés la réfection du corps [Charles le Téméraire] donnoit réfection à l'âme et employait ses jours, non pas en fole vanité ou mondain spectacle, mais en saintes escriptures, hystoires approuvées et de haulte recommandation, souverainement en l'art de musicque dont il estoit amoureux que nul plus . . . Et, comme le roy Charlemaine avoit honnouré celle science en son temps, lors qu'il avoit mandé les expers musiciens de Rome pour enseignier ceulx de France en vraye modulation, le duc Charles recoeilloit les plus famez chantres du monde et entretenoit une chapelle estoffée de voix tant armonieuses et délitables que, après la gloire celeste, il n'estoit aultre léesse.[38]

Perhaps it was Charles' preoccupation with music that prevented him from acquiring the political savoir-faire that characterized his father. In any case, his own reign as Duke of Burgundy was a brief and stormy one, and he is usually regarded by political historians as an inept individual whose blustering imperialistic policy ultimately destroyed the power of the Burgundian duchy.

35. Houdoy, *Histoire artistique*, p. 87.
36. Marix, *Histoire de la musique*, p. 19.
37. Ibid., p. 19, n. 3.
38. Albert Vander Linden, "La musique dans les Chroniques de Jean Molinet," *Mélange Ernest Closson* (Brussels, 1948), p. 167.

Charles was evidently neither warrior nor statesman. He was a humanist, and his interests are reflected not only in his love of music but also by the fact that the additions to the Burgundian library under his aegis were among the most valuable and the most discriminating of all the acquisitions.

Molinet's reference to Charles' splendid chapel and to his surrounding himself with the most famous singers of the world is tantalizing, and it is curious, too, since the ducal registers during his reign (1467–77) include hardly any of the names of composers who are known to have been outstanding exponents of the new style. Binchois is the only one whose name appears consistently in the official records. The names of Morton and Busnois frequently do not appear in the roster at times when they are known through other sources to have been there. Dufay's name never appears in the court register of accounts, even though he had been attached to the Burgundian court since 1446, at least, and must have had rather close connections.

One possible explanation of these lacunae is that Charles' greatest activity as patron of the arts had taken place before he succeeded his father as Duke of Burgundy. Certainly Busnois served him before 1467, while Charles still bore the title of Count of Charolais, for in the text of *In hydraulis,* Busnois refers to himself as "illustris comitis de Chaulois indignum musicum." The capacity in which Busnois served must have been distinct from that of the regular chaplains in the ducal retinue. Charles also seems to have exhibited some predilection for English musicians. Robert Morton, the English chaplain, received permission from Philip to spend three months with Charles in 1464 on the condition that he accept no payment from Charles, since he was already receiving "VIII sols royaulx par jour" from Philip. The following year Morton again spent three months serving Charles.[39] It is an account book of Charles, not of Philip, that records the entry of Morton, as well as that of Hayne van Ghizighem, into Burgundian circles in 1457.[40] Their names do not appear in the official ducal registers of payments until 1467, when Charles actually became Duke.

Since the records of Charles' musical activities prior to 1467

39. Marix, *Histoire de la musique,* pp. 209–10.
40. Ibid., pp. 205–06.

are scanty, it is impossible to know the exact nature of the service rendered him by Busnois, Hayne, and Morton. But it is known that as early as 1454, when he was just twenty-one years of age, Charles had been made master of several large rural domains, and "tout comme il a son propre domaine, Charles a désormais sa propre Maison, ses chambellans, ses écuyers, ses secrétaires." [41] With an equipage such as this, it is almost certain that he had a small chapel, and possibly a large and important one.

Charles was renowned for his interest in music by the time he was twenty-four. He was presented with some music books by a Dutch priest in 1457, and in the same year he also received some music from a Scottish cleric on his way to Rome.[42] All these reports suggest that Charles cultivated music far more actively in the years preceding his father's death than has been thought. In view of Charles' sympathetic attitude toward the English and his connection with such important musical figures as Dufay, Binchois, and Busnois, it seems highly probable that his patronage was an influential factor in the fusion of artistic ideals which took place during the third quarter of the fifteenth century. The decades of the 'fifties and 'sixties were important ones, and it was during those years that Charles, then the Count of Charolais, was employing musicians on his own initiative and even borrowing composers from his father's court. There were many composers whose works appear in Burgundian manuscripts but whose names appear nowhere in the ducal registers of accounts. Some of them are now known to have been English, and they were very probably in the employ of Charles. The works of these composers are of especial importance, for they illustrate the English style with which Netherlands composers between 1450 and 1475 presumably had direct contact.

41. Bartier, *Charles le Téméraire,* p. 19.
42. Pirro, *Histoire de la musique,* p. 115.

CHAPTER 2

Walter Frye: Biography and Bibliography

ONE OF the English composers whose works are known chiefly through manuscripts related to the Burgundian court is Walter Frye. There are relatively few works attributed to Frye, but those few seem to have been widely known. At least one of his compositions, the *Ave Regina,* must have been enormously popular, for it survives in thirteen manuscripts as well as in two paintings in which fragments of the discant and tenor are portrayed. Two of his chansons similarly enjoyed a considerable success; the rondeau *Tout a par moy* has been found in nine manuscripts, and the ballade *So ys emprentid* in eight, of which one has two copies. Frye's music was certainly well known to the Netherlands composers at the end of the century. Le Rouge wrote a Mass on the tenor of *Soyez aprantiz* (one of the corrupt versions of *So ys emprentid);* Agricola, Tinctoris, and Josquin all drew upon his *Tout a par moy;* [1] and Obrecht used the *Ave Regina* for his own motet on that text, as well as for a Mass.

There is very little biographical information about Frye. His name does not appear in the archives of the Burgundian court. In the absence of documentary evidence it has been conjectured that he was the same person as the Gualterius Liberti represented in the Bodleian Ms. *Canonici* 213,[2] and at one time it was thought that he was German, because many of his motets were preserved in the Schedel Liederbuch with the German spelling of his name, "Frey." Recent research, however, has revealed

1. Josquin's *Missa Faysant regrets* is based on this chanson, citing the entire superius in the "Agnus Dei III," but deriving its title from the IIa pars, of which the opening motive provides an ostinato. See Reese, *Music in the Renaissance,* p. 244.
2. Ibid., p. 93.

18

several documents which incontrovertibly prove his English nationality. One of these is the bede roll of a London guild of musicians, in which Frye's name is entered among the clerks in 1457.[3] Another is a copy of a will, the existence of which was discovered by Sydney Charles. The will, in the name of one Walter Frye, is preserved at Somerset House and was made on August 12, 1474, and proved on June 5, 1475, in the Prerogative Court of Canterbury.[4] It is headed by the inscription: "St. Gregory, Allhallows the Less, London, Certesey, Surrey." It is not informative with regard to his profession, but suggests that he was a traveler, since he apparently had no fixed residence. Among his bequests is a small one to a brother, John Frye, in Wells, and one to the nearest Carthusian house for his Requiem Mass. He also requests that his letters of fraternity with the Friars Preachers be sent to their convent in London, but does not specify which one. Curiously enough, the London Guild of Musicians does not list Frye among its deceased members at any time between 1474 and 1476. Possibly he had severed connections with the Guild for a sojourn on the Continent.

Two other documents, found at Ely Cathedral, suggest that Frye was affiliated with Ely for about ten years before he went to London. These documents are less conclusive than the others, for they do not give the surname but refer only to "Walter, the Cantor," who was paid an annual stipend of thirteen shillings and fourpence, in 1443–44 and again in 1452–53.[5] Ely was searched because of the elusive character of the *cantus firmus* in Frye's *Missa Flos regalis*. *Flos regalis* was not a common liturgical text, and the *Alleluia Flos regalis vernans rosa* in a thirteenth-century Sarum Gradual is not the source of Frye's tenor. There is, however, an antiphon beginning *Flos regalis Etheldreda* for the birthday of St. Etheldreda on June 23, preserved without music in a fifteenth-century prayer book from a Carthusian monastery at Cologne.[6] St. Etheldreda is the patron saint of Ely Cathedral

3. Hugh Baillie, "A London Guild of Musicians," *Proceedings of the Royal Musical Association*, 83d Session (1956–57), p. 20.

4. Somerset House, 19 Wattys.

5. "Et in stipendi Waltero Cantoro per annum xiii s iiii d," Ely Cathedral, Dean and Chapter, Custos Capellae rolls," 22 Henry VI. "In stipendi Walteri cantori per annum xiii s iiii d," Custos Capellae rolls, 31 Henry VI.

6. G. M. Dreves, *Analecta Hymnica* (Leipzig, 1886–1922), 7, Pt. XXVIII, 293.

in Cambridgeshire. One of the most popular of the Anglo-Saxon women saints, she lived in the seventh century and founded a monastery on the Isle of Ely. She is widely venerated on her birthday in the York, Sarum, and Hereford liturgies and in the Benedictine mythologies. The translation of her relics is celebrated on October 17 in both the Sarum and Hereford calendars. The text of the antiphon from Cologne is as follows:

> Flos regalis Etheldreda
> Sponsa, virgo, vidua
> Monialis, abbatissa
> Regina dulciflua
> Mente, carne non marcessis
> Vivens neque mortua
> Famulorum sis tuorum
> Adiutrix assidua.

Such an eight-lined rhymed antiphon is typical of the memorials sung to local saints and inserted, according to Benedictine rule, after Lauds or Vespers.[7] But these were invariably taken from the office in the Breviary, and the text *Flos regalis Etheldreda* does not appear in the one extant monastic Breviary from Ely. (Thirteenth century, Cambridge University Library, Ms. Ii-IV-20.) The liturgist, J. B. L. Tolhurst, believes that the text is more likely to have come from the Processional and that it may have been used on Sundays and more important feasts, when special antiphons were sung before High Mass and Terce.[8] Unfortunately no Ely Processional survives.

The monastic community at Ely of course had a particular affection for St. Etheldreda, and the cathedral is decorated throughout with various carvings of scenes from her life. In the fifteenth century, the iconography of St. Etheldreda seems to have flourished anew, for one of the outstanding examples of English painting of that period is an altarpiece, originally from

---

This manuscript, which was compiled by the Bishop of Treves ("auctoris, Episcopi Trevirensis," fol. 221v'), contains in addition the offices for many other English saints: Osmundus, Thomas of Lancaster, Edmund, Edward, and others.

7. J. B. L. Tolhurst, *The Monastic Breviary of Hyde Abbey*, vol. 6, *The Henry Bradshaw Society, 80* (1942), 101–02.

8. Ibid., p. 142. The specific suggestion about the *Flos regalis* text was communicated by personal correspondence from J. B. L. Tolhurst.

Ely, depicting four scenes from her life.[9] It is very possible that the same spirit prompted the composition of a rhymed antiphon in her honor at that time and that its melody served as the *cantus firmus* for a Mass by a composer at Ely. No trace of either text or chant is to be found at Ely today, nor are there any other extant Ely books besides the Breviary.[10]

The lack of conclusive proof with regard to Frye's *Missa Flos regalis* is discouraging, but nevertheless the references to a "Walter, the cantor" are striking, and prove to be interesting. They are found in the records of the custodian of the Lady chapel, entered in the rolls for the twenty-second and thirty-first years of the reign of Henry VI. The rolls for the intervening years are missing, but since annual stipends were paid it seems safe to assume that the cantor was there continuously from 1443–52. If the cantor was indeed Walter Frye, the dates are perfectly compatible with those of the London Guild of Musicians and the will. Probably he left Ely some time between 1453 and 1457, when he appeared in London. There are no rolls extant from the last nine years of Henry's reign.[11]

The reference of 1443–44 (22 Henry VI) is the first mention of the office of cantor in all the rolls.[12] The cantor was an extremely important figure in the development of English choral polyphony. "Walter" himself, whether Frye or not, is described by Seriol Evans as "the forerunner of the 'Organist and Master of the Choristers' of Henrician statutes given to the 'Newe Colleges of the Holie and Undivided Trinity of Ely' after the Dissolution." [13] His role was quite distinct from that of the precentor, who was charged with the musical service in the choir of a monastic cathedral. The precentor was a cleric first and a

9. See John Harvey, *Gothic England* (London, 1947), p. 83. The altarpiece is now at the Society of Antiquaries in London.

10. An Antiphonal and Gradual were available to James Bentham when he published the supplement to the second edition of his history of Ely in 1812.

11. The cantor named in 1465–66 (5 Edward IV) is Johann Rede de Scotia; in 1467–68 (7 Edward IV) Joh. Wedenby; and in 1470–71 and 1478–79 (10 and 18 Edward IV) Rich. Harryngton.

12. A few more rolls than are extant today were available to the Rev. J. H. Crosby, precentor of the cathedral, who made a handwritten transcript of all the obedientary rolls in about 1907, but he cited this as the first.

13. "Ely Almonry Boys and Choristers in the later Middle Ages," in *Essays presented to Sir Hilary Jenkinson*, ed. J. Conway Davies (London, 1957), p. 161.

musician second. His duties involved plainsong only, and his choir consisted of the monastic community, not of boys or outside singers. The cantor, on the other hand, was a professional musician, and not necessarily a cleric. There is no ecclesiastical title affixed to the name of Walter, the cantor, nor to Walter Frye's name in the London bede roll, although he may have been a friar, since his will refers to his fraternity with the Dominicans. The cantor was charged with the secular liturgy, i.e. with the services held outside the monastic choir, in the nave or the Lady chapel, and he was concerned with polyphony.[14]

There is no document at Ely defining the duties of the new cantor, but there is one at Durham, where a cantor named John Stele was appointed several years later, in 1447. Stele was required to teach " 'playnesange, prikenot, faburdon, dischaunte et countre,' to some monks and eight secular boys, play the organ, and sing the tenor part in polyphonic music at Mass and Vespers in Choir." [15] Worcester, too, had cantors associated with the Lady chapel, the first of whom was one Richard Grene in 1480.[16] A deed of 1522 from Worcester lists similar duties for Grene's successor, Daniel Boyse, who was to "keep the Lady Mass in the Lady Chapel daily with plain and broken song and with organs . . . Besides this he is to teach eight boys of the chapel in plain and broken song especially in the Lady Masses, the Mass of the name of Jesus and those of the principal feasts. He is also to teach them to sing Vespers and the customary antiphons of the daily office." [17]

The records of the Lady chapel at Ely, while scant, are informative. They show particularly elaborate celebrations of the Feast of the Translation of Relics of St. Etheldreda, and of Lady Masses, and they show the use of boys and extra singers, presumably drawn from outside the monastic community for the celebration of special occasions. The boys and extra singers are mentioned in the roll that contains the first reference to the cantor: "Et datis clericis [cantantibus] in capella tempore translationis et depositionis Scte. Etheldreda . . . Et datis diversis

14. Harrison, *Music in Medieval Britain,* p. 40.
15. Ibid., pp. 40 and 187.
16. Seriol J. A. Evans, "Ely Almonry Boys," p. 161.
17. Ibid., p. 161.

clericis cantantibus organum ad missam Bte. Maria Virginis
. . . et aliis amicis ecclesiae et cantantibus in capella." [18] Later
references, in 1452–53, 1467–68, 1470–71, and 1478–79, show
consistent use of outside singers for the celebration of the translation of Etheldreda's relics and, in the last case, during the
reign of Edward IV, the borrowing of singers from the Duke
of Norfolk.[19]

Until the last twenty years of the fifteenth century, the musical organization of the Lady chapel at Ely seems to have been
entirely distinct from that of the regular monastic order. The
cantor, paid by the custodian of the Lady chapel, often had his
lodgings in the almonry. But his functions were different from
those of the precentor, and his boys were not those who were
cared for by the almonry school. When Richard Harryngton
was the cantor and John Downham the almoner in 1473–74, a
reference in the almonry rolls calls the singers "Harryngton's
boys," not "Downham's boys." [20] There is no evidence at Ely
with regard to the care and education of these young singers,
although at Worcester they are known to have been provided
with food and clothing, and possibly also with a general as well
as musical education.[21]

The establishment of this song school at Ely, like those of
other monastic cathedrals, is always connected with the Lady
chapels and inextricably related to the Marian cult which enjoyed such a new flowering in fifteenth-century England. The
Lady chapels, established with a monk as warden, the *custos
capellae,* secular clerks, and boy choristers, had been maintained
at Worcester from the fourteenth century, and payments had

18. Custos Capellae rolls, Ely Cathedral, 22 Henry VI.
19. "Datis clericis in capella auxiliantibus tempore translat. et depositionis
Scte. Etheldreda . . . Et datis diversis in capella cantant . . . et datis extraneis
in capella cantant," 31 Henry VI. Later, in 7 Edward IV, "Salutem clericis in
capella auxiliantibus in tempore translacionis et depositionis Scte. Etheldreda
cum tempore indulgencie et aliis temporibus . . . In denariis datis cantoribus
domine Episcopi Eliensis ad translationis Scte. Etheldreda." In 10 Edward IV,
"Datis Ambrosi [?] Cantori Harryngton Mendam et aliis per vices auxiliantibus in
capella," and in 18 Edward IV, "Datis clericis cantantibus auxiliantibus in capella
tempore translationis et depositionis Scte. Etheldreda . . . In denariis datis fratri
Wendham et cuidem servienti domini Ducis Norfolch cantanti in festo translationis Etheldreda."
20. Evans, "Ely Almonry Boys," pp. 162–63.
21. Ibid., p. 162.

been made to clerks and outsiders (*clerici extranei*) who stayed in the hostelry and sang polyphonic music in the Lady chapel.[22] John Alcock, Bishop of Worcester from 1476–86, endowed the Lady chapel there and gave one hundred pounds for singing services.[23] (Alcock left Worcester to become Bishop of Ely, where he died in 1500. He is commemorated by a tomb festooned with elaborate cocks.) At St. Albans Abbey, Abbot John Wheathamstead had the Lady chapel painted during his first tenure as abbot (1420–40) and instituted daily polyphonic Lady Masses by singers outside the cathedral. In 1423 he decreed that at least two stipendiary singers of polyphony (*organistae*) were to be engaged for Lady Masses, Vespers, and for High Mass in the choir on Sundays and festivals.[24]

The Lady chapel at Ely is unequaled anywhere for size and splendor. It has a forty-six-foot single span roof, and was built between 1321 and 1349 by the "flower of craftsmen" (*flos operarum*), Alain de Walsingham, off the north transept of the cathedral. The construction was interrupted by the collapse of the great central tower—a disaster which prompted the building of one of Ely's most famous architectural features, the octagon and lantern, also conceived by the brilliant imagination of Walsingham. Walsingham was a virtuoso, and the Lady chapel, no less than the octagon, is a tribute to his genius. Originally its walls were completely lined with carvings and niches separated by slender columns of Purbeck marble. Although it was once filled with elaborately carved statues—which were all beheaded and otherwise mutilated by the zeal of the Puritan reformers—and painted in the most brilliant hues (of which only faint traces remain), the chapel now seems desolate, cold, and very white. The roof bosses alone are intact, and they are unique for the fourteenth century—with all the curious grotesques, animal masques, Passion symbols, and figures of the Virgin and of the translation of relics of St. Etheldreda. They have been described as "combining a naïveté and crudeness with an undeniable skill in carving." [25]

22. Harrison, *Music in Medieval Britain*, p. 40.
23. Ibid., p. 40.
24. Ibid., pp. 41–42.
25. C. J. P. Cave, "The Roof Bosses in Ely Cathedral," *Second Annual Report of the Friends of Ely Cathedral*, quoted in Raymond Birt, *The Glories of Ely Cathedral* (London, n.d.), p. 25.

Before the building of the Lady chapel at Ely, the sacrist was entrusted with the care of the altar to the Virgin. But as soon as the chapel was begun, the altar was placed under a new officer, the *custos capellae Beate Marie,* and from that time on the records were kept separately. The first custodian was John de Wisbech (d. 1349), although the earliest rolls kept date only from 1364–65 (38 Edward III).[26] It was here that the cantor performed his duties. There was evidently no cantor appointed in the fourteenth century, even though there is reference to singers *(clerici cantantes)* in the Lady chapel as early as 1364–65.[27] The role of the cantor, while less glorious than that of the precentor in the eyes of the church, was a more important one musically. The type of services held in the Lady chapel belonged to the secular liturgy. In some cathedrals they were held in the nave, in others in the Lady chapel, but in either case they were open to the laity. The records at Ely show that laymen were even drawn in as singers. The chorus of the Lady chapel there, in fact, drew upon many resources to enhance the musical aspects of the service, even to the point of borrowing virtuoso singers from the Duke of Norfolk. It was here, as in other Lady chapels of England, that sacred choral polyphony developed very rapidly with the maintenance of large choirs for the services, independent of the monastic liturgy.

The Marian cult, which flowered so abundantly all over England in the fifteenth century, was the primary cause of much of the new polyphony, particularly in the educational foundations and secular liturgies. *The Eton Choirbook,* consisting as it does entirely of Marian motets, and other manuscripts containing great numbers of Lady Masses (i.e. the Lambeth Palace manuscript) are evidence of the zeal with which English composers responded to the institution of daily Marian rites. Eton College at Windsor and King's College, Cambridge, were the two royal colleges "of our Ladie" founded by Henry VI.[28] King's College was founded in 1441; Eton was formally opened in 1443—the same year in which a cantor first appeared at Ely—and its statutes

26. James Bentham, *History and Antiquities . . . of Ely Cathedral* (Norwich, 1812), Supplement, pp. 65–67.

27. Custos Capellae rolls, Ely Cathedral, 38 Edward III.

28. Canon E. C. Ratcliffe, Ely Professor at Cambridge, suggests that Frye's *Flos regalis* may have been from the *Flos regalis anglici* in the special service for Henry VI.

of 1444 provide specifically for a clerk proficient in polyphonic music.[29] King's College, fifteen miles distant from Ely, shows some similarity of repertory with Eton, for an inventory of 1529 lists a book containing motets by Dunstable and Lambe, both of whom were originally represented in *The Eton Choirbook*.[30]

The cantor named Walter at Ely may or may not have been the same person as Walter Frye. Even if the two cannot be conclusively identified, the musical organization at Ely and the specific duties of the English cantor in the mid-fifteenth century illustrate the kind of professional experience that a composer of Frye's generation must have had. If they were indeed the same person, then the presence of Frye's motet for St. Nicholas, *Sospitati dedit*, in the Pepys Ms. 1236 (Magdalene College, Cambs.) is easily understandable. This collection contains a large number of motets in honor of St. Nicholas, including other settings of *Sospitati dedit*, and it is possible that the manuscript was compiled for King's College, which was originally "The Collegiate Church of Saints Mary and Nicholas." The proximity of Ely to Cambridge, as well as to Bury St. Edmunds, suggests that an Ely cantor was very close to the center of English polyphony in the fifteenth century.

There remain a good many questions unanswered with regard to Frye and his relations with Ely. One, of course, is whether the melody of *Flos regalis Etheldreda* is actually the one used by Frye. There is no trace of it at Ely today. Canon E. Ratcliffe, formerly canon of Ely and Ely professor at Cambridge, is familiar with the antiphon but knows of no source for it. The melody used by Frye is in the seventh mode and is very similar to, though not identical with, many of the seventh mode antiphons in the Sarum Gradual and Antiphonal. It bears a particularly close resemblance to the chants for the feast of the octave of the Epiphany, specifically to *Tu qui in spiritus*.[31] All the chants for this office are very much alike, and one of them, *Veterem hominem*, served as the *cantus firmus* for one of the early English cyclic masses preserved in the Trent codex 88.[32]

29. Harrison, *Music in Medieval Britain*, p. 34. See also Harrison, ed., *The Eton Choirbook* (London, 1956), *1*, preface, xv.

30. George Williams, "Ecclesiastical Vestments, etc., in King's College," *The Ecclesiologist*, 24 (1863), 102.

31. W. H. Frere, ed., *Antiphonale Sarisburiense* (London, 1901–25), *1*, 95.

32. Nos. 404 (KYRIE), and 199 through 202.

St. Etheldreda was also venerated in the metropolitan sees of both Cologne and Treves. The Cologne manuscript containing the text of *Flos regalis Etheldreda* is not a particularly significant source, but it was copied by the Bishop of Treves, and liturgical books, particularly from Treves, from the tenth century on contain the office of St. Etheldreda.[33] It is possible that Treves or Cologne provides the link between the *Flos regalis* antiphon and a Mass utilizing its melody as a *cantus firmus* in a manuscript of the Burgundian court, since Burgundy had close connections with both sees in the mid-fifteenth century. Philip the Good had assigned his natural brother to the bishopric of Treves and his nephew to that of Cologne, and Charles the Bold went to Treves in 1475 to try to effect a reconciliation with the Roman Emperor Frederick III.[34]

If Walter Frye himself did go to the Continent, his activities there remain shrouded in mystery. He is mentioned by the English Carmelite monk, John Hothby, in a list which includes Continental and English composers known in Europe:

> In quamplurimis . . . aliis cantilenis recentissimis quarum conditores plerique adhuc vivunt, Dunstable anglicus ille, Dufay, Leonel, Plumere, Frier, Busnoys, Morton, Octinghem, Pelagulfus, Micheleth, Baduin, Forest, Stane, Fich, Caron.[35]

The most convincing indication of a European sojourn by Frye is provided by the sources of his music, of which the overwhelming majority are Continental manuscripts. There is only one complete composition of Frye's known from an English manuscript, the motet *Sospitati dedit;* the Ashmole manuscript (Bodleian) contains only a fragment, textless and anonymous, of his secular song *So ys emprentid.* The two most important single sources for his work are the Ms. 5557 in the Brussels Biblio-

33. See Max Keuffer, *Beschreibendes Verzeichnis der Handschriften der stadtbibliothek zu Trier* (Trier, 1888–97), Nos. 358, 469, 470. See also Peter Miesges, *Der Trierer Festkalender* (Trier, Lintz, 1915).

34. Ruth Hannas, "Concerning Deletions in the Polyphonic Mass Credo," *JAMS, 5* (1952), 160, 168.

35. *Dialogus Johannis Ottobi,* Florence Biblioteca Nazionale Centrale, Ms. Magliab. XIX, 36, fol. 82v'. See Albert Seay, "The *Dialogus Johannis Ottobi Anglici in arte Musica,*" *JAMS, 8* (1955), 95.

thèque Royale and the Mellon chansonnier, both of which appear to have originated in Burgundian circles (See Chapters 3 and 4). Yet there is no mention of Frye's name in the Burgundian archives.

The three Masses of Frye all appear in a single source, the Brussels manuscript, with attributions. The chansons and motets published in the *Collected Works of Walter Frye* [36] (edited by this author) include the French rondeau *Tout a par moy;* three English ballades, *Alas, alas, So ys emprentid,* and *Myn hertis lust;* and five motets, *Ave Regina, O florens rosa, Sospitati dedit, Trinitatis dies,* and *Salve Virgo mater.* This last motet, though anonymous, was included because of the apparent parody relationship to Frye's *Missa Summe Trinitati* (see below).

Among the chansons, there are conflicting attributions of authorship for *Tout a par moy* (Binchois) and *So ys emprentid* (Bedingham). *Myn hertis lust* has no real attribution to Frye, but is assigned to Bedingham in one of its later incarnations by the same scribe who gave Bedingham *So ys emprentid.* It is virtually impossible to distinguish stylistically between Frye and Bedingham, but since the ascription of *So ys emprentid* is to Frye on the only English-texted copy, which must be the most authentic, it has been assumed that all three English ballades are by Frye (see Chapter 4). For purposes of stylistic investigation, at least, they are so similar that a discussion of all these chansons together seems justifiable even in the face of the possibility that evidence of Bedingham's authorship may appear in the future.

One other ballade, which was discovered by Dragan Plamenac after the publication of the *Collected Works,* is a textless two-voiced piece in the Prague codex (Strahov D.G. IV. 47).[37] This piece bears an inscription which Plamenac reads as "Watlin Frew" and believes to be a corruption of "Walter Frye." It is stylistically very similar to the two-voiced structure of discant and tenor in Frye's known works, and it shows the typical ballade musical form, with similar closing measures for the two

36. American Institute of Musicology, 1960.
37. "Browsing through a Little-Known Manuscript," *JAMS, 13* (1960), 104–07 and 109.

main sections. The only unique feature of the piece is the passage from measures 33–36 in which first the tenor is completely silent for two measures, then the discant is silent while the tenor repeats the phrase an octave lower. This is a rather more Italianate technique than is usual for Frye. Still another work, tentatively ascribed to Frye, is the Italian chanson *Che faro io* in the Oporto chansonnier. The ascription is to one Galfridus, whom Bukofzer believed to have been an English composer and Gilbert Reaney suggests may be the same Walter as Frye.[38]

The transmission of Frye's music in Continental sources and the interrelationship between motets and chansons will be discussed further in Chapters 3 and 4, but two important identifications made by Bukofzer with regard to Frye's work should be mentioned here. Two motets in the Trent codex 88 borrow their *cantus firmi* from pieces by Frye: *Stella coeli extirpavit* (No. 204) uses the tenor of *So ys emprentid,* while *Salve Virgo mater* (No. 240) not only uses the tenor of Frye's *Missa Summe Trinitati* but also shows a very clear parody relationship with the Mass.[39] Bukofzer suggested that this might be one of the earliest examples of a parody Mass. Since the time when Bukofzer wrote on this subject, however, parody Masses or Mass movements have been revealed from considerably earlier sources. Kurt von Fischer finds that Antonio Zacara of Teramo used some of his ballate for Mass movements,[40] and Suzanne Clercx has shown that Ciconia used his motet *Regina gloriosa* as a model for a GLORIA and CREDO.[41]

What is perhaps more interesting in the Frye pieces is the possibility that the parody relationship worked the other way around, i.e. that the motet is the parody, and not the Mass. This suggestion comes to mind because the *cantus firmus* of the Mass is so eminently legitimate. The Mass tenor is labeled *Summe trinitati,* and the melody is clearly that of the chant accompanying that text in the Sarum usage. The text *Salve Virgo mater* has not been identified, and no melody is known for it. Thus, of the two compositions, the Mass seems more likely to have been com-

38. *New Oxford History of Music, 3* (London, 1960), 132–33.

39. *MGG*, article "Frye, Walter."

40. "Origins and National Aspects of the Quodlibet," *International Musicological Society, Report of the Eighth Congress, 2, Reports* (New York, 1962), 56.

41. *Johannes Ciconia* (Brussels, 1960), *1*, 128ff.

posed first, in the normal tradition of a borrowed liturgical
cantus firmus, and it is the motet that must be a parody. No
other examples of parody motets are known to this author, and
yet there was one practice with regard to *cantus firmi* which
might explain the phenomenon—a practice which was more
common in England than on the Continent.

The importance of the Marian cult, particularly in England,
resulted in a profusion of Marian motets, and composers began
to range far and wide for their *cantus firmi,* no longer restricting
themselves to the appropriate chants. The composers of *The
Eton Choirbook* utilized a great variety of chant melodies, only
some of which have so far been identified. The *Salve Regina* was
a particularly important text, composed countless times, and
there is only one of the settings in *The Eton Choirbook* which
uses the chant belonging with that text.[42] Browne, for example,
used the melody *Maria ergo unxit,* an antiphon for the *Man-
datum* on Holy Thursday. Richard Hygons even used the famous *Caput* melody, embedded in the second verse, for his *Salve
Regina.*[43]

What appears to be the case is that for English composers the
Marian motet had something of the character which the Ordinary of the Mass had for Continental composers. They were
composed in such quantities that musicians simply used different
cantus firmi for the sake of variety, and perhaps also wrote
parody motets. The English almost never used a secular *cantus
firmi* for a Mass Ordinary—*Western Wynd* is a rare exception.
Perhaps just as the Continental composers borrowed secular
and sacred sources alike for their Mass settings English
composers incorporated secular songs or inappropriate chant
melodies in their motets to the Virgin. The two motets from
Trent 88, *Stella coeli extirpavit* and *Salve Virgo mater,* are both
composed to Marian texts. Both are anonymous in Trent and
not known from any other source. Bukofzer suggested that they
may have been composed by Frye. Stylistically they are very
similar to Frye's work, and in any case are very probably

42. Josquin, although he frequently used foreign *cantus firmi,* and even secular
ones, never did so when the motet text had its own chant melody. See Jacquelyn
A. Mattfeld, "Liturgical Motets of Josquin des Pres," *JAMS, 14* (1961), 177–79.
43. Frank Ll. Harrison, "An English Caput," *ML, 33* (1952), 203.

English. Their discovery, therefore, contributes further specific knowledge of English works known in Europe around 1450.

English music was apparently much more widely known and copied in Europe around 1450 than has been supposed. Because there is so little known about the life of Walter Frye, and because the actual activities of English composers on the Continent are still obscure, it has seemed worth while to study the sources of Frye's compositions closely in order to determine the circumstances and chronology of their compilation. The Brussels manuscript, the unique source for his three Masses, will be studied first, and then the manuscripts containing motets and chansons will be studied together.

Part II: The Manuscript Sources of Compositions by Walter Frye

CHAPTER 3

The Masses of Frye:
The Brussels Manuscript 5557

THE THREE polyphonic Masses of Walter Frye are known only through the manuscript listed as No. 5557 in the Bibliothèque Royale de Belgique. This manuscript is an important one, for it contains a highly representative selection from the repertory of northwestern Europe between 1450 and 1475. Of the composers whose works are brought together in the manuscript BR 5557 (Dufay, Ockeghem, Busnois, Regis, Frye, Cockx, and Heyns), at least four were outstanding figures in that transitional period. The presence of works by young Franco-Netherlandish composers, by English composers, and by Dufay in one manuscript implies that the circumstances of its compilation may have been related in some way to the actual exchange of artistic ideas which took place around the middle of the fifteenth century. It does not follow, of course, that the composers whose works are brought together here were as closely linked as the gatherings of the manuscript, although Dufay and Regis are known to have been closely associated. But unlike many of the contemporary sources which represent large and heterogeneous anthologies of mid-fifteenth-century repertory, the Brussels manuscript reflects a certain degree of personal choice and selection on the part of the owner.

Charles Van den Borren has published a brief stylistic analysis of the compositions in BR 5557,[1] as well as a descriptive inventory of the manuscript.[2] At the time his inventory was made, the foliation was confused. Since then the volume has been rebound,

1. *Etudes*, pp. 144–251.
2. "Inventaire des manuscrits de musique polyphonique qui se trouve en Belgique," *AM*, 5 (1933), 66, 120, 177, and 6 (1934), 23, 65, 116.

and, at the request of the Bibliothèque Royale, Van den Borren has restored the major portion of it to the original order.[3] The first folio of the manuscript bears the arms of the Dukes of Burgundy—more specifically, those of Philip the Good and Charles the Bold. (This particular emblem was not used by Charles' daughter, Marie of Burgundy, nor by Philip the Handsome.) Thus the manuscript must have been acquired before the death of Charles in 1477, and it may be supposed that a record of its acquisition can be found among the inventories of the ducal library.

J. Marchal, in his catalogue of the Burgundian Library published in 1842,[4] identifies this manuscript with one which appeared in the inventory of 1467.[5] The book described in that inventory was a parchment manuscript beginning after the table of contents with the words "Et in terra" and ending with "Ergo beata," and it is known to have been acquired in 1435 from Hainaut.[6] The description does not fit BR 5557, which is of paper and contains a repertory of at least fifteen or twenty years later than 1435.[7] There seem to be no entries in the inventories of 1467 or 1487, nor in that of Sanderus in 1644, which describe this particular choir book, but the inventory of Viglius in 1577 lists, in addition to the book bought in Hainaut in 1435, "autre vielz livre de musique en pappier couvert de parchemin Intitulé 'Livre de musique,' commenchant au second feuille ET IN TERRA PAX." [8] While this description is not very precise, it does at least meet all the requirements, as far as it goes. Furthermore, the use of the word "vielz" in an inventory written in 1577 makes an identification of this book with BR 5557 even more justifiable.

3. References here are to the new foliation.

4. *Catalogue des manuscrits de la Bibliothèque royale des ducs de Bourgogne* (Brussels, 1842), *1*, "Resumé historique," p. cclix.

5. Published by J. Barrois, *Bibliothèque protypographique, ou Librairies des fils du roi Jean, Charles V, Jean de Berri, Philippe de Bourgogne et les siens* (Paris, 1830), No. 1110, p. 169.

6. Léopold Devillers, *Cartulaire des comtes de Hainaut*, *5*, 335–36 (cited in part by J. Marix, *Histoire de la musique*, pp. 19–20).

7. See Sylvia W. Kenney, "Origins and Chronology of the Brussels Manuscript 5557 in the Bibliothèque Royale de Belgique," *RB*, *6* (1952), 75–77.

8. Brussels, Bibliothèque Royale, Ms. 11675–11676, No. 408. The original numbering of the manuscript is used here rather than the revised penciled numbering.

It seems curious that a manuscript bearing the arms of the Dukes of Burgundy should appear nowhere in the inventories before 1577. The omission can perhaps be explained by the fact that BR 5557 is not an elaborately illuminated manuscript like the *Liber Missarum* of Pierre de la Rue or the Antiphonal of Marguerite of Austria. Furthermore, it is exceedingly accurate. Scribes' errors are rare, and are generally corrected. It may be assumed that it was a manuscript actually used in the chapel rather than as a display piece in the fabulously rich Burgundian library. Certainly, in comparison with the exquisite illumination of the Books of Hours or the *Chronique de Hainaut,* this manuscript is rather poor and unpretentious—so unpretentious, in fact, that it may never have been deemed worthy of mention among the real treasures. The inventory made at Bruges in 1504 does mention the following:

> Item, plusieurs et divers LIVRES DE CHANT servant à la chapelle, de petite valeur; ensemble pluiseurs [*sic*] quayers de diverses choses, tous rassamblez et mis ensemble en ung coffre à part.[9]

Since BR 5557 must have been compiled before the death of Charles the Bold in 1477, it might well have been tucked away in just such a coffer as this until Viglius restored it to the dignity of a separate listing in 1577.

So far, any certainty which might previously have existed with regard to the acquisition of BR 5557 has been dispelled. Very little more definite information is forthcoming from the registers of expenses, since, as Marix has pointed out, the purchase of music books was included among the expenses of the chapel and details were seldom given.[10] It is known that a number of Masses were commissioned by Philip the Good for the ceremonies of the *Toison d'Or,* and that Alexandre Colombe was paid 1½ gros for binding one such book in 1431 and 1 franc for writing and illuminating another in 1436. One Sancy, also a chaplain of Sainte-Chapelle at Dijon, was paid for notating the latter.[11] It is also known that a book "plain de nouvelles chante-

9. Barrois, *Bibliothèque protypographique*, No. 2210, p. 313.
10. Marix, *Histoire de la musique,* p. 19.
11. Ibid., pp. 33–34.

ries comme messes, mottes et plusieurs autres choses . . . pour servir en la chapelle" was bought at Malines in 1446, and that in 1468 three Masses were "nouvelles nottés es livres de ladite chapelle," [12] but there is no precise mention of the contents of any of these manuscripts.

The manuscript BR 5557 is not a homogeneous one. There are four different kinds of paper used, examples of which are found dating from 1459 to 1480, and there are at least five different types of handwriting. Probably then the manuscript was compiled over a period of years, gatherings being added to the original corpus as they were acquired. The Registres des Chambres de Comptes show frequent payments for rebinding of books and additions of new leaves,[13] and it seems very likely that a choir book such as BR 5557, which was in actual use in the chapel, would have had new compositions added in the course of time.

The particular fashion in which the manuscript BR 5557 was compiled casts some light on the chronology of the compositions contained in it. It comprises twelve gatherings, of which the first four appear to have been a homogeneous unit, written at one time, and probably forming the original manuscript (folios 2–49 inclusive). They are written in a completely uniform hand, all on the same kind of paper, and with regular gatherings of twelve folios each. Furthermore, this section contains five settings of the Ordinary of the Mass (three by Frye, one by Cockx, and one anonymous [14]), which overlap between gatherings, frequently starting in the middle of one gathering and ending in the next. All but one of the Masses in this section are written for three voices. These factors, as well as stylistic considerations, imply a common origin for the first five compositions of BR 5557.

From folio 50 to the end, the additions seem to have been made gathering by gathering. Each of the major compositions begins on the first verso of a gathering and does not continue into

12. Ibid., pp. 19–20, 130.

13. In 1464 a man was paid to rebind some "livres des evangiles et y mettre aucuns nouveaulx feuillets." Marix, *Histoire de la musique*, p. 130.

14. This Mass is attributed to Binchois in the manuscript, but the handwriting is clearly a later addition. Van den Borren considers an attribution to Busnois more probable, but, in lieu of further evidence, refers to the composer as Pseudo-Binchois. See his *Etudes*, pp. 206 and 210.

the next. (The only exception to this is in the case where the beginning discant and tenor parts were copied onto the last verso of the preceding gathering.) The fifth gathering contains Dufay's *Missa Ecce ancilla;* the sixth, an anonymous Magnificat; the seventh, a Magnificat of Busnois; the eighth, Ockeghem's *Missa Quinti toni;* the ninth, an anonymous *Missa Sine nomine;* the tenth, Heyns' *Missa Pour quelque paine;* the eleventh, Dufay's *Missa Ave Regina;* and the twelfth, Regis' *Missa Ecce ancilla—Ne timeas.*[15] The following diagrams show how each of the gatherings is put together. The heavy line through the middle of each gathering indicates the binding string, while the lines at the left serve to connect corresponding folios on either side of the string. Since the seventh gathering is wrongly bound, a second diagram is included in order to show the original order of the folios.

Of these twelve gatherings, all but the seventh, eighth, and twelfth are made up of the same kind of paper, which bears a watermark of three fleurs-de-lys and a pendant initial "P." Examples of this paper have been found at Troyes, dated 1459, while variants of it are found to have been used at Damme (1460–80), Grammont (1461–72), and at Paris (1460–74).[16] Gathering 7, which contains the Busnois Magnificat, bears a crescent watermark, of which examples have also been found at Troyes (1468) and Damme (1470) as well as Amsterdam (1474).[17] The eighth gathering, which includes the Ockeghem Mass and motets by Busnois, has an anchor watermark, the only other known example of which is from Paris, dated 1479.[18] The last gathering, that containing the Regis Mass, also bears a distinct watermark—this time in the form of a hunting horn. This filigrane is not so easily identified in Briquet's dictionary, but the closest approximation is with a document from Azeglio in Italy (1474).[19] The Italian origin of this paper does not necessarily imply that it was written in Italy, for maritime commerce was

15. Dufay's *Missa Ecce ancilla* and Ockeghem's *Missa Quinto toni* are without attributions here.

16. C. M. Briquet, *Les Filigranes: Dictionnaire historique des marques du papier* (Geneva, 1907), vol. *1,* No. 1740.

17. Ibid., No. 5185.

18. Ibid., No. 393.

19. Ibid., No. 7828.

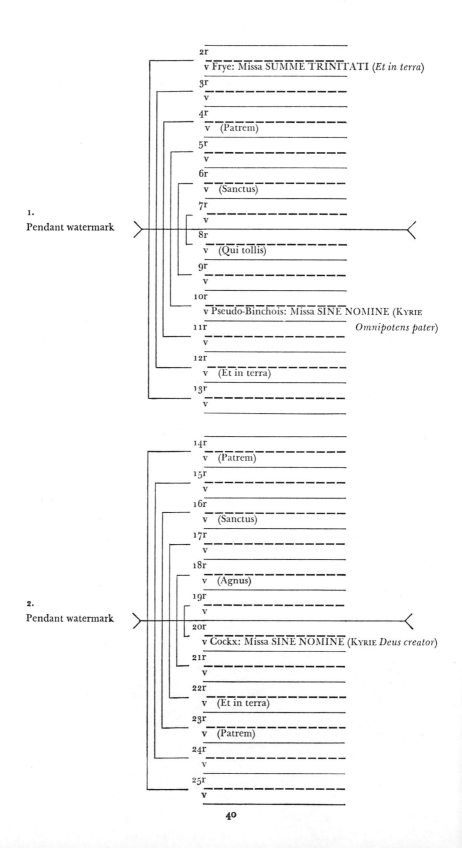

2r
v Frye: Missa SUMME TRINITATI (*Et in terra*)
3r
v
4r
v (Patrem)
5r
v
6r
v (Sanctus)
7r
v
8r
v (Qui tollis)
9r
v
10r
v Pseudo-Binchois: Missa SINE NOMINE (Kyrie
Omnipotens pater)
11r
v
12r
v (Et in terra)
13r
v

1.
Pendant watermark

14r
v (Patrem)
15r
v
16r
v (Sanctus)
17r
v
18r
v (Agnus)
19r
v
20r
v Cockx: Missa SINE NOMINE (Kyrie *Deus creator*)
21r
v
22r
v (Et in terra)
23r
v (Patrem)
24r
v
25r
v

2.
Pendant watermark

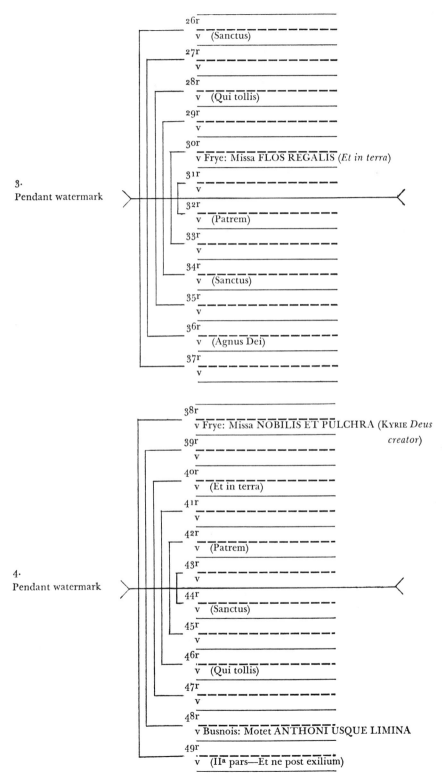

3.
Pendant watermark

26r
v (Sanctus)
27r
v
28r
v (Qui tollis)
29r
v
30r
v Frye: Missa FLOS REGALIS (*Et in terra*)
31r
v
32r
v (Patrem)
33r
v
34r
v (Sanctus)
35r
v
36r
v (Agnus Dei)
37r
v

4.
Pendant watermark

38r
v Frye: Missa NOBILIS ET PULCHRA (Kyrie *Deus creator*)
39r
v
40r
v (Et in terra)
41r
v
42r
v (Patrem)
43r
v
44r
v (Sanctus)
45r
v
46r
v (Qui tollis)
47r
v
48r
v Busnois: Motet ANTHONI USQUE LIMINA
49r
v (II^a pars—Et ne post exilium)

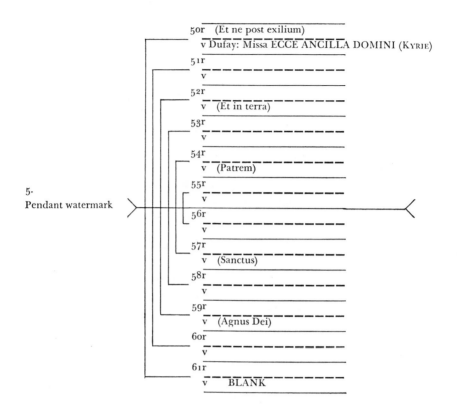

5.
Pendant watermark

50r (Et ne post exilium)
v Dufay: Missa ECCE ANCILLA DOMINI (KYRIE)
51r
v
52r
v (Et in terra)
53r
v
54r
v (Patrem)
55r
v
56r
v
57r
v (Sanctus)
58r
v
59r
v (Agnus Dei)
60r
v
61r
v BLANK

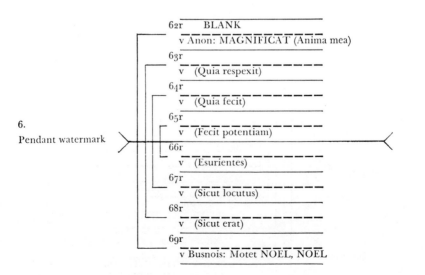

6.
Pendant watermark

62r BLANK
v Anon: MAGNIFICAT (Anima mea)
63r
v (Quia respexit)
64r
v (Quia fecit)
65r
v (Fecit potentiam)
66r
v (Esurientes)
67r
v (Sicut locutus)
68r
v (Sicut erat)
69r
v Busnois: Motet NOEL, NOEL

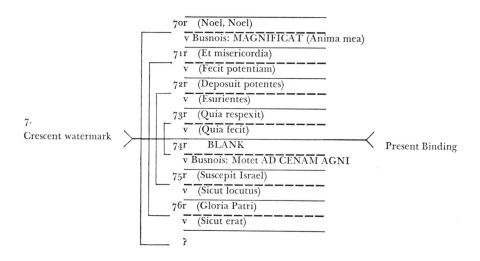

7.
Crescent watermark

70r (Noel, Noel)
v Busnois: MAGNIFICAT (Anima mea)
71r (Et misericordia)
v (Fecit potentiam)
72r (Deposuit potentes)
v (Esurientes)
73r (Quia respexit)
v (Quia fecit)
74r BLANK
v Busnois: Motet AD CENAM AGNI
75r (Suscepit Israel)
v (Sicut locutus)
76r (Gloria Patri)
v (Sicut erat)
?

Present Binding

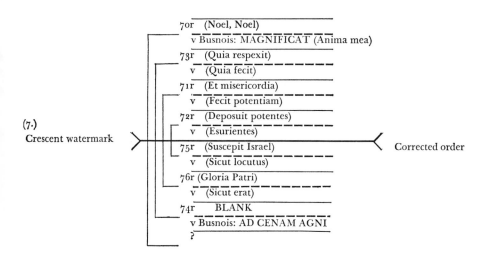

(7.)
Crescent watermark

70r (Noel, Noel)
v Busnois: MAGNIFICAT (Anima mea)
73r (Quia respexit)
v (Quia fecit)
71r (Et misericordia)
v (Fecit potentiam)
72r (Deposuit potentes)
v (Esurientes)
75r (Suscepit Israel)
v (Sicut locutus)
76r (Gloria Patri)
v (Sicut erat)
74r BLANK
v Busnois: AD CENAM AGNI
?

Corrected order

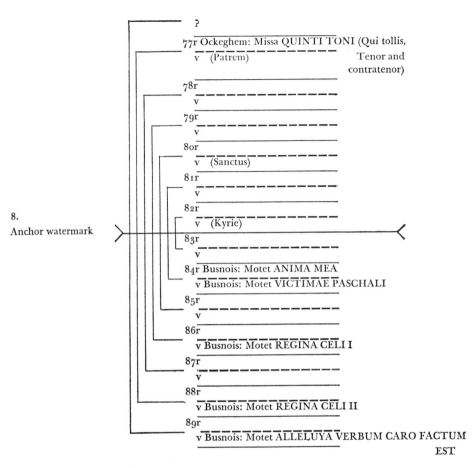

?

77r Ockeghem: Missa QUINTI TONI (Qui tollis,
v (Patrem)   Tenor and
                                              contratenor)

78r
v

79r
v

80r
v (Sanctus)

81r
v

82r
v (Kyrie)

83r
v

84r Busnois: Motet ANIMA MEA
v Busnois: Motet VICTIMAE PASCHALI

85r
v

86r
v Busnois: Motet REGINA CELI I

87r
v

88r
v Busnois: Motet REGINA CELI II

89r
v Busnois: Motet ALLELUYA VERBUM CARO FACTUM
                                              EST

8.
Anchor watermark

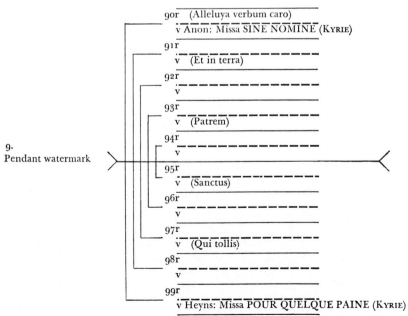

90r (Alleluya verbum caro)
v Anon: Missa SINE NOMINE (KYRIE)

91r
v (Et in terra)

92r
v

93r
v (Patrem)

94r
v

95r
v (Sanctus)

96r
v

97r
v (Qui tollis)

98r
v

99r
v Heyns: Missa POUR QUELQUE PAINE (KYRIE)

9.
Pendant watermark

44

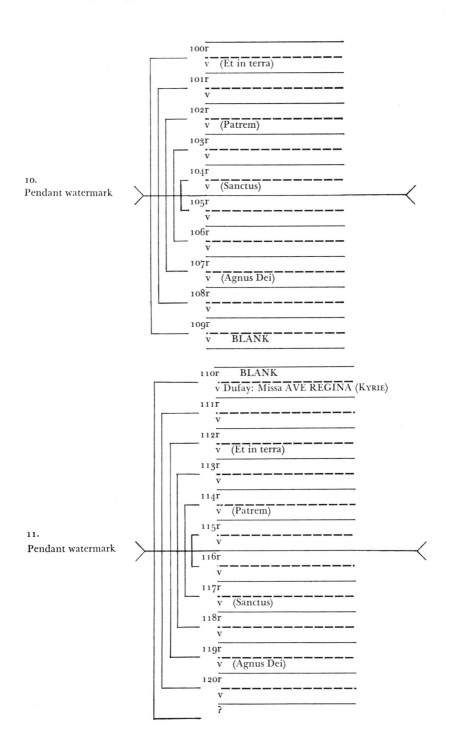

10.
Pendant watermark

100r
v (Et in terra)
101r
v
102r
v (Patrem)
103r
v
104r
v (Sanctus)
105r
v
106r
v
107r
v (Agnus Dei)
108r
v
109r
v BLANK

110r BLANK
v Dufay: Missa AVE REGINA (KYRIE)
111r
v
112r
v (Et in terra)
113r
v
114r
v (Patrem)
115r
v
116r
v
117r
v (Sanctus)
118r
v
119r
v (Agnus Dei)
120r
v
?

11.
Pendant watermark

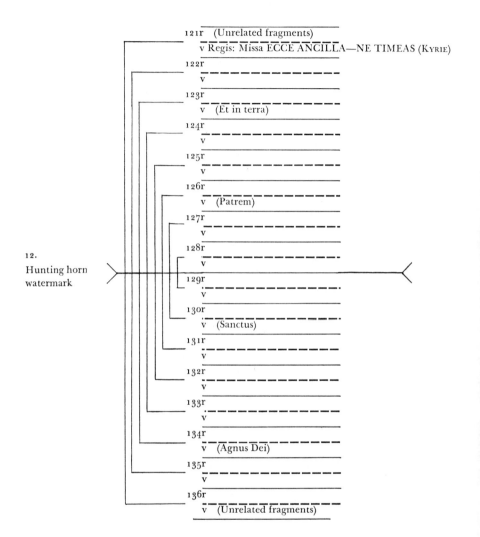

121r (Unrelated fragments)

v Regis: Missa ECCE ANCILLA—NE TIMEAS (Kyrie)

122r

v

123r

v (Et in terra)

124r

v

125r

v

126r

v (Patrem)

127r

v

128r

v

12.

Hunting horn
watermark

129r

v

130r

v (Sanctus)

131r

v

132r

v

133r

v

134r

v (Agnus Dei)

135r

v

136r

v (Unrelated fragments)

highly developed, and examples of Italian paper have been found in the Netherlands and Normandy even quite close to local centers of paper manufacture.[20]

The musical handwriting of the manuscript may be classed in five main categories. The first five Masses (by Frye, Cockx, and Pseudo-Binchois) are clearly written by the same hand, A. Dufay's *Ecce ancilla* Mass and the anonymous *Sine nomine* Mass are written in a hand, A', which, though not identical with A, probably came from the same workshop. Another variant of the same handwriting, A'', appears in Dufay's *Ave Regina* Mass and Regis' *Missa Ecce ancilla — Ne timeas* of the last two gatherings. While the text writing accompanying A and A'' is very similar, that of A' is much less cursive. An entirely different hand, B, is used for the five motets of Busnois that fill up the eighth gathering, and it is the same as that found in the motet *Anthoni usque limina* and the hymn *Ad cenam agni*. The Busnois Magnificat of the seventh gathering is in still another hand, C, as are also the anonymous Magnificat, D, and Ockeghem's *Missa Quinti toni*, E.

It can be seen from the diagrams that the short compositions, all of which are by Busnois, are scattered throughout the manuscript, but in a rather significant fashion. The large group of five motets (*Victimae paschali, Anima mea liquefacta est, Regina celi* I and II, and *Alleluya verbum caro factum est*) fills up the second half of the eighth gathering, of which the first part is devoted to Ockeghem's *Quinti toni* Mass. The others are all entered in the manuscript either at the end of a gathering, where a few folios may have been left blank, or in such a way that they serve to connect those gatherings which were separately written and then added to the manuscript. The first recto and last verso of a single gathering (or of a group of gatherings) were nearly always blank because of the practice of writing the discant and tenor voices of a composition on a verso and the contratenor and bass on the opposite recto. Hence, whenever an already written gathering was added to the manuscript there resulted a consecutive blank verso and recto, and it is at these points that the other compositions of Busnois are found in BR 5557. His

20. Ibid., 2, 419.

motet *Anthoni usque limina,* for example, starts on ff. 48v and 49r. The second part is written on 49v, the last folio of the fourth gathering, and 50r, the first folio of the fifth gathering. The motet *Noel, Noel* appears on the last verso of the sixth and the first recto of the seventh gathering (ff. 69v–70r). Similarly, the hymn *Ad cenam agni* falls at the end of the seventh gathering, after the Magnificat which fills all but the last folio.

The position of *Ad cenam agni* is not apparent as the volume is bound now. Because one folio of that gathering is misplaced, the verses of the Magnificat do not follow consecutively and the beginning of the hymn falls in the middle of the Magnificat. This gathering is unique in the manuscript, for it is the only one in which all the voices are written on one side of each folio instead of being placed opposite one another on verso and recto. Since each verso or recto contains all the voice parts of a particular section and it is not necessary that a certain verso be opposite a specific recto, the folios could easily have been juxtaposed in the binding without separating the voice parts of any one given section.[21] If the correct order is restored, as illustrated in the diagram, the verses of the Magnificat follow in perfect order and the two voice parts of the hymn fall at the end, on the verso of the last folio.

It is apparent that one folio must have been deleted at the end of the seventh gathering, not only because there are but two voices of *Ad cenam agni* but also because folio 77 is not the complement to folio 70. It bears the anchor watermark and therefore belongs in the eighth gathering. This gathering is also incomplete, although the deletion appears at the beginning, directly following the gap at the end of gathering 7. The recto of folio 77, in fact, starts with the tenor and contratenor of "Qui tollis" (from the GLORIA) of Ockeghem's *Quinti toni* Mass. (The KYRIE is at the end.) The folio missing from the end of gathering 7 probably contained the other voices of *Ad cenam agni* on the recto side and the superius of Ockeghem's "Et in terra" on the verso. The missing folio at the beginning of the eighth gathering presumably contained the contratenor and

21. The gathering contains only four sheets (i.e. eight folios), but in the binding one of them, corresponding to folios 73 and 74, was placed on top instead of next to the bottom.

tenor of the "Et in terra" and the superius of "Qui tollis" on recto and verso respectively. The last of the Busnois motets in the eighth gathering continues on the first recto of the ninth, this time, however, apparently recopied from a previous gathering, for it is in a hand different not only from what follows it but also from the first part of the same motet.

The ninth gathering, containing the anonymous *Missa Sine nomine,* may have been written in close conjunction with the tenth, for the *Missa Pour quelque paine* of the tenth gathering begins on the last verso of the ninth, and is written by the same hand. The last two gatherings, which contain Dufay's *Missa Ave Regina* and Regis' *Missa Ecce ancilla — Ne timeas,* were evidently added separately, with no overlapping or filling in at the ends and beginnings of gatherings. The first recto of the Dufay gathering is blank, while the last verso reveals the relatively rare case of grouping all four voices of the last AGNUS on one side of a folio. The first recto of the Regis gathering contains an unrelated discant part of an AGNUS DEI and the monophonic hymn *Vexilla regis.*

It seems as though the manuscript could not have been compiled over a very long period of time, since the same paper and similar, if not identical, handwriting reappears toward the end of the book in those gatherings which are among the latest additions. The compositions may be divided into four categories, however, on the basis of their positions in the manuscript. First there are those which were clearly written as a group and formed the original nucleus of the manuscript (the Masses of Frye, Cockx, and Pseudo-Binchois). A second group is comprised of those large works which fill the major parts of gatherings by themselves and were, in all probability, added to the manuscript one by one (the two Magnificats, Dufay's *Missa Ecce ancilla,* and the Masses of Ockeghem, Heyns, and the anonymous composer). A third group may be formed by those short compositions which were added to fill in the blank spaces between gatherings (the Busnois motets and hymn). The fourth group consists of the two Masses which fill entire gatherings, like those of the second group, but which are not followed by short compositions at the ends or between the gatherings (Dufay's *Missa Ave Regina* and Regis' *Missa Ecce ancilla*).

This grouping reveals an obvious chronological order in the compilation of the manuscript. There was first the nucleus, then the second group, then the compositions of Busnois—which occupy spaces between gatherings of both the first two groups— and finally the late Masses of Dufay and Regis, which seem to have been added subsequently to the entering of the Busnois compositions.

The Masses in the earliest part of the manuscript, those by Frye, Cockx, and Pseudo-Binchois, are almost certainly of an earlier date than those of Dufay and Regis. They all show specific evidence of English origin. Nothing is known about the composer Ricquardus Cockx, although Striels claims that he was a pupil of Barbireau at Antwerp.[22] Van den Borren questions this, because De Burbure makes no mention of such a composer in his research on the archives of the Antwerp cathedral.[23] It seems likely that Cockx, like Frye, was English, for the Mass by Cockx in BR 5557 and Frye's *Missa Nobilis et pulchra* both use the KYRIE trope, *Deus creator omnium,* which was an English favorite for polyphonic settings as well as plainsong performance. There are four KYRIES using this trope in the Trent codices (three anonymous and one by the English composer Benet). No. 404 (Trent 88) is that of the *Missa Veterem hominem,* which appears separate from the remaining movements of the Mass (Nos. 199, 200, 201, and 202). The KYRIE of Dufay's *Caput* Mass also uses the same trope and is also preserved separately in Trent 88 (see below, p. 66). Bukofzer has suggested that the only movement of Dufay's *Caput* Mass to be written independently of the English tradition was the KYRIE, because omission of the KYRIE was characteristic of English polyphonic Mass Ordinaries.[24] Yet it was equally characteristic to include a KYRIE so lavishly troped that it became one of the longest movements of the Mass. Those of *Veterem hominem* [25]

22. G. Striels, "De Zangkapel van de Kathedral van Antwerpen," *Musica Sacra* (Flemish edition), *41* (1934), 37.
23. *Etudes,* p. 208.
24. *Studies,* p. 258, n. 90.
25. Laurence Feininger, ed., *Monumenta Polyphoniae Liturgicae Sanctae Ecclesiae Romanae, Ordinarium Missae* (Rome, 1951), ser. 1, tomus 2, 1.

and Dufay's *Caput* are longer than the GLORIAS, while Frye's is the longest of the entire Mass. Of the remaining Masses from this first section of BR 5557, the other two by Frye omit the KYRIE, while that of Pseudo-Binchois uses the trope *Omnipotens pater.*

All three of Frye's Masses are cyclic, with a recurrent tenor *cantus firmus* appearing in all movements. The tenor of his *Missa Summe Trinitati* is a responsory, and is to be found in the Sarum usage.[26] That of his *Missa Nobilis et pulchra* is also a responsory (for St. Catherine of Alexandria), and similarly is to be found in Sarum Antiphonals and choir Breviaries.[27] The other two Masses from this older portion of BR 5557 are not in cyclic form. The tenors do not recur in the other movements, and they have not been identified with any known liturgical melodies.

Another feature which seems to have been characteristically English, and which is common to all the Masses of the early part of BR 5557, is the omission of certain parts of the CREDO text. The CREDOS of two of Frye's Masses, *Nobilis et pulchra* and *Summe Trinitati,* are considerably abbreviated, coming to an end with the words "non erit finis," with varying parts of the preceding text omitted. The other Masses, and also the anonymous Mass of folio 90v, leave out different sections, but all conclude with the final: "Et vitam venturi saeculi." Dom Anselm Hughes thinks that this practice may have been a later development of the procedure followed by Dunstable of "telescoping" the text in such a way that consecutive parts of the text are sung simultaneously in order to shorten the musical setting.[28] This arrangement is found in many of the CREDO settings of the Old Hall manuscript (Damett, folio 60v; Lyonel, folio 70v; Swynford, folio 73v; and Typp, folio 74v). Hughes thinks that while Dunstable frequently set the lines "Et resurrexit" and "Et ascendit" simultaneously, later composers simply omitted the

26. W. H. Frere, ed., *Antiphonale Sarisburiense* (London, 1901–25), 2, 292, and 3, 572.

27. Oxford, Bodleian Library, Ms. 948 and London, British Museum Ms. Lansdowne 461. Facsimile of the Bodleian Ms. in Frere, *Antiphonale Sarisburiense,* Vol. 3, Plate X.

28. "Text Omissions in the Creed," introduction to *Missa "O quam suavis,"* ed. H. B. Collins (Burnham, 1927), p. xxxiii.

"Et ascendit." The fact that the Mass of "Johannes Dunstable Anglicanus" in the Bologna manuscript (Conservatorio G. B. Martini, Ms. Q 15) [29] reveals both telescoping and omission of other parts, however, suggests that the two traditions existed independently. A similar arrangement is seen in the Frye Mass *Flos regalis* of the Brussels manuscript, in which the text is written out fully only in the superius. The other voices merely have phrase incipits at periodic intervals. One of these incipits is for a section which is completely lacking from the superius text. Other deletions from the text are not accounted for by this type of implied telescoping.

Ruth Hannas, who has been particularly interested in this question, has advanced the theory that certain deletions were the result of the crusading fervor at the Burgundian court, while others are attributable to the revival of the Virgin cult during the fifteenth century.[30] Her explanation is based largely on developments which took place on the Continent, and therefore implies that English composers who set the Mass text were influenced by Continental attitudes. Yet these omissions occur most frequently in the works of English composers. Hughes has found that among fifty-five English Masses from the time of Dunstable to the end of the sixteenth century, only two contain complete CREDO texts.[31] The omissions varied considerably during the early period of polyphonic Masses, too much so, in fact, to permit as rigid an interpretation as Miss Hannas has given. Even up to the time of Henry VIII, English composers fairly generally adopted the practice of stopping after "non erit finis," and going on directly to "Et vitam" or to the "Amen." [32] Frye's *Missa Flos regalis* is among those that include "Et vitam."

W. K. Ford has taken issue with Miss Hannas' theory on other grounds. After giving a brief survey of the history of the Creed, he writes that:

> development tends to lengthen a creed rather than to shorten it, and thus the fundamental assumption of Dr. Hannas's theory, *viz.,* that the Mass creed was shortened, is

29. John Dunstable, *Works,* ed. Manfred Bukofzer, vol. 8 of *Musica Britannica* (London, 1953), No. 8.

30. "Concerning Deletions in the Polyphonic Mass Credo," p. 155.

31. "Sixteenth Century Service Music," *ML,* 5 (1924), 152.

32. Dom Anselm Hughes, "Chant versus Polyphony for a Thousand Years," *Musical Times 87* (December 1946), 363.

open to question. Moreover, I doubt whether any omission from any creed could be made, even in the Middle Ages, for purposes of conciliation; creeds, by their very nature are to serve as guides to orthodox beliefs, and the medieval Church stuck close to tradition—how else could it convict heresy? [33]

There seems to be no historical explanation of the CREDO deletions apart from musical practice. Hence it must be assumed that it was done for purely musical, or practical, reasons, and undoubtedly, as Hughes suggests, in order to shorten the musical setting. In any case, it is a practice which is identifiable primarily with works of English composers.

Another English characteristic found in the Masses of the oldest part of BR 5557 is seen in the handling of the AGNUS DEI. In all but one of them (Frye's *Flos regalis*) the first two words are omitted, and the polyphonic setting begins with "Qui tollis." The opening words were undoubtedly sung in plainchant, like those of the CREDO. While English practice in this respect is not clearly defined, it is fairly safe to attribute it to English liturgical traditions. Of the seventeen Agnus Dei settings in Old Hall, only three start the polyphonic version with "Agnus Dei" (Chirbury, f. 104v; Lyonel, f. 106; anon., f. 106v). In all the others, the words "Agnus Dei" are chanted. In the Trent codices, the settings attributed to Dunstable–Leonel and Bedingham are entirely polyphonic. The majority of those which appear with a plainsong intonation of "Agnus Dei" are anonymous. That they are probably the work of English composers is suggested by the fact that one of them (Trent codex 90, No. 963) is also found in an English manuscript, Cambridge, cod. Ii. V. 18 (fol. 251). The settings by Binchois, who had close affiliations with the English, invariably give the first two words in plainsong. It should be mentioned, however, that this feature is also found in the Mass of Arnold de Lantins published in *Polyphonia Sacra*. So far as we know, this composer had no connections whatsoever with the English.

Still another English technique, the practice of writing rests of one breve simultaneously in both voices of a duo section, is found in four of the Masses in the first section of BR 5557 as well as in the anonymous Mass on folio 90. While there are no such rests in the duos of the Pseudo-Binchois Mass, the two voices frequently come together on a cadence held for one breve. This device produces essentially the same result as the rests, for although there is no actual cessation of sound, there is a definite halt of the usual continuous rhythmic flow. Apel is at a loss to explain this strange interruption, but suggests that it may have had liturgical significance.[34] Bukofzer mentions it as a typically English device but does not explain it.[35] The fact that it occurs nearly always at the same points in the text does indeed imply a liturgical explanation. In the Frye Mass on *Nobilis et pulchra* it appears in all movements except the KYRIE, but its use in the SANCTUS and second AGNUS DEI is common to all of the Masses in this first section of BR 5557. It appears most consistently in the "Pleni sunt," just before the word "gloria." In the "Benedictus" it comes after the first word, before "qui venit," and also between "qui venit" and "in nomine." In the second AGNUS, the interruption occurs just before "qui tollis" and before "miserere." In the anonymous *Missa Sine nomine* on folio 90, the practice of writing a full breve rest alternates with the use of a double bar at these points. Full rests occur between "Benedictus" and "qui venit" and between "Agnus Dei" and "qui tollis." The double bar is used between "terrae" and "gloria" in the "Pleni sunt," between "venit" and "in nomine" of the "Benedictus," and before "miserere" of the second Agnus. In either case, the intention is the same—to bring both voices to a temporary halt. While this sort of pause seems somewhat logical from a textual point of view in the AGNUS DEI, the interruption of the phrases "Pleni sunt coeli et terrae gloria tua" and "Benedictus qui venit in nomine domini" is curious, to say the least, and certainly seems to imply an explanation outside the realm of aesthetic considerations.

Denis Stevens, in an article on a fourteenth-century music fragment found in an Exchequer book, points out that the text is broken at exactly the same places in these earlier English Mass sections. Stevens claims that "a rest of one measure is just sufficient to allow the lungs to be refilled with God's good air,

34. *The Notation of Polyphonic Music* (Cambridge, Mass., 1945), p. 118.
35. *Studies*, p. 188.

as our Exchequer clerks realized only too well." [36] Considering the length of some of the melodic lines in the works of Ockeghem, for example, it is difficult to believe that composers of the late fifteenth century were motivated by any such humane considerations for the welfare of the singers. Even other movements from Frye's own works show a fine disregard for the necessity of breathing, as can be seen by the discant part, measures 17–25, of the KYRIE in the *Missa Nobilis et pulchra*. These rests, in any event, have been found to be characteristic of English music. Possibly they represent a tradition peculiar to the Anglican liturgy.

From this survey of various features such as omission or troping of the KYRIE, intoning of the first words of the AGNUS DEI, deletions from the CREDO texts, and the use of simultaneous rests, it can be seen that the entire nucleus of BR 5557 was devoted to works by English composers. Where they were working, and how their works came to be included in a Burgundian manuscript are still unanswered questions. But it is possible to attach a fairly precise date to them by means of the other compositions in the manuscript, for there is pertinent information available with regard to the Masses of Dufay, and also in connection with Busnois' biography.

It is known that Dufay's *Missa Ecce ancilla* was copied at Cambrai in 1463, for in that year Simon Mellet was paid "pour avoir escript et notté es nouveaulx livres deux fois la messe que a fait M. G. du Fay sur ecce ancilla domini ct. XI feuilles." [37] The copy of this Mass in BR 5557 occupies exactly eleven folios of the fifth gathering. The other known copy of the Mass, in the codex 14 of the Sistine Chapel archives, also fills eleven folios, but it is thought that the manuscript was not copied before 1481. [38] It is very likely that the fifth gathering in BR 5557, then, is one of the copies made by Mellet in 1463. It clearly existed as a separate gathering at one time, for it is joined to the preceding gathering only by the motet of Busnois, copied in by a different hand, and it has no connection whatsoever with the gathering

---

36. "A Recently Discovered English Source of the 14th Century," *MQ, 41* (1955), 34, n. 20.

37. Houdoy, *Histoire artistique*, p. 194.

38. Franz X. Haberl, *Bibliographischer und thematischer Musikkatalog des päpstlichen Kapellarchives im Vatikan zu Rom* (Leipzig, 1888), pp. 6–7.

following it, for the last verso is blank. The date of this Dufay
Mass enables us to postulate at least a terminal date for the
composition of the English Masses in the Brussels manuscript.
Dufay's *Ecce ancilla* Mass was the first composition to be added
to the original manuscript, and, if it is indeed the copy made
by Mellet in 1463, the preceding compositions in BR 5557 were
probably composed and copied prior to that date.

The copy of Dufay's Mass was no doubt commissioned, and
most probably the commission came from Charles, the Count of
Charolais. The Duke of Burgundy himself, Philip the Good,
remained in or near Brussels in 1462 and 1463, but Charles was
around Cambrai on October 19–20 and December 21–22 of 1462,
and nearby at Quesnoy almost continually from January through
July of 1463.[39] This in itself would not be conclusive were it not
for the fact that Charles is known to have had close connections
with Dufay. It has been mentioned that Dufay may have given
Charles instruction in music. But more substantial proof is supplied by documents relating to Dufay's testament and to the
Missa Ave Regina, which also appears in BR 5557.

In the testament of Dufay, the following items appear as part
of the inventory:

> Pour six livres de diverses chanteries que avoit donnés le
> dit deffunct à tres-excellent prince M. S. le duc de
> Bourgogne ad cause que ce don fut fait en son vivant et
> n'avoit retenu que l'usance d'iceulx n'ont point esté prises
> et pour ce icy . . . riens.[40]

In connection with this part of Dufay's testament, Houdoy also
lists the package of books sent to Charles at Doullens at the time
of Dufay's death in 1474 as follows:

> I petit livre en vermeille couverture à agrape de keuvre;—
> item, IIII livres d'une grandeur de diverses chanteries;—
> item I petit livre de chansons;—item I livre des louanges de
> musique et la messe *Ave Regina caelorum.*[41]

39. Herman Vander Linden, *Itinéraires de Philippe le Bon, Duc de Bourgogne
(1419–1467) et de Charles, Comte de Charolais (1433–1467)* (Brussels, 1940), years
1462–63.

40. Houdoy, *Histoire artistique,* p. 268.

41. Ibid., p. 88.

The relationship between these two excerpts from the archives of Cambrai is not quite clear, for Houdoy does not indicate the exact origin of the latter. The first book, however, the "petit livre en vermeille," is not specified as music. Neither does the "louanges de musique" belong in the category of "chanteries." The six remaining items then—"IIII livres . . . de diverses chanteries," the "petit livre de chansons," and "la messe *Ave Regina caelorum*"—might certainly have been the six books of "diverses chanteries" referred to in the testament, as Houdoy infers. It is tempting to accept the theory that the *Ave Regina* Mass was among those works which were written and given to Charles earlier but sent to him only at the time of Dufay's death, for its position at the end of BR 5557, clearly as a separate addition but on the same kind of paper as the first part of the manuscript, would tend to confirm such a hypothesis. It is known to have been copied by Simon Mellet in 1473,[42] and could very well have been added at about the same time as the last gathering of the manuscript, which follows it and contains the Mass of Regis written on paper of a somewhat later date than the rest of the manuscript (1474). A close relationship between these two composers is to be expected, since Regis worked as Dufay's secretary at Cambrai from 1463–74.[43]

Another aspect of the Brussels manuscript which serves to link it with Charles the Bold is the position of the Busnois works. The predominance of Busnois' religious compositions is striking, for in no other manuscript is so large a group of his sacred works gathered together. (The Cambrai codex of 1475, which contained compositions of the Mass, Magnificat, and Lamentations by Busnois, is mentioned in the archives of Cambrai, but it has never been found.[44] Practically nothing is known about the early life of Busnois except for the fact that he probably came from Artois, near Hainaut.[45] The fact that he served in the Burgundian chapel until at least 1481 is proven

42. Ibid., p. 200.

43. C. W. H. Lindenburg, *Het leven en de werken van Johannes Regis* (Amsterdam, 1938), p. 4.

44. See Houdoy, *Histoire artistique*, pp. 84, 201.

45. C. L. W. Boer, *Het Anthonius-Motet van Anthonius Busnois* (Amsterdam, 1940), p. 7.

by the register of accounts. The information relative to his service with Charles before 1467 is provided by his own motet *In hydraulis* (see above, p. 16). In the light of this known fact, the position of the Busnois motets in the Brussels manuscript assumes considerable importance. These works could not have been entered in the manuscript any earlier than 1463, for one of them, the *Anthoni usque limina,* appears as a "filler" between the original section of the manuscript and Dufay's *Ecce ancilla* (which was copied only in 1463). Most of the Busnois compositions were copied in the same hand, and presumably at the same time. This suggests that the occasion for the sudden appearance of so many of his works in the Brussels manuscript was Busnois' own sudden appearance in the chapel of Charles in about 1463 or 1464.

The gathering which contains Busnois' Magnificat is quite distinct from the rest of the manuscript, and even from the other works of Busnois. It bears a different watermark, the handwriting appears nowhere else in the manuscript, and the practice of writing all the voice parts on the same folio is peculiar to this gathering (save for the end of Dufay's *Ave Regina* Mass, where it was obviously done merely to save paper). These factors seem to indicate that the Magnificat was composed at a slightly earlier date and that the gathering was added to BR 5557 only after Busnois entered the service of Charles. His other compositions were probably written during his service with the Count of Charolais. Thus they may be dated fairly precisely, between 1463 and 1467.

All the evidence taken together makes it appear quite certain that this Brussels manuscript did belong to Charles, and not to Philip, and that it was started sometime before 1463, but probably not very much earlier. With the exception of the last two gatherings, which were probably added only at the time of Dufay's death in 1474, the rest of the manuscript was probably the work of musicians associated with the chapel of the Count of Charolais. Frye, Cockx, Pseudo-Binchois, and the anonymous composer might all have been attached to Charles' own retinue.

It is possible that Cornelius Heyns, too, was a singer in Charles' chapel. The only biographical facts known about Heyns are that he was "maître de chant" at St. Donatien in Bruges in

1452 and again from 1462 to 1465.[46] There is no record of his ever having served the Dukes of Burgundy, but Van den Borren suggests a possible identification of Heyns with Hayne van Ghizeghem, who is known to have been a member of the Burgundian chapel intermittently and to have received his first payment in 1457 from the accounts of Charles.[47]

The presence of Ockeghem's *Quinti toni* Mass in BR 5557 is a little puzzling. This inclusion cannot be so easily explained by the assumption that the composer was a member of Charles' chapel, because Ockeghem was already in the service of King Charles VII of France by 1452, when Charles of Burgundy was only nineteen years of age. It is doubtful that there was much exchange of music or musicians between the King of France and either Charles or Philip during the 'fifties, for their political relations were becoming more and more strained. Hence it is not likely that Ockeghem's Mass should have come into the hands of Charles directly from the chapel royal of France. It may have come from the Duke of Bourbon, whom Ockeghem served from 1446 to 1448, since Charles' first marriage in 1454 was to Isabelle of Bourbon. The paper on which the Ockeghem *Quinti toni* Mass is written is also of a different type from the largest part of the Brussels manuscript, and it may be that its inclusion was due to entirely external circumstances. Possibly it was brought by Isabelle herself, and only added to the existing corpus at a later date. For various reasons, however, this explanation is not wholly satisfactory.

The Ockeghem Mass raises some questions which are related to the larger issues of the manuscript and of the period as a whole. Certain features of this particular Mass imply a common origin with the English Masses in BR 5557, specifically the position of the KYRIE at the end of the Mass. Admittedly the mass is preserved in a fragmentary form in BR 5557. The AGNUS DEI is lacking, and the first part of the GLORIA is also missing. But the placing of the KYRIE at the end can not be laid to misbinding or to any of the other hazards that beset com-

46. A. C. de Schrevel, *Histoire du Séminaire de Bruges* (Bruges, 1895), pp. 155, 157.

47. Marix, *Histoire de la musique*, pp. 205–06.

pilers of manuscripts. It must have been deliberately copied that way, since the KYRIE begins on the verso of the folio which contains the concluding portion of the SANCTUS. This suggests that the Mass was written originally in the English tradition, without the KYRIE, or that the KYRIE was placed at the end for optional use.

Manfred Bukofzer has pointed out a similar situation in regard to the *Caput* Mass of Ockeghem, in which the KYRIE stands distinctly apart from the other four movements. It has the same *cantus firmus*, but the motto beginning which links the other movements is lacking from the KYRIE. In his *Studies in Medieval and Renaissance Music*, published in 1950, Bukofzer attributed this to the influence of English Mass settings.[48] Shortly afterward, however, when he had found an English source for the AGNUS DEI of Dufay's *Caput* Mass, Bukofzer revised his views and concluded that it was only Dufay who had been subjected to English influence—that Ockeghem merely used Dufay's Mass as a model and hence was only indirectly affected by English practices. The KYRIE of Dufay's Mass is known to have existed apart from the rest of the Mass, and Bukofzer suggests that Ockeghem may have been acquainted with only the last four movements of Dufay's *Missa Caput*.[49] This may be true in the case of the *Caput* Mass, but the appearance of Ockeghem's *Quinti toni* Mass in BR 5557 suggests that he was influenced independently by the same tradition. There are, furthermore, certain stylistic features which relate the Ockeghem Mass to those of Frye, and particularly to the *Missa Summe Trinitati*, since both of these Masses are written entirely in tempus imperfectum. Duple time was rarely used for an entire Mass composition as early as the middle of the fifteenth century.

Bukofzer's recent findings with regard to the English composers of the mid-fifteenth century have considerable bearing on this study in general. Most significant is his discovery of the *Caput* melody in a Sarum Gradual. The implication that there was an English model for the polyphonic *Caput* Masses of Dufay, Ockeghem, and Obrecht suggests that English Masses of the 1450s and 1460s were of more importance to the Netherlands

48. Page 279.
49. "Caput Redivivum," *JAMS*, 4 (1951), 105.

composers than has hitherto been thought. The KYRIE of Dufay's *Caput* Mass was copied at Cambrai in 1463, the same year as his *Ecce ancilla* of BR 5557, and, like the Masses of Frye and Cockx, uses the trope *Deus creator omnium*. Bukofzer called attention to various other English features of the *Caput* Masses which are also characteristic of the Masses in BR 5557—e.g. the simultaneous breve rests in both voices in duo sections of Ockeghem's *Caput* Mass and omissions of certain parts of the CREDO text—and the many points of contact between the Brussels English Masses and the *Caput* Masses are significant. The hypothetical English *Caput* Mass must have been composed before 1463, at about the same time as the Masses by Frye, Cockx, and Pseudo-Binchois. Possibly it was the work, if not of Frye or Cockx, at least of one of the composers in this group associated with the Count of Charolais. Charles' court indeed appears to have been a central point of contact between English and Continental composers in the third quarter of the fifteenth century, and this Brussels manuscript, containing the repertory of his chapel, seems to reflect the chronology of the international stylistic merger which was taking place at that time.

CHAPTER 4

The Motets and Chansons

A. *The Continental Sources*

IT IS CUSTOMARY to discuss chansons and motets under separate
headings. They belong in distinctly different spheres, and this
differentiation is generally reflected in the musical style. The
sources of Frye's works, however, reveal a certain amount of
confusion with regard to these two categories. His chansons are
unquestionably real chansons, but some of his motets belong to
that hybrid species known as the "chanson motet." The term
"chanson motet" is one which has been applied by modern historians to a motet which appears to have been written in the
style of a chanson. Such a composition by itself is indistinguish-
able from another type—the contrafactum, in which a Latin
sacred text has been substituted for the vernacular, secular
poem for which the music was originally written. These two
forms, the chanson motet and the contrafactum, are stylistically
identified with the chanson and are frequently found in chansonniers. They will therefore be discussed in conjunction with
the secular songs.

Walter Frye's chansons and motets, unlike his Masses, made
their way into a large number of Continental manuscripts, and
with various changes of text. The two principal sources, however, are the Mellon chansonnier,[1] which contains the three
English ballades and the French rondeau, and the Schedel Liederbuch,[2] which contains all the motets but *Sospitati dedit* and

1. Yale University, Beinicke Library.
2. Munich, Bayerische Staatsbibliothek, codex 810 (Cim 315ᵃ; Mus. 3232; Schedel
Liederbuch).

the questionable *Salve Virgo mater*. Both *Sospitati dedit*, an authentic English motet, and *Salve Virgo mater* use *cantus firmi*, but none of the motets in Schedel's book show a trace of *cantus firmus* treatment.

A comparison of these two main sources of Frye's motets and chansons immediately brings to light a feature of the copying of Frye's music which not only explains the absence of a *cantus firmus* in the motets but also has considerable significance for the investigation of English works in foreign manuscripts in general. Schedel includes among the works attributed to one "Frey" a motet *O sacrum convivium*. But it appears that this piece is not a bona fide motet. It is not even a chanson motet. It is simply a contrafactum of the chanson *Alas, alas* in the Mellon chansonnier.

Alas, alas is not the only English ballade in the Mellon manuscript to be converted into a motet. All three of them appear eventually as chanson motets, although the other two pass through intermediate incarnations as French ballades. *So ys emprentid* and *Myn hertis lust* both appear consecutively in the manuscripts Escorial IV a 24, Pixérécourt, and Florence 176, with the English texts discarded in favor of French ballades—*Pour une suis desconforté* and *Grant temps*.[3] Both pieces are attributed to Bedingham in the Florence manuscript, although the English form of the latter, *Myn hertis lust,* is anonymous in Mellon and had been tentatively ascribed to Frye by Bukofzer on stylistic grounds. In Trent 90, where there is a whole series of motet contrafacta which are labeled with their original French incipits, these two ballades appear again, this time as *Sancta Maria succurre* and *Beata es*.[4] *Beata es* has the French incipit given, although *Sancta Maria succurre* does not. Thus we know not only that a considerable number of chanson motets in Trent are actually contrafacta but also that at least three such motets of the mid-fifteenth-century repertory can be traced back to English models:

3. See Sylvia W. Kenney, "Contrafacta in the Works of Walter Frye," *JAMS, 8* (1955), 184–86.

4. *Sancta Maria succurre* appears twice, as No. 990, with text, and No. 1029, textless. *Beata es* is No. 1140.

ENGLISH	FRENCH	LATIN	
Mellon	Escorial Pixérécourt, and Florence 176	Trent 90	Schedel
Myn hertis lust	*Grant temps*	*Beata es*	
So ys emprentid	*Pour une suis desconforté*	*Sancta Maria succurre*	
Alas, alas			*O sacrum convivium*

The process of text substitution seems clearly to have been from English to French to Latin. There is of course no question about the priority of the French texts in the Trent motets where they are so plainly labeled. But it is also apparent, for several reasons, that the English versions of Mellon preceded the French ones. Obviously French scribes would have been far more likely to substitute French for English texts than vice versa at a time when the English language was hardly well-known on the Continent. One Continental scribe, in fact, made a valiant attempt to make the words "So ys emprentid" into French, for the piece appears in the Laborde chansonnier and the Monte Cassino manuscript 871 as *Soyez aprantiz.* Once over this initial hurdle, however, the unfortunate scribe was at a loss for further "transliterations" and had to content himself with merely inserting chivalric phrases such as "ma belle dame" here and there. But on stylistic grounds also there seem to be good reasons for assuming that the music, at least that of *Alas, alas,* was written originally for that particular English text. The sequential treatment of the lines "For peyne" and "and woo [woe]" and then again for "the more long" and "the more byting" has considerable significance for the English poem but none at all for the substitute text.[5]

One interesting aspect of the contrafactum question is the

5. The text reading is according to Robert J. Menner, "Three Fragmentary English Ballades in the Mellon Chansonnier," *Modern Language Quarterly, 6* (1945), 381. The relationship of text and music is not apparent in the transcription published by Bukofzer in *MQ, 28* (1942), 42. Bukofzer has misread the text, and he has not followed the exact placing of the words as they appear under the music in the manuscript.

fact that so many of them are ballades. The ballade form is rather suspect in a way because it was so out of date on the Continent by the middle of the fifteenth century. Dufay's ballades all date from his early period, and Busnois' only ballade setting is also his only Flemish piece, *In mijne sin*, which is preserved in a single source with only the text incipit.[6] English composers, on the other hand, seem to have remained attached to this form. In addition to the Mellon English songs there is one other known English-texted piece in contemporary Continental manuscripts, *The Princesse of Youth*.[7] *The Princesse* is a ballade, and so also apparently is the two-voiced textless piece attributed to "Watlin Frew" in the Prague codex.[8] Still another ballade which turns out to be by an English composer is the Italian *Gentil madonna*, which appears between Frye's *So ys emprentid* and *Myn hertis lust* in Mellon. Plamenac has identified *Gentil madonna* with the chanson *Fortune élas*, which is attributed to Bedingham in the Schedel Liederbuch.[9]

The practice of fairly systematic text-substitution appears to have been an eminently logical one at the time. While English music was enjoying great favor abroad in the mid-fifteenth century, neither the English texts nor the archaic ballade forms could have been particularly well-received. The only one of Frye's secular pieces to pursue a Continental career unmolested was, significantly, his only non-ballade form, the rondeau *Tout a par moy*, which has survived intact in nine extant manuscripts. (The slight deviation of "Tant apart" in the Buxheimer Orgelbuch can be laid to a German scribe's ignorance of French.) The text of *Tout a par moy*, moreover, appears in the *Jardin de plaisance* and the Rohan chansonnier, while the ballade texts are not to be found there. They may have been drawn from an earlier source, no longer currently used.

The Latin texts inserted in Frye's ballades are among those which were widely known and not limited to one particular

6. Catherine Brooks, "Antoine Busnois, Chanson Composer," *JAMS, 6* (1953), 114.

7. Manfred Bukofzer, "The First English Chanson on the Continent," *ML, 19* (1938), 119.

8. Dragan Plamenac, "Browsing Through a Little-Known Manuscript," 104–07.

9. Dragan Plamenac, "A Reconstruction of the French Chansonnier," *MQ, 38* (1952), 246.

66   THE MANUSCRIPT SOURCES OF COMPOSITIONS

usage.[10] Two of them are antiphons to the *Magnificat*.[11] One of these *Magnificat* antiphons, *Sancta Maria succurre,* appears in both Roman and Sarum books, but the Sarum version, which is used in the Frye piece, is an abbreviated one. It was a popular text during the middle years of the fifteenth century; there are, in the Trent codices, several polyphonic settings of it, one of which is by Dunstable and also has the shorter Sarum form. The scribe of Trent 90 may have drawn on the Dunstable motet when he inserted the text in the Frye chanson. In any case, all three of these texts must have been easily available to scribes, either through liturgical books or through other polyphonic settings.

The insertion of Latin motet texts in the ballades alters the musical structure only insofar as the repetition of the first half is eliminated; the form becomes simply AB instead of AA'B. The open and close endings of the first part had been a characteristic feature of the musical ballade form, and in fact one fifteenth-century source distinguishes the three chanson types, ballade, rondeau, and virelai, solely on the basis of these endings. A newly-discovered manuscript containing a Benedictine regula from ca. 1440 has also a musical tract which defines the ballade specifically as having open and close endings "in primo versu," the virelai as having them "in secundo versu," and the rondeau as not having them in either.[12] Originally the first ending was a substantial musical section which was omitted from the repetition (A') in favor of the second. But in the period of

10. One of these texts even varies considerably in its liturgical function. *Beata es* is given as a chapter in a Sarum Devotional (J. H. Blunt, ed., *The Myroure of Oure Ladye* [London, 1873], p. 155); as a combination of two antiphons in the *Liber Usualis* (Tournai, 1934), p. 1686; and as a responsory in the *Processionale Monasticum* (Solesme, 1893), p. 260.

11. *O sacrum convivium* is an antiphon to the Magnificat for the Feast of Corpus Christi and is found in both Roman and Sarum usage. See W. G. Henderson, ed., *Processionale ad usum insignis ac praeclarae Ecclesiae Sarum* (Leeds, 1882), p. 128. It was used frequently for polyphonic settings. There are several anonymous fifteenth-century motets on this text, based on the chant: Rome, Capella Sistina cod. 14, fol. 143; Trent 88, No. 489 (the thematic index in *DTO*, 7, is misleading, for it omits the intonation which has the first nine notes of the chant); and the Glogauer Liederbuch, No. 27 (erroneously entitled *O sacrum mysterium*). *Sancta Maria succurre* is also a Magnificat antiphon in both Roman and Sarum usage. See Blunt, *The Myroure of Oure Ladye*, p. 203, Frere, *Antiphonale Sarisburiense, 3, 530,* and *Antiphonale Sacrosanctae Romanae Ecclesiae* (Rome, 1912), p. [82].

12. University of Pennsylvania Library, Ms. lat. 36, fol. 207°.

the Frye ballades the "ouvert" ending was sometimes treated as no more than a kind of half cadence with fermata indicating the point at which their performers should go back to the beginning. In these cases, no music is skipped when A is repeated; both open and close endings are sung. Frye's ballades, as well as *The Princesse of Youth,* are all constructed in this fashion. Disregarding the repeat sign, then, does not constitute a serious abuse, since the musical line is in no way distorted. The music, if simply sung straight through as it appears in the manuscript, is that of A'B. Thus there was no problem for the scribes when they substituted Latin texts which were not in the form of A A'B. They merely ignored the implied repetition and reduced the musical form, quite legitimately, to a through-composed form.

Any doubt that both open and close endings are to be sung in the second A of these ballades is dispelled by a comparison of the A and B sections. One of the characteristic features of the ballade is a musical rhyme between the first and second sections. In fifteenth-century ballades this rhyme frequently begins well before the "ouvert" ending, and since the music returns in the B section with both "ouvert" and "clos" included, the repetition of A is unquestionably to be sung in the same fashion. This recurrent section, when it becomes as long as eight or nine measures, ceases to be merely a musical rhyme and partakes rather of the character of a refrain. The two sections, A and B, may be subdivided therefore, and the resultant form is A (x y) B (z y). These refrains, varying from five to nine measures in length, appear in all of the English ballades under discussion, including the three from the Mellon chansonnier, *The Princesse of Youth,* and the textless piece in the Prague codex.

From the standpoint of musical structure, Frye's famous *Ave Regina,* which has long been regarded as the typical chanson motet, now begins to look very suspicious. This composition gives every indication of being a contrafactum, especially in view of what is now known about the fate of Frye's other English-texted chansons. The *Ave Regina* appears, with *O sacrum convivium,* in the Schedel Liederbuch. The association in this manuscript is noteworthy, since it is the Schedel Liederbuch which gives the only attributions of both these compositions to Frye, and we now know that one of them is not a bona fide motet but a transformed ballade. Wolfgang Stephan, who first called attention to this chanson motet and pointed out that it was the model for Obrecht's motet and Mass on *Ave Regina,* thought it probable that the tenor was based on a chorale melody.[13] Frye's tenor, however, is not the liturgical melody associated with this text. Furthermore, the particular phrase with which the tenor melody begins was one extensively used in the chanson repertory of the fifteenth century. Jeppesen also describes it as "Gregorian-influenced" when he gives a list of examples of similar phrases in the secular songs of Binchois, Caron, Dunstable, Molinet, Ockeghem, and even from Bedingham's (Frye's?) *Grant temps.*[14] Nevertheless, the tenor is not, by any possible stretch of the imagination, identifiable with a chorale melody, and the triadic formula which appears so frequently is more likely a feature of the English style. It was undoubtedly freely composed by Frye, and most probably for a secular song, since the use of a *cantus firmus* was foreign to the chanson tradition. What is most striking about this *Ave Regina,* however, is the fact that its form is identical with that of the English ballades when, in their motet guises, the repetition of the A section is disregarded. A comparison in terms of measures of the *Ave Regina* with the other ballades shows an exactly parallel refrain structure:

	A		B	
	x	y	z	y
Ave Regina	12	9	14	9
Myn hertis lust	12	7	16	7
So ys emprentid	12	7	20	7
Alas, alas	17	4	24	4
The Princesse of Youth	13	9	18	9
Textless piece in the Prague codex	15	5	18	5

When the repetition of A is eliminated by the insertion of Latin texts, there is, of course, no longer any significance to the "ouvert" ending. Nevertheless the half cadence is still there in the music, even if it is not functional. And in the *Ave Regina* there is a clear suggestion of such a vestigial "ouvert" ending at measure 15. The seven-measure "clos" ending which follows is

13. Wolfgang, Stephan, *Die Burgundisch-niederländische Motette,* p. 53, n.
14. *Der Kopenhagener Chansonnier* (Leipzig, 1927), "Einleitung," p. xxi.

rather long, but not impossibly so; that of *The Princesse of Youth* is even longer (eight measures).

The phrase structure of the entire *Ave Regina*, moreover, is very closely related to that of the ballades. In all of the Mellon ballades there is a final cadence at the end of the first line of text, a little less than half way through the first section (m. 9 of *Alas, alas;* m. 7 of *Myn hertis lust;* m. 8 of *So ys emprentid*). This cadence appears in the *Ave Regina* at measure 8. The *Ave Regina* also has in common with *Alas, alas* a half cadence with fermata after the first few bars (mm. 4 and 5 respectively). Musically, then, this Marian motet is identical in form with the English ballades which became motets, and the similarity speaks strongly for a secular origin of the *Ave Regina* as well.

One thing that differentiates the *Ave Regina* from the known contrafacta of Frye chansons is the fact that in some sources the third and fourth lines of text are repeated at the end to correspond with the recurrence of musical material. The complete six-line text is as follows:

x	Ave, Regina coelorum
	Mater regis angelorum
y	O Maria, flos virginum
	Velut rosa vel lilium
z	Funde preces ad filium
	Pro salute fidelium.

The second part of the music starts with "Funde preces" and at the conclusion the two lines: "O Maria, flos virginum,/ Velut rosa vel illium" are sung again, with the result that both musical and textual forms are x y z y. It has been suggested that this form is an example of responsorial structure.[15] Since it was customary to repeat the last part of a plainsong responsory after the verse, composers of the sixteenth century adopted the practice of using both responsory and verse and including this repetition in the polyphonic settings, with the resultant x y z y form of text and music. The *Ave Regina,* however, is not commonly found as a responsory and verse. It is given in the Sarum Processional and, with a long list of sources, in Chevalier's *Reper-*

15. Gustave Reese, *Music in the Renaissance*, p. 94.

torium Hymnologicum as an antiphon,[16] and it is included as a shorter antiphon among the formulas for grace after dinner in the York Primer.[17]

The confusion about the nature of this text arises from a statement by Mone, who calls it first a responsory and then an antiphon. After discussing another Marian chant, *Ave coelorum regina,* Mone says: "Ein Responsorium auf diese Antiphone steht in einer Hs. des 14. Jahr. zu Lichtenthal und lautet also:

> Ave, regina coelorum
> Mater regis angelorum

Mone gives the complete text and then continues: "Die marianische Antiphone *Ave regina coelorum* wird in den Vespern von der Complete der Lichtmesse bis zum grünen Donnerstag gesungen." [18] In any case, the settings of this particular text do not seem to be related to the sixteenth-century responsorial settings. Adrian Willaert, who is best known for polyphonic responsories using the refrain structure, also set this *Ave Regina,* but he did not treat it as a responsory.[19]

The repetition of text, moreover, does not occur in all the sources of the *Ave Regina.* Admittedly, text placing in fifteenth-century manuscripts leaves a good deal to be desired and cannot be taken as a completely reliable criterion. But neither can it be totally disregarded. The wide variation in text underlay in this one composition, in fact, suggests not only that there was no inherent connection between musical and liturgical form but that the text did not really belong to that music in the first place. Of the eleven texted versions of the *Ave Regina,* only five have the third and fourth lines repeated. These are Laborde, Schedel, Trent (no. 1013), Florence, Riccardiana 2794, and Speciálník, none of which is a primary source for Frye's work. Laborde has *So ys emprentid* already transformed to *Soyez aprantiz;* Schedel has *Alas, alas* changed to *O sacrum convivium;* Trent has contrafacta of *So ys emprentid* and *Myn hertis lust,* the Florence manuscript is obviously a later source—containing

16. (Brussels, 1892–1921), No. 2072.
17. Richard L. Greene, *The Early English Carols,* p. lxxxv.
18. Franz J. Mone, *Hymni Latini medii aevi* (Freiburg im Breisgau, 1854), 2, 202.
19. Adrian Willaert, *Opera omnia,* eds., H. Zenck and W. Gerstenberg (American Institute of Musicology, 1950–), 2, 35, Motet No. 6.

works by Josquin, Agricola, and Compère—and Speciálník a peripheral one. A comparison of these sources also shows the normal variation of text placing to be expected in manuscripts of this period. Trent, No. 1013, for example, has the words "pro salute fidelium" repeated as well as the third and fourth lines.

The other six sources reveal as many different ways of underlaying the text. In Perugia, for example, the text is completely confused, an Alleluia is added at the end, and the "Funde preces" begins before the *secunda pars* of the music. Florence 112 bis, one of the earliest manuscripts, repeats only the final word "Fidelium." Wolfenbüttel merely extends the last two lines over the whole *secunda pars*. The scribe of Trent No. 1086 evidently found the whole problem very troublesome, for he had already written "ad fili," then thought better of it when he saw how little text he had to fit with the remaining music, and moved the phrase "ad filium" on to a further point. He was obliged nevertheless to spin out the final "fidelium" for a long melisma. Obviously this particular text is too short for the music, and all the manuscripts reflect the attempt to adapt it either by repetition or by excessive melismata. Had the music originally been set to an eight-line ballade, the discrepancy would be quite understandable, for obviously two more lines were needed than were provided by the six-line *Ave Regina*. The repetition of the third and fourth lines was most certainly an ingenious way of supplying the two additional lines. The problem of text length is not evident to the same extent in *O sacrum convivium, Beata es,* and *Sancta Maria succurre* because they are prose texts and therefore more flexible than the poetical Marian antiphon. But even in *O sacrum convivium* the text ends six measures before the music, and the final word "datur" is copied in again on the penultimate measure.

Certainly melismata at the ends of text lines were characteristic of ballade settings, especially for the "clos" ending of the *prima pars*. But here, oddly enough, the scribes who inserted Latin texts ran the text right up to the final cadence, thus expending it when they might well have conserved it. The text placing of the *Ave Regina* is handled in the same fashion as are those of the known contrafacta. The first two lines correspond to the first two of the hypothetical ballade text. But the third and fourth lines of the antiphon fall in the "ouvert" and "clos" endings, whereas the third and fourth lines of the ballade would be sung to the same music as the first two. Line 5 of the antiphon starts with the *secunda pars,* just as the fifth line of the ballade would begin, and the cadence at the end of it is appropriate to both texts. The sixth line brings the end of the antiphon text, and hence the repetition of the third and fourth.

While it is tempting, in view of the structure and text placing of the *Ave Regina,* to conclude that it too is a contrafactum, it must be admitted that the composition is preserved in thirteen sources with its Latin text or title, and no secular model seems to be forthcoming. At best one may conclude that a secular version was contained in a manuscript which is no longer extant. In the case of the usual French chansons which were converted into motets, the majority of sources have the authentic vernacular text, while there may be only one or two with the motet version.[20] But with the English songs, the situation is reversed; they appear only once, in the Mellon chansonnier, with English texts, and in numerous other manuscripts with either French or Latin texts. The metamorphoses through which Frye's chansons passed were undoubtedly due in part to Continental requirements, and since Latin forms were acceptable in French-, German-, Italian-, or Flemish-speaking countries, there is little reason to suppose that the original text would survive in more than one manuscript or be restored by other copyists. It would, then, have required but one motet-minded scribe to perpetuate Frye's composition as *Ave Regina.*

It may well have been the scribe of the Florence manuscript 112 bis who was responsible for making the piece into a motet. There are many Marian motets in this manuscript, some based upon chant melodies and others not. On folio 24' there is an *Ave Regina I.*[21] It is lavishly troped and does not use the chant. It is followed by another *Ave Regina I* (Dunstable's), which is

20. Helen Hewitt and Isabel Pope, eds., *Harmonice musices Odhecaton A* (Cambridge, Mass., 1946), "The Significance of the Literary Texts," pp. 39–40.

21. The designations *"Ave Regina I"* and *"Ave Regina II"* will be used hereafter to differentiate the two texts. The first will refer to the more common antiphon, "Ave regina coelorum,/Ave domina angelorum," while the second will indicate the text used in Frye's famous chanson-motet, "Ave regina coelorum,/Mater regis angelorum."

based on the chant melody. The next folio contains Frye's *Ave Regina II*, which is followed by another *Ave Regina II*, also without the chant. Then, further on in the manuscript, are to be found *Gaude Maria, Salve Regina,* and *Regina coeli laetare* (Dunstable's). The scribe was obviously interested in Marian texts and might well have drawn on other forms than bona fide motets for the realization of his aims. Many of the compositions are, in fact, in the category of chanson motets.

Three of the sources for Frye's *Ave Regina* are notable for their inclusion of contrafacta: Trent 90, Glogauer, and Schedel. The Germans in particular indulged in the practice of substituting texts, both Latin and German, in French chansons, as is demonstrated by the presence in Glogauer and Trent of secular works of Busnois, Caron, Dufay, and Binchois, converted into motets. The chanson manuscripts from which Trent and Glogauer drew most heavily for the purpose of creating motets are Escorial IV a 24 (and to some extent also V 3 24), Pixérécourt, Florence 176, Porto 714, and Florence Riccardiana 2356, all of which contain works by English composers. The composition *Beata es* was probably taken from Florence 176 and not from the original English Mellon version, for the French text incipit is given as well as an attribution to Bedingham. Presumably *Sancta Maria succurre* was also drawn from Escorial, Pixérécourt, or Florence 176, and not from Laborde or Monte Cassino 871, because it follows the same pattern as *Myn hertis lust—Grant temps—Beata es*. In addition to works by Frye, Trent 90 also drew from Escorial and Pixérécourt, *Unicus dei filius* (Le Grant's *Las! Je ne puis);* and from Escorial alone, *Globus igneus* (Pyllois' *Quelquechose*) and *O Beata* (Anon. *De Madame*).

There were several routes along which the Frye chansons traveled. *So ys emprentid* and *Myn hertis lust* accompanied each other to Mellon, Escorial, Pixérécourt, and Florence 176, and thence to Trent 90. *Alas, alas* appears in Mellon but was not chosen by the scribes of Escorial, Pixérécourt, Florence, or Trent. It went instead to Schedel's Liederbuch, which seems to represent a different chain, even though it has some compositions in common with Trent 90. The *Ave Regina,* which appears in both Schedel and Trent 90, is not to be found in Mellon,

Escorial, Pixérécourt, Florence 176, nor in any of the other manuscripts from which French chansons were frequently taken and made into motets. Whatever the original text of the *Ave Regina* may have been, it may be that it was never given a French one, but was converted directly into Latin, like *Alas, alas,* at an early date in its Continental career. The *Ave Regina* traveled generally, though not exclusively, with Frye's *Tout a par moy.* They were both entered in Wolfenbüttel, Seville, Berlin, and Laborde as well as in the Buxheimer Orgelbuch. The scribes of these manuscripts were apparently less given to changing texts, and not even the French rondeau was turned into a motet in those sources.

Another explanation, and perhaps a more plausible one, for the ballade-like form of the *Ave Regina* is that the original secular song received its Latin text before it left England. The practice of singing Latin sacred texts to the music of secular songs was not by any means limited to the need for comprehensible words. Nor was it peculiar to the mainland, for it was widely practiced in England, probably for the same reasons that contrafacta of French chansons were made in France. Richard L. Greene, in his study of the English carol, writes:

> Interesting testimony as to the practice of writing sacred Latin words to fit the music of profane songs is given by the "Red Book of Ossory" in which are written, in a fourteenth-century hand, sixty Latin lyrics, several being preceded by lines of English and Anglo-Norman songs, to the tunes of which the Latin words were to be sung.[22]

There is a good deal of evidence, moreover, to suggest that this particular text, *Ave regina coelorum,* originated in England. Certainly it was a popular one for English polyphonic settings. There are two motets on this text in the Bodleian manuscript, Seldon B 26, and one in the Ritson manuscript (B.M. Addit. 5665). It was set by Binchois, who had close relationships with the English, and there is a two-voiced setting of this *Ave Regina* in the eleventh fascicle of W[1].[23] All its lines, furthermore, were used in macaronic carols by John Ryman (ca. 1492). In one

22. *The Early English Carols,* p. cxviii.
23. Bukofzer, *Studies,* p. 19.

carol, the first line of the antiphon provides the first line of the burden, while the other five serve as closing lines for each of the five stanzas. In another, the last four lines of the antiphon alternate with English lines to make up the third stanza. And in a third carol, the line "Pro salute fidelium" serves as a refrain for the burden as well as for the eight stanzas.[24]

Bukofzer presents some interesting evidence that the origin of the chant belonging to this text may be traced to an even more specific locality in England. The two fourteenth-century motets from a manuscript at Bury St. Edmunds, which he discussed at length in his *Studies,* are both based on a tenor *cantus firmus, Ave rex gentis.* Bukofzer points out that not only is this chant identical with that of *Ave regina coelorum* but that the words are the same except for the substitution of names and attributes:

Ave rex gentis Anglorum
Miles regis angelorum
O Edmunde, flos martyrum
Velut rosa vel lilium
Funde preces ad Dominum
Pro salute fidelium.[25]

Sources for both Edmundian and Marian forms go back to the thirteenth century. Bukofzer debates the priority of the two texts, suggesting that the Edmundian form may have been composed first and that the chant was then adapted to more general use by the substitution of the Marian text before it became known on the Continent. Antiphons in honor of local saints were not usually newly composed for the Sarum usage, however, but were more commonly substituted for the texts in pre-existent chants. The analogies with roses and lilies, more commonly associated with Marian poetry, also suggests that the Marian form was the original model, and that the Edmundian form for local use was the substitute. But the rhymed form is indicative of local usage and supports the position held by

24. Greene, *The Early English Carols,* Carols Nos. 201, 218, and 62. See also p. lxxxv.
25. Bukofzer, *Studies,* p 18.

Bukofzer. Both forms, for Edmund and the Virgin, were used in carols.[26]

There is another variant of this antiphon, *Ave prothomartyr Anglorum,* this time honoring Saint Alban, in a Sarum Breviary of 1531.[27] And still another, for Edward, is to be found in the Cologne Prayer Book, cod. 28. The appearance of both Edwardian and Edmundian forms of this antiphon in the Cologne manuscript may be significant for the work of Frye, since it is in this same manuscript that is found the text *Flos regalis Etheldreda,* which is presumably the text indicated by the incipit of one of Frye's Masses. Saint Alban, Saint Edmund, and Saint Etheldreda were all venerated particularly in one small quarter of England. The towns of St. Albans, Bury St. Edmunds, and Ely (where Etheldreda founded a monastery) are all very close together and it is a reasonable assumption that one chant which was well-known in a particular community should have been adapted by neighboring dioceses in accordance with their Proprium Sanctorum. Certainly if Frye was working at Ely from 1443–53, one of his songs might well have been given a motet text which was familiar in that region before it was exported to the Continent.

The connecting link between Frye's activities in England and the wide circulation of his works in European circles remains obscure. Of the Continental sources for his work it is perhaps the Schedel Liederbuch which points most directly towards the original manuscript of the Frye chansons. Even though it contains a later version than does the Mellon chansonnier (see below), we know something about the circumstances of its compilation. Copied personally by Dr. Hartmann Schedel, it has two outstanding characteristics: (1) It has attributions not found in any other sources, e.g. Frye's *Ave Regina* and *O sacrum convivium* and Bedingham's *Fortune élas — Gentil madonna* (2) It is highly inaccurate musically and could not have served as the parent source for other manuscripts, even supposing that Schedel's private Liederbuch was accessible to other scribes. It is equally evident that the Mellon chansonnier is not the parent source for Schedel. Apart from the fact that Mellon seems to

26. Greene, *The Early English Carols,* Carol No. 312. See also p. lxxxiv.
27. Bukofzer, *Studies,* p. 19.

have been compiled at a later date than the Liederbuch, Schedel could not have taken the attribution to Frye for *Alas, alas — O sacrum convivium* from Mellon, for it has none. Both Schedel and the scribe of Mellon must have had access to authoritative sources, Schedel because of the attribution and the Mellon scribe because of the English texts. The fact that the Mellon manuscript retained the English instead of substituting French texts may be explained by its relationship to the Burgundian court, specifically to that of Charles the Bold, who is known to have spoken English fluently.

The authoritative sources were in all probability Italian. The Mellon chansonnier, even though devoted almost exclusively to works by Burgundian composers, is thought to have been copied in Italy,[28] and the presence of Tinctoris' *O virgo miserere*, dedicated in this manuscript to Beatrice of Aragon, suggests Neapolitan provenance. The Schedel Liederbuch was copied at least in part in Italy. There are three dates in the manuscript— 1461, 1465, and 1467. Dr. Schedel, a physician and humanist, was born in Nuremberg in 1440, attended the University of Leipzig from 1456 to 1461, and spent three years in Italy (Padua), from 1463 to 1466.[29] On the basis of Schedel's handwriting during his student years, as well as the contents of the manuscript, Stauber claims that the manuscript was started in Leipzig, but that a small part of it came from his Padua sojourn.[30] It seems very likely that at least the addition of Frye's works dates from the Italian period.

A further indication that Frye's works were known first in Italy is provided by the testimony of the English Carmelite monk, John Hothby, who went to Italy around 1440 and settled there, first at Florence and then at Ferrara. In 1467 he went to Lucca and in 1486 was recalled to England where he died shortly afterward.[31] If Hothby had left England as early as 1440 he

28. Leo Schrade and Geneviève Thibaut believe that the style of illuminations indicates Italian provenance.

29. Richard Stauber, *Die Schedelsche Bibliothek* (Freiburg im Breisgau, 1908), p. 2. For Robert Eitner's views, see "Das deutsche Lied des XV. und XVI. Jahrhunderts," *MfM, 12* (1880), 3.

30. Stauber, *Die Schedelsche Bibliothek*, pp. 42–43.

31. U. Kornmüller, "Johann Hothby, eine Studie zur Geschichte der Musik im 15. Jahrhundert," *KJ, 8* (1893), 2–4.

could hardly have known Frye's compositions there, for they do not appear in any of the English manuscripts of the early part of the century, such as Oxford, Canon. misc. 213, Old Hall, or the Fountains fragment. Neither does Frye's music appear in Italian sources before about 1450. The Aosta manuscript and Bologna (Conservatorio G. B. Martini, Ms. Q 15), while representing a good many English musicians of Dunstable's generation, do not yet include Frye's work in the repertory. Hothby remained at Florence until 1467, however, and Frye's *Ave Regina* and all but one (*Alas, alas*) of his secular songs appear in Florentine sources of that period. The *Ave Regina* appears in three other Italian manuscripts as well. Frye's works generally appear in company with those of other English composers, usually Dunstable, and sometimes Lyonel Power and Morton. In general, his companions in manuscript are those listed by Hothby in his Dialogus (see above, p. 27). The works of Dunstable are, of course, late ones, especially *O rosa bella,* which accompanied Frye chansons to such diverse manuscripts as Escorial, Pixérécourt, Berlin, Wolfenbüttel, Monte Cassino, and Trent 90.

The tryptich of Polizzi Generosa, which shows a banderole containing part of the tenor of Frye's *Ave Regina,* is a peripheral source, but it lends weight to the theory that Frye's works were well-known in Italy and perhaps made their Continental debut there. The missing Italian source from which Schedel copied would perhaps prove illuminating for the entire question of English composers on the Continent. At all events it might well be expected to shed some light on the other two compositions of Frye which are found, with attributions, in the Schedel Liederbuch—*Trinitatis dies* and *O florens rosa.*

Trinitatis dies might conceivably be a contrafactum. It is not a ballade like *O sacrum convivium* and the other two contrafacta found in Trent, but it is very brief, has no evidence of a *cantus firmus,* and is generally very close in style to Frye's chansons and quite unlike his motet *Sospitati dedit.* The phrases are short and concise, and the piece has exactly the same medial cadence on A (with a fermata) and final on G as does Frye's rondeau *Tout a par moy.* Perhaps it too was originally a rondeau.

O florens rosa is an extended composition in three sections and is probably a bona fide motet, although it does not have a recognizable *cantus firmus*. There is another copy of it in Trent 90 (no. 1087) on the folio directly following Frye's *Ave Regina II*. The scribe of Trent has bestowed a different text upon it, and the text he chose adds to the general confusion concerning Frye's texts, since it is that of the more common Marian antiphon, *Ave Regina I*. Thus on consecutive folios of Trent 90 one finds two *Ave Regina* settings by Frye. Probably the Schedel text, *O florens rosa* is the authentic one, since the piece also appears twice in the Prague codex (Strahov D.G. IV. 47) with that text, although this is not a very strong guarantee and there is no way of identifying the piece by a *cantus firmus*. The *Ave Regina I* in Trent is not the variant of Sarum usage. The *O florens rosa* is found in a Neumarkt chant book,[32] which might have been known to Schedel, and also in *The Myroure of Oure Ladye,* a devotional book of the Sarum liturgy.[33] It is also the text used by Touront.[34]

In general, the texts found in Schedel's Liederbuch were well known in Germany and seem to reflect local usage. *O sacrum convivium, Ave Regina II,* and *O florens rosa* were used as devotional pieces, and all three texts appear in the Glogauer Liederbuch. It is conceivable that Schedel merely copied the music of the Frye compositions while he was in Italy and added the familiar texts when he returned home. Or perhaps he had with him in Italy a German Breviary from which to draw texts.

It can be seen from a comparison of musical aspects of the manuscripts that Schedel's source had already departed from the original in some respects. The freedom with which fifteenth-century scribes edited the music they were copying is demonstrated by a comparison of the Schedel copies with the earlier versions, found in both Mellon and Trent, of Frye's pieces. The changes are slight, but they are important in the light of the stylistic development which took place between 1450 and 1475. *O sacrum convivium* and *O florens rosa* show consistent deviations from their counterparts in Mellon and Trent, and always

32. Heribert Ringman and J. Klapper, eds., *Das Glogauer Liederbuch* (Kassel, 1936–37), 2, 76.

33. J. H. Blunt, ed., p. 220.

34. Trent codex 88, fol. 301 (No. 426). Published in *DTO,* 7 (1900), 217.

in the direction of simplification, both melodic and rhythmic. This is particularly striking at cadence points, where the melodic under-third form of the old Landini cadence is eliminated in Schedel's version. In almost all cases a more nervous and jerky rhythm is replaced in Schedel by a smoother and simpler rhythmic flow. (See Example 1.) It is difficult to believe that Schedel made these emendations himself; it is more likely that they were already in the book from which he copied.[35] Perhaps this source had even provided the new texts and Schedel was entirely blameless in the affair. In any case, the stylistic comparison plainly suggests that even the manuscript from which Schedel copied was not an original source. The scribes of Mellon and Trent must have had access to earlier ones.

This investigation of the Frye chansons and motets in Continental manuscripts raises several questions. The first of these concerns the chanson motet. The question arises whether, after all, there was such a thing, whether the pieces we call "chanson motets" might not all be traced back to chansons if all the sources were still extant. It has been shown that three compositions which were supposedly motets were originally English songs, and a fourth gives all the indications of being a contrafactum and not simply a motet composed in the style of a chanson. The term "chanson motet" is a modern invention for the sake of convenience in stylistic distinction, but it may be that there is no basis in historical fact for assuming that motets were actually written in this fashion. All that is really known is that motets were sometimes created artificially by changing the texts of chansons.

A second question concerns the relationship of contrafacta or chanson motets to the English style. It is probably not a coincidence that three of the so-called chanson motets have proved to be derived from English-texted chansons. The contrafactum is closely linked with the whole question of English influence on the Continent, for it was during the middle years of the fifteenth century that the English played an important role, and it was also during this period that contrafacta and

---

35. These emendations were not made in Schedel's version of the *Ave Regina*, which appears in an earlier part of the Liederbuch, before the folio on which the date 1461 is inscribed.

EXAMPLE 1

a) *Alas, alas—O sacrum convivium,* mm. 36–37

b) *Alas, alas—O sacrum convivium,* mm. 28–29

c) *Ave Regina I—O florens rosa,* mm. 45–48

d) *Ave Regina I—O florens rosa,* mm. 21-23

chanson motets appeared in very considerable numbers. There are perhaps a good many more English works disguised in similar fashions in Continental manuscripts than has been supposed. Thurston Dart has suggested recently that many of the texts in the Strasbourg codex M.222.C.22 which have been called "Flemish" and even some which were supposedly French, may have been English. Spellings of such words as "Apurille" are related to the English "April" rather than to the French "avril." [36] Certainly the logical and systematic text-substitution which is evident in the dissemination of the Frye chansons implies that the pattern might be a quite general one, and that other works which are thought to be chanson motets, or even French ballades, may prove on closer examination to be Continental adaptations of English works. Many compositions in manuscripts such as Pixérécourt, Escorial, and Florence 112 bis which have a strong stylistic affinity with the works of Frye are perhaps traceable to English composers.

The specifically English idiom exemplified by the works of Frye was distinct enough to be recognized by his Continental contemporaries. The discernment of the scribes in this respect is apparent even in their errors. One might better say "especially by their errors," for conflicting attributions in the case of Frye's works are only to Bedingham and Binchois. While it is true that Binchois was not English, he was the first of the Continental composers to be affected by the English style, and conflicting attributions of his motets are only to English composers (Dunstable, Lyonel, Sandley).[37] Because Frye's songs lost their textual identity in Continental manuscripts they are difficult to trace. But the fact that they were recopied so often and provided with more suitable texts proves that the favor enjoyed by English musicians in Europe did not cease with the death of Dunstable.

B. The English Sources

Although Frye's English nationality has now been established, the fact remains that he is far more widely represented in Euro-

---

36. "Une contribution anglaise au manuscrit de strasbourg?" *RB*, 8 (1954), 123.
37. See the concordance of Binchois' works given in Marix, *Histoire de la musique*, pp. 233–34.

pean manuscripts than in English ones. There is no documentary proof of a sojourn by Frye on the Continent, but it is certainly possible that he was among the large group of composers who worked at some time in Continental circles—perhaps at the court of Charles, Count of Charolais. The question then arises of how truly his style may be said to represent purely English traditions. It has been assumed that many of the English composers who went to the Continent, especially in the middle years of the fifteenth century, were themselves influenced by European composers. Various features of Dunstable's style have been explained in this fashion. Morton has been thought to have adopted Continental practices to such an extent that his nationality no longer has any stylistic significance. And even Bedingham has been said to have succumbed to Burgundian influence in his secular music. It is small wonder, then, that it has been difficult to determine the essentially English characteristics of the mid-fifteenth century as long as these works which were known on the Continent are considered to be unrepresentative. The works of Frye do not permit this latitude of interpretation, for the English sources of his work, few as they are, convey important information with regard to where and in what tradition he was writing. All three categories of his compositions are related in some way to strictly English traditions.

Frye's Mass compositions are decisive in one respect, even though they are not represented in English manuscripts. Certain features such as deletions from the CREDO text, writing of full breve rests, and omission of the KYRIE from polyphonic Mass settings, might have been retained by an English composer writing on the Continent. Some of them, in fact, were imitated by Dufay and Ockeghem in their Mass compositions. But it is unlikely that Frye would have composed a Mass on the *cantus firmus Flos regalis* anywhere but at a place where the melody was known, or at least easily accessible. All the evidence available to date suggests that that place was Ely. Judging by the difficulty of finding the melody at all, it is most improbable that Frye would have had access to it elsewhere. The four-voiced *Missa Flos regalis*, moreover, appears to be stylistically the most advanced of Frye's three Masses. Thus it would seem as though all three of them must have been written before he left England.

Frye's motet *Sospitati dedit* must also be related to England and not to the Continent. The only source in which it is preserved, the Pepys manuscript 1236 (Cambridge, Magdalene College) contains an exclusively English repertory. Included in the Pepys manuscript are works by Corbronde, Banastir, Nesbet, Hawt, Fowler, Garnesey, and Frye. Many of the motets in Pepys 1236 are written, like Frye's *Sospitati dedit,* in alternate two- and three-voiced sections. There are five other settings in the Pepys manuscript of *Sospitati dedit* (see above, p. 26), which is a Processional Prosa for the end of Matins on the Feast of St. Nicholas in the Sarum usage. It is to be found in the Sarum Processional, as is also the tenor of Frye's *Missa Summe Trinitati.*[38]

Stylistically this motet of Frye's is quite unlike the motet *O florens rosa* attributed to him in the Schedel Liederbuch. *O florens rosa* has no *cantus firmus,* and it does not utilize the alternate two- and three-voiced writing of the English motet style. It is entirely in compact three-voiced writing, with very few rests in any voice. It might conceivably have been written after Frye left England and became acquainted with Continental motet style. But if this is so, *O florens rosa* is the only one of Frye's works which can be said to have been stylistically affected by a Continental sojourn. (His rondeau has a French text, but it is in no way differentiated stylistically from his other secular works.) It is barely possible that *O florens rosa* is a contrafactum, compounded of three different songs. The individual sections are short and very much in the style of Frye's chansons. There is no known precedent for this, however, and since the piece appears in three sources, with two motet texts, it does not seem a very likely explanation. But whatever doubts there may be with regard to *O florens rosa,* there can be no question about the provenance of *Sospitati dedit* and its relationship to English liturgical and musical practices.

It is equally apparent that behind Frye's chansons there was a tradition of secular song writing in England, even though this category was not cultivated as actively there as on the Continent. The fact that Frye's songs originally had English texts is evidence of this. Heinrich Besseler denies the existence of any such

38. W. G. Henderson, ed., *Processionale ad usum,* p. 172.

tradition in England. In his article on Bedingham in *MGG* he says that because of the lack of any secular song tradition in England Bedingham adopted the Continental manner for his chansons and that all of them are in "ballade style," with a leading discant and two accompanying instrumental parts. Included among the works he attributes to Bedingham is *Grant temps,* which is now known to be the same composition as *Myn hertis lust.* To be sure, Besseler did not know of this concordance with an English song, but the style is nevertheless quite distinct from that of the earlier French chansons. None of the English songs in the Mellon manuscript are in the pure "ballade style" known on the Continent during the early years of the fifteenth century. On the contrary, they show a close relationship to the few secular songs known from fifteenth-century England, and specifically to those of the Ashmole manuscript 191 which have been published in *Early Bodleian Music* (vol. *1,* plates XXX–XXXVI; 2, 66–73).

On the last folio of this Ashmole fragment, part of the discant of Frye's *So ys emprentid* has been copied (without text). Bukofzer has pointed out, furthermore, that Frye's *Alas, alas* is modeled both textually and musically on a song in this same manuscript—*Alas, departynge is ground of woe.*[39] Stylistically there is an even closer relationship between the part songs of Ashmole 191, which are dated about 1445, and the English ballades of the Mellon chansonnier. The tenor part of that same song, *Alas, departynge,* begins almost note for note like the discant of Frye's *So ys emprentid,* save that one is in tempus perfectum and the other in imperfectum. The similarity continues for nine or ten notes. The song *O kendly creature*[40] demonstrates beyond any doubt the close relationship between the two groups of compositions, for nearly every phrase in it can be found in one or the other of the Mellon ballades or in other works of Frye. It is apparently not accidental, then, that a fragment of *So ys emprentid* is included in this manuscript.

There is a difference in notation, for Frye's chanson is notated with a breve tactus while the other six songs in Ashmole 191

39. "An Unknown Chansonnier of the 15th Century" *MQ, 28* (1942), 45.
40. John Stainer, ed., *Early Bodleian Music* (London, 1901), vol *1,* Plate XXXI; vol. 2, 67.

have the semibreve as the basic unit. The difference may be due to chronological factors, but since notational practices were far from consistent in England at that time they do not provide a good criterion for dating. Six of the songs in the Ashmole manuscript, including *So ys emprentid,* are in black notation, while only one, *Luf wil wt variance,* is in white. Here again, it is doubtful what inferences may be drawn concerning the date of copying. Bukofzer has said that black notation was used later in England than on the Continent. Curiously enough, however, his justification for this statement is the Ashmole manuscript, which he dates in the second half of the century on the basis of the inclusion of Frye's *So ys emprentid.*[41] We now know that Frye's works were known and copied by Schedel in the early 1460s from a source which was probably already at least once removed from the original. Probably Frye's chansons can be dated earlier than they have been, and perhaps the Ashmole manuscript too may be placed in the early 1450s. At all events, it is obvious that the chansons of Frye are to be related to these English songs, and not to the influence of Continental chanson style.

The fact that Frye was so widely known through Continental sources and that his works seem to have appeared first in Italian manuscripts does not seem to warrant his being identified with the Gualterius Liberth (Liberti) who was in the papal chapel in 1428 and is represented in the Bodleian Ms. Canon. Misc. 213.[42] The style of the compositions attributed to Gualterius in the Bodleian manuscript, *Se je me plains sans rayson,* a "fuga quatuor tempora," and *De tristesse de deuil,* is far removed from anything in the known works of Frye. They are both in tempus imperfectum, prolatio maior, with frequent examples of hemiola and a general character of rhythmic complexity which is quite foreign to anything we know of Frye's works. Frye's music is generally distinguished by its smooth, rhythmic character and its simplicity. It is possible, of course, that his style changed in the same manner as Dufay's. But if Frye had left England as early as 1428 it is difficult to explain his dependence on the Sarum usage for his Masses and motets as well as the

41. Bukofzer, *Studies,* p. 94.
42. Reese, *Music in the Renaissance,* p. 93.

appearance of *Sospitati dedit* in a late English manuscript, the
Pepys Ms. 1236. Bukofzer dated the Pepys manuscript variously
at circa 1475 and 1480.[43] Greene points out that it can be dated
no earlier than 1465.[44] Frye's motet may have been entered in
the Pepys manuscript some time after his departure for the
Continent (if he did indeed go there), since his works begin to
appear in Continental manuscripts by 1460, at the latest. This
particular motet was undoubtedly included in the English
manuscript because of the text in honor of St. Nicholas, and
English copyists might well have searched back ten or fifteen
years for compositions on this text, but they would hardly have
gone back as far as 1428. And stylistically, Frye's motet cannot
be separated by forty years from the other works in the Pepys
manuscript. The inclusion of a fragment of *So ys emprentid* in
the Ashmole manuscript also implies that Frye must have been
still in England considerably later than 1428.

A quite justifiable confusion exists between Frye and Bedingham, both Englishmen and both of a generation a little younger
than Dunstable's. Quite a number of attributions to Bedingham
in mid-fifteenth-century sources are conflicting: *Durer ne puis* is
variously attributed to Bedingham and Dunstable; *Mon seul
plaisir* to Bedingham and Dufay; *O rosa bella* to Bedingham and
Dunstable; and *So ys emprentid* to Bedingham and Frye. *Grant
temps (Myn hertis lust)* is attributed to Bedingham in Florence
176 and Trent, but these attributions are a bit suspect. The
earlier one is in Florence 176, from which Trent drew, and since
the same scribe attributed *Pour une suis desconforté (So ys
emprentid)* to Bedingham in Florence 176 it may be assumed
that he was wrong on both counts. Other attributions in this
Florence manuscript have also been found to be erroneous.[45]
Since there is no conflicting attribution for *Grant temps,* even in
Mellon, one is not justified in ignoring Bedingham's claim to it,
particularly since it is the ballade *Gentil madonna* (attributed to
Bedingham in Schedel) which falls between *So ys emprentid* and
Myn hertis lust in the Mellon manuscript. It would be hazardous

43. Bukofzer, *Studies,* p. 117 (circa 1475) and p. 94 (circa 1480).
44. "Two Medieval Musical Manuscripts: Egerton 3307 and Some University of
Chicago Fragments," *JAMS* 7 (1954), 12.
45. Bukofzer, "An Unknown Chansonnier," p. 25.

to try to distinguish between Frye and Bedingham on the basis of style alone, for they were obviously very close. Whether or not they can be distinguished, however, there are some important points which emerge even from the confusion of authorship.

It becomes increasingly clear that the works of men like Frye, Bedingham, and Morton represent a body of musical literature which had a distinct character of its own. They are not merely illustrative of the general merger of styles which characterized the transitional period in the middle of the century. They represent, rather, one of the elements which went into that merger. Frye, at least, cannot be dismissed as a composer who wrote partly in the English tradition and partly under the influence of Burgundian composers. His works, which were in great demand on the Continent, are the products of a purely English musical training.

The manner in which composition was taught in England is described best in the theoretical treatises. In these musical treatises, the basic rules of English composition are set forth concisely and, for the most part, clearly. The theory of discant in England has been variously interpreted, however, and in some instances dismissed as being irrelevant to the art of music of the fifteenth century. This fact, coupled with the tendency to attribute Continental influence to many English composers, is responsible for much of the confusion regarding English music of the fifteenth century. A reinterpretation of those treatises may cast some light on the distinctive quality of the English works which found their way into Continental manuscripts.

Part III: The Theoretical Literature

CHAPTER 5

The Theory of Discant

ONE OF THE most troublesome questions in the history of fifteenth-century music is that of discant, or more specifically, what is called "English discant." Throughout the thirteenth and fourteenth centuries, discant had meant simply counterpoint—that is a note-against-note style in which one discanting voice was set for the most part in contrary motion against the tenor. In view of the unanimity of theoretical opinion with regard to this simple but precisely defined technique, it seems curious that such a thing as a three-voiced improvisatory procedure based on strictly parallel motion should have been dignified in the fifteenth century with the name "discant." Nevertheless, the common interpretation today of fifteenth-century English discant technique is of a succession of chords analogous to first inversions of triads. This form has inevitably become confused with the practices of faburden and fauxbourdon. The *Harvard Dictionary of Music,* for example, defines "English discant" under the heading of fauxbourdon, which is equated with faburden, as follows:

> Here only one part, the tenor, is notated, and the other two singers improvise melodies resulting in sixth chords with occasional open triads (1-5-8) . . . The result is a sixth-chord harmony with the cantus firmus in the lowest part.

A few scholars, notably Thrasybulos Georgiades, have interpreted the English discant theory in an entirely different fashion, one that is in complete accord with the traditional meaning of the term "discant." [1] But the consecutive-sixth-chord

1. *Englische Diskanttraktate aus der ersten Hälfte des 15. Jahrhunderts* (Munich, 1937). See also Rudolf von Ficker, "Epilog zum Faburdon," *AM,* 25 (1953), 129.

interpretation has attracted many more followers, in spite of the fact that it is full of inconsistencies.

There is, first of all, the fundamental contradiction in the application of the term "discant" to an improvisatory three-voiced technique of parallelism. But even more disconcerting is the discrepancy between this technique and the actual music written by fifteenth-century English composers. In speaking of the Old Hall manuscript, for example, Bukofzer said: "The scarcity of English discant is especially striking because most of the treatises describing it stem from precisely the time of Old Hall, the early fifteenth century." [2] The author of one of these treatises, Lyonel Power, was among the foremost composers of the fifteenth century. Yet the music of Power reveals no trace of such a style of consecutive sixth chords. Thus we are confounded above all by the fact that the theory of English discant, if interpreted in such a fashion, has very little relevance to the study of the music itself. A theory of music completely detached from practice, even from preceding practice, is sufficiently irregular to warrant a re-examination of the entire subject.

Historians who have adopted the sixth-chord interpretation of the English treatises have had, perforce, to minimize the importance of discant theory in the development of fifteenth-century music in general. In 1936 Bukofzer described it as relating to primitive folk practices,[3] while Johannes Wolf wrote, in 1939, that: "Rules—nothing more—are given for singing at sight . . . The result is a manner of singing in thirds and sixths, apparently popular in origin." [4] It seems strange, to say the least, that English theorists should have been devoting themselves to the question of folk music at a time when English music itself was of great importance. Research into Medieval English music, however, had been rather neglected at the time Bukofzer and Wolf were writing in the 1930s. Only recently, with the publication of important studies in fourteenth- and fifteenth-century English music, has some of the mystery surrounding English theory been dispelled.

2. Manfred Bukofzer, *Studies*, p. 49.

3. *Geschichte des englischen Diskants und des Fauxbourdons nach dens theoretischen Quellen* (Strasbourg, 1936), p. 18.

4. "Early English Musical Theorists," *MQ*, 25 (1939), 422.

Much of the confusion between discant and fauxbourdon has arisen from the Medieval English use of a term "faburden," which is related to the "sights" of discant but apparently not very closely connected with Continental "fauxbourdon." The philologist Hermann Flasdieck maintains that the two words "faburden" and "fauxbourdon" are not from the same derivation, and recent research into the background of both terms has shown a tendency to separate the two practices sharply until the late fifteenth century, when the distinction between them was obscured.[5] Ernest Trumble, who has done extensive work on Continental fauxbourdon, thinks that there was no specified faburden in England until after 1450, but Ernst Apfel believes that a passage in the fourteenth-century treatise of Pseudo-Tunstede (CS, 4, 294), which Bukofzer interpreted as referring to discant, really describes an early form of English faburden.[6] While earlier definitions have maintained a distinction between the two forms in stating that the English form had the *cantus firmus* in the tenor while the Continental composers placed it in the superius, most of the recent scholars see a greater difference and relatively independent traditions behind them.

Ernest Trumble is convinced that authentic fauxbourdon originated in Italy, among French-speaking Italians (hence the Gallic term).[7] Trumble also draws an interesting distinction between canonic and improvisatory fauxbourdon, the canonic being the earlier. By canonic, or composed, fauxbourdon he means those pieces of which the cantus and tenor were fully notated, as they appear in most Continental manuscripts, and the contratenor derived exactly by rule.[8] This type of piece, as he points out, is really fully composed from the start. Even though one part is not notated, its course is entirely prescribed from the outset. Improvisation, whereby parts could be invented extemporaneously from a chant book containing only the plainsong, is obviously a different matter, and it is more descriptive of

5. Hermann M. Flasdieck, "Franz. fauxbourdon und frühneuengl. faburden," *AM*, 25 (1953), 111, and Brian Trowell, "Faburden and Fauxbourdon," 44–46.

6. Ernest Trumble, "Authentic and Spurious Fauxbourdon," *RB*, 14 (1960), 4; Ernst Apfel, *Studien zur Satztechnik der mittelalterlichen englischen Music* (Heidelberg, 1959), 1, 84–85.

7. "Authentic and Spurious Fauxbourdon," pp. 8–9.

8. *Fauxbourdon, An Historical Survey* (Brooklyn, 1959), pp. 22–23.

faburden, although Trumble relates it to fauxbourdon. Thus the difference in techniques which Trumble points up seem to suggest the most basic distinction between fauxbourdon and faburden.

Brian Trowell, who has provided the most lucid account of English faburden, emphasizes the relationship of faburden to "sights" and the practice of popular improvising. Thus Johannes Wolf's definition as well as that in the *Harvard Dictionary* probably refer to faburden, rather than to discant proper. Trowell sees faburden as a phenomenon which has not as much relevance for the sophisticated art music of the fifteenth century as for the semi-popular form of the carol.[9] Since fauxbourdon now appears to have been a strictly Continental affair, it is not immediately germane to this discussion. But faburden is related to the question of "sights," which were an exclusively English invention, and which will be touched on in connection with the sights transposition as it is discussed in the treatises on discant.

"English discant" is considered a development peculiar to the fifteenth century. Nevertheless, it is important to understand the original implications of the term "discant," since it must have had certain connotations for the English composers of the fifteenth century. Leaving aside for the moment the select group of fifteenth-century English treatises dealing with the subject, it can be said that the theory of discant from the twelfth through the fourteenth centuries exhibited several clearly de-fined characteristics.[10] It is essential to establish at the outset that discant theory was concerned primarily with two voices only. That is not to say that compositions in discant style were always limited to two parts. But discanting, by definition, was the art of setting one voice against another, and it was always taught and explained by means of two voices only—the cantus and dis-cantus. In the *Speculum Musicae* the word is traced to the Greek "dyaphonie," based on "dya" (two) and thence to the Latin form of "discantus." [11] The author points out that the term was used for three-voiced compositions, but adds: "And yet in prin-ciple, in discant, there were but two melodies, that which is called tenor, and the other, which discants above the tenor and

9. Trowell, "Faburden and Fauxbourdon," pp. 55–57.
10. See Manfred Bukofzer's article, "Discantus," *MGG, 3*, 559–77.
11. *CS, 2*, 387a.

which is called discantus." [12] The triad is never discussed as such, and the problem of adding third or fourth parts is always dismissed cursorily with the injunction that the same general principles are to be observed as for the first discanting voice.[13]

The theoretical basis for the composition of any one voice against the tenor remained essentially unchanged throughout the thirteenth and fourteenth centuries. Discant style, in the strictest sense, involved rhythmically equal voices in a note-against-note relationship, in contrast to the melismatic technique of many notes in one voice set against one in the tenor. The theory of discant was governed by two general principles: first, it was concerned with consonances only and made no real provision for the use of dissonances; second, discant was always characterized primarily by the principle of contrary motion.[14]

Discant, as a style of note-against-note writing, is distinguished from the melismatic style as early as the twelfth century in the circles of St. Martial. The anonymous *Tractatus de Musica* published by De la Fage states that:

> The difference between discantus and organum is that discantus accords with the cantus firmus always through some consonance or unison and by means of an equal number of notes, while organum is made to agree with its cantus firmus not with an equal number but with an infinite multiplicity of notes and with a certain wonderful flexibility.[15]

William Waite has pointed out that this distinction was maintained in the thirteenth century as well, for the treatise of Johannes de Garlandia discusses the difference between discant and organum while also including a third style, copula, which partakes of the characteristics of both discant and organum.[16]

During the fourteenth and early fifteenth centuries, the distinction still existed between melismatic and discant style, but

12. *CS*, *2*, 386a. See also the anonymous treatise published by De la Fage in *Essais de diptʜérographie musicale* (Paris, 1864), I, 349.

13. See the treatise of Anon. I in *CS*, *3*, 306b, and the *Speculum Musicae*, *CS*, *2*, 386b.

14. Richard L. Crocker, "Discant, Counterpoint, and Harmony," *JAMS*, *15* (1962), 2–3. Mr. Crocker's formulation is an improvement over this author's original statement in " 'English Discant' and Discant in England," *MQ*, *45* (1959), 28.

15. William G. Waite, *The Rhythm of Twelfth-Century Polyphony* (New Haven, 1954), p. 107.

16. Ibid., pp. 108 and 111.

the latter came to be known as counterpoint (from "punctus contra punctum"). Discant is specifically equated with counterpoint in many of the treatises,[17] and the terms were eventually used synonymously; but whichever term was used, the theorists always maintained that strictly speaking it referred to a note-against-note style. Prosdocimus de Beldemandis mentioned that there was a kind of melismatic counterpoint but that it was not true counterpoint. What he called *Contrapunctus vero proprie sive stricte*, on the other hand, "is the placing of only one note against any other note in any cantus, and . . . this is rightfully called counterpoint." [18]

The first principle of discant that was accepted from the earliest times was the exclusive use of consonance. This held true even though the views concerning the handling of perfect and imperfect consonances did change. The anonymous writer from St. Martial, in the excerpt cited above, said that the discant always accorded with the tenor through consonance or unison; the thirteenth-century Anonymous II writes that "discant is composed principally of consonances and only incidentally of dissonances," [19] and the same definition appears in countless other treatises.[20] Dissonances, in short, were to be avoided, and the treatises such as *De Discantu et consonantiis* reveal, even by their titles, how exclusively discant was identified with the use of consonances.

The defense of consonances is presented most eloquently by the author of the *Speculum Musicae,* Jacques de Liège, who launched a veritable polemic, solely on the grounds of their use of dissonance, at the composers of his day who claimed to write discant. He gives several definitions of discant, among them: "He who makes discords is not discanting," and then attacks these misinformed composers mercilessly in a chapter entitled "De ineptis discantoribus":

> How does it happen that now discords are introduced, that composers either jumble the concords of discant or mutilate,

17. Johannes Wolf, "Ein Beitrag zur Diskantlehre des 14. Jahrhunderts," *SIMG,* 15 (1913–14), 508; De la Fage, *Essais, 1,* 241 and 335; CS, *3,* 60b.

18. *Tractatus de Contrapuncto,* CS, *3,* 194a.

19. CS *1,* 311b.

20. See Simon M. Caserba, O.P., *Hieronymus de Moravia O.P. Tractatus de Musica* (Regensburg, 1935), p. 192; GS, *3,* 306a–b; CS, *4,* 281a.

destroy or dash them to pieces? Even if they arrive at a con-
cord with the tenor these composers, through ignorance of
the art, do not know how to remain there but speedily lapse
into discord. Ah misery! Nowadays some of them attempt to
gloss over their defects by quoting silly rules, saying that it
is a new way of discanting, that is, using new consonances.
They offend the intellect of those who recognize their fail-
ings. They offend the senses! O foolish maxim! O miserable
disguise! Irrational excuse! O dreadful abuse! O terrible
crudity! O profound stupidity! . . . O, if the ancient
doctors of music should hear such discanters, what would
they say? What would they do? [21]

The colorful tirade of Jacques de Liège was directed toward
composers of discant. But dissonances were used freely enough
in other types of composition outside the realm of discant. They
belonged in the style known variously as *cantus fractibile, floratura, diminuto,* or *figurativa*—in other words, in the florid
melismatic style. This relegation of dissonances to the small
nonessential melodic tones of the florid style is found in all the
treatises from the fourteenth century on,[22] and even Tinctoris,
writing in the second half of the fifteenth century, maintained
that in strict counterpoint dissonances were simply and abso-
lutely prohibited.[23]

The second principle of discant theory was that of contrary
motion. The admonition to move in contrary motion recurs
unfailingly throughout all the treatises on discant. In one of the
earliest, the thirteenth-century *Tractatus de discantu* of Anonymous II, it is stated that when the *cantus firmus* rises the discant
falls.[24] The phraseology varies, but from the thirteenth century
on there appears with monotonous regularity at the beginning
of each treatise the rule that when the tenor ascends the discant
descends, and vice versa.[25] Once this rule was stated, certain
exceptions were allowed if the beauty of the sound justified it.[26]

21. *CS, 2,* 394a.
22. *CS, 3,* 27a, 197a, 463a.
23. *CS, 4,* 134b.
24. *CS, 1,* 311b; De la Fage, *Essais,* p. 358.
25. See *CS 1,* 156b; *CS, 2,* 388b; De la Fage, *Essais,* p. 241; *CS, 3,* 60a; *CS, 4,* 281a.
26. *CS, 1,* 311b; *CS, 2,* 388b.

These exceptions, at first, have to do with similar—not parallel
—motion. The author of *De discantu et consonantiis* allows the
discant to move *with* the tenor from any imperfect interval to a
perfect one,[27] but Guglielmus Monachus permits similar motion
between perfect intervals, provided they are not of the same
kind (A to G in the discant over D to G in the tenor, for
example).[28] The rule for this voice-leading is stated clearly by
Anonymous VIII thus: "If the *cantus firmus* ascends by one note,
the discant may ascend by four, and if the *cantus firmus* ascends
by four steps the discant may ascend by one, as much from
imperfect as from perfect intervals." [29] It is clear, then, that
similar motion was allowed by these earlier writers, provided
that one voice moved stepwise while the other leaped. Nevertheless, every one of the theorists began firmly and unequivocally with the injunction that contrary motion was the rule, and
similar motion was treated as an exception.

This summary description of discant theory is necessarily
simplified. It is the intention of this writer not to deny that any
change took place between the twelfth and fifteenth centuries,
but merely to establish that certain traits remained constant, and
that by the beginning of the fifteenth century there was a long
and deeply rooted tradition attached to the term "discant."
Among the theorists quoted there were English as well as Continental musicians. The accepted meaning of discant, then, was
not limited to French or Italian circles but was generally and
universally understood. The question arises, therefore, whether
the fifteenth-century English writers merely ignored the formidable body of literature of their predecessors or whether they
actually built upon that foundation bequeathed to them from
the thirteenth century.

There is extant a large group of fifteenth-century English
musical treatises. Several of them were edited independently,
but almost simultaneously, between 1935 and 1937 by Sanford
B. Meech, Manfred Bukofzer, and Thrasybulos Georgiades.[30]

27. *GS, 3,* 307a.
28. *CS, 3,* 290b.
29. *CS, 3,* 410b–411a; see also Anon. XI, *CS, 3,* 463b.
30. Sanford B. Meech, "Three Musical Treatises in English from a Fifteenth-
Century Manuscript," *Speculum, 10* (1935), 235–69; Bukofzer, *Geschichte;* Georgiades, *Englische Diskanttraktate.*

THE THEORY OF DISCANT

Meech published a transcription and paraphrase in modern English of three treatises in English from the Lansdowne Ms. 763 of the British Museum. They are all mid-fifteenth-century copies by one John Wylde, of Essex, although they are by different authors. The first is by Lyonel Power, the second anonymous, and the third by Chilston. The anonymous treatise was ascribed to Chilston by Riemann, and the author has been known since as Pseudo-Chilston. The first two of these treatises were also published by Georgiades and Bukofzer, but Georgiades gives, in addition, the British Museum Ms. Add. 21455, Nos. 8 and 9. Bukofzer's study includes all of these, plus No. 10 of the Ms. 21455, the treatise of Johannes Torkesey (B.M., Lansdowne Ms. 763, No. 12), that of Richard Cutell (Oxford, Bodleian, Ms. 842), an anonymous tract from Cambridge (Corpus Christi Ms. 410, II), excerpts from Nicholai Burtius' *Musices Opusculum* of 1487, and an anonymous Scottish treatise (B.M., Ms. Add. 4911).[31]

The theory has been advanced most convincingly by Bukofzer that the fifteenth-century English treatises, unlike those of the thirteenth and fourteenth centuries, are simply lessons in improvisation. Yet the treatise of Power states specifically that the author was not confining his attention to improvisers. It opens with the statement that it is directed to "hem that will be syngers or makers or techers."[32] "Makers" are surely composers, as Georgiades has pointed out,[33] and Power appears to have been setting down rules for discanting which might be applied either by singers in improvisation or by composers. The author of the French treatise *Qui veult savoir l'art de dechant* similarly addresses himself to both composers and improvisers when he writes: "ne doilt on point faire ne dire."[34]

Power uses the term "counterpoint" in the strict sense of "point against point," just as did the *Ars Nova* theorists. Like them, he is discussing the problem of setting one voice against the tenor. His theory does not preclude three- or even four-voiced writing, but it is set forth in terms of one discanting

31. Meech's edition of the treatises will be used wherever possible for citations.
32. Meech, "Three Musical Treatises," p. 242.
33. Georgiades, *Englische Diskanttraktate*, p. 31.
34. *CS, 3,* 497a.

voice only. That Power could not have been ignorant of the earlier writings on discant is apparent even from the order of his presentation, for he approaches the problem in exactly the same fashion as did his predecessors.

IIe starts by listing the possible intervals, dividing them into perfect and imperfect, then enunciating the general rule banning consecutive fifths and octaves:

> For the ferst thing of alle thei must knou hou many cordis of discant ther be . . . ther be 9 acordis of discant: the vnisoun, 3de, 5te, 6te, 8te, 10the, 12the, 13the, & 15the. Of the whech 9 acordis 5 be perfite and 4 be inperfite. The 5 perfite be: the vnisoun, 5te, 8te, 12the, & 15the. The 4 inperfite be: the 3de, 6te, 10the, & 13the. Also thu maist ascende & descende with almaner of cordis excepte 2 acordis perfite of one kynde, as 2° vnisouns, 2° 5tis, 2° 8tis, 2° 12this, 2° 15this. With one of these thu maist neythir ascende neythir descende, but thu must cunsette thes a-cordis to-gedir & medele hem wel, as I shal enforme the.[35]

This was the standard opening formula in all discant treatises, with the exception that the earliest ones do not forbid consecutive fifths and octaves. In the thirteenth-century treatises, the opening paragraph usually comprises a list of the intervals, divided into perfect and imperfect consonances and dissonances,[36] while in the fourteenth century this list is invariably followed by the rule forbidding parallel fifths and octaves.[37] Crocker emphasizes the point, in this connection, that the ban is not on parallelism as such, but on the sound of consecutive perfect intervals, and thus shows Medieval concern with the progression of vertical sonorities.[38]

Up to this point, then, Lyonel Power's systematic method of approach shows him to have been thoroughly conscious of the traditional order of presentation. He was following a formula that was established in the early treatises on discant and shows no deviation from the conventional definitions. He next pro-

---

35. Meech, "Three Musical Treatises," p. 242.

36. See CS, 1, 311b–312a, 356b.

37. See Bukofzer, "Discantus," p. 571; GS, 3, 306b; CS, 3, 497a; CS, 4, 281a; De la Fage, Essais, pp. 141, 241, 335.

38. "Discant, Counterpoint, and Harmony," p. 11.

poses to show how, in discanting a given tenor, thirds and fifths may alternate, or sixths and octaves, or tenths and twelfths, etc. But before doing so he introduces the matter of "sights," and in this respect he does deviate from the pattern established by his European predecessors.

It is partly through a misunderstanding of the function of sights that some authors have arrived at their preoccupation with parallelism in the English discant treatises. The discussion of sights is peculiar to the English treatises, and while there is some difference in how they are defined by the various writers, their function is always the same. The sights are simply a means of visualizing transposition. A discanting part, though actually having a range a fifth or an octave higher than that of the tenor, is visualized by transposition on the same staff as the *cantus firmus*.

Power's discussion of sights certainly implies nothing more than a difference in range. He starts by saying that there are three sights—the mene, treble, and quadreble—but actually he discusses only two, the treble and quadreble, both of which are read at the transposition of an octave. They are visualized, that is, an octave below the actual pitch. He describes the process thus:

> Ferst to enforme a childe in his counterpoynt, he most ymagyne his vnisoun the 8te note fro the playnsong benethe, his 3de the 6te note benethe, his 5te the 4the note benethe, his 6te the 3de note benethe, his 8te euyn with the playn-song, his 10the the 3de note aboue, his 12the the 5te note aboue, his 13the the 6te note aboue, his 15the the 8te note aboue the playnson[g].[39]

Power then goes on to explain which intervals are permitted to these sights above each note of the scale. To the quadreble may belong the tenth, twelfth, thirteenth, or fifteenth, according to the degree of the scale. To the treble may belong the unison through the twelfth.

Pseudo-Chilston's explanation of the sights is rather more complicated and involves transposition at the fifth as well as the

39. Meech, "Three Musical Treatises," pp. 242–43.

octave. It is, furthermore, more methodical than Power's. There are no loose ends or intervals, and everything is taken care of with formidable thoroughness. Pseudo-Chilston defines the sights thus:

> Also it is to wete that ther be 3 degreis of descaunt scilicet the quatreble sight, and the treble sight, and the mene sight. The mene be-ginnyth in a 5te aboue the plain-song in vois & with the plain-song in sight; the trebil be-ginnyth in a 8te a-boue in voise & with the plain-song in sight; the quatreble be-gynnyth in a 12e aboue in voise & with the plain-song in sight.[40]

It can be seen from this that all parts are visualized as beginning in unison with the *cantus firmus* ("with the plain-song in sight") while actually in sound ("in vois") the mene is a fifth above the tenor, the treble an octave above, and the quadreble a twelfth, or octave and fifth. Pseudo-Chilston then goes on to explain that: "To the mene longithe propreli 5 a-cordis, scilicet vnisoun, 3de, 5te, 6te, & 8te; to the treble longith propreli 5 a-cordis, scilicet 5te, 6te, 8te, 10te, & 12te; to the quatreble longith propreli 5 a-cordis, scilicet 8te, 10e, 12e, 13e, and 15e." [41] These are the intervals "in voice" or actual sound and are distributed among the three sights according to the distance of the discant from the *cantus firmus*. Pseudo-Chilston's theory is a much tidier one than Power's, in that he assigns exactly one octave to each sight, allowing an overlapping of exactly three intervals between adjacent sights. Nevertheless, the sights serve the same purpose in both treatises. They enable one to visualize, or to write, intervals that would normally exceed the range of the staff on which the tenor is written. The mene sight intervals, for example, begin with the unison and extend up to the octave. Even supposing that the tenor never rises above the middle of the staff, an octave above it could not well be visualized or written on the same staff without liberal use of ledger lines. While there is one ledger line in Power's treatise, the first systematic use of such lines is not found until 1523. The alternative, then, is transposition. And transposition at the fifth is the mene sight.

Bukofzer has concluded that this group transposition makes

40. Ibid., pp. 258–59.
41. Ibid., p. 259.

sense only if the distance of the discanting voices from the *cantus firmus* remains constant, "in other words, if parallel motion prevails." [42] Yet it does not really follow that parallel motion must prevail. The discanting voice is not compelled to maintain a constant intervallic relationship with the tenor. It is free to expand this distance to an octave or contract it to a unison. By definition, the mene sight has at its disposal the unison, third, fifth, sixth, and octave—in short, all the consonant intervals. The same is true of the other two sights, the only difference being that of what later came to be called "open" or "close" position in harmony.

Lyonel Power's introduction of sights at an early point in his treatise has sometimes been regarded as an unsystematic digression.[43] Actually it has considerable relevance for the understanding of his musical examples. By transposing the discant, it is possible not only to visualize but also to write it on the same staff as the tenor, thereby obviating the need for another staff to illustrate the discant. Where two staves were used to illustrate the discant and tenor in older treatises, Power needed but one. His examples are all given by means of numbers on the tenor staff, but at the treble sight—i.e. they must be transposed up an octave. The sights, then, were not only a device for improvisation. They had a didactic purpose, and an eminently practical one at that.

Much too much furor has been aroused over the question of sights. They have been taken to mean something more significant than is implicit in their actual use by fifteenth-century musicians. The sights terms, "mene," "treble," and "quadreble," do not appear in choir books or part books where the parts are written out at pitch on different staves and no transposition is necessary. They were not used in the same sense as the terms which designated parts as "triplum," "motetus," or "quadruplum," but are found only in theoretical literature, for illustrative purposes or for improvisation. Their principal function was transposition.[44]

42. Bukofzer, *Geschichte,* p. 26.

43. Ibid., pp. 29–30.

44. Transcription at the octave was also described in the *Compendium Discantus* ascribed to Franco. See Crocker, "Discant, Counterpoint, and Harmony," p. 8.

The English method of transposition by means of sights is
related to the question of faburden and improvisation. Pseudo-
Chilston's treatise is devoted solely to the sights of discant,
counter, countertenor, and faburden. Faburden he describes as
the least (or humblest) of the family of sights but one that is so
natural and common that an explanation is in order.[45] According to Brian Trowell's interpretation, which is by far the most
plausible explanation to date, the faburden always involved
transposition at the fifth, sounding a fifth lower than visualized,
and it had only two actual intervals: the third and the fifth
below the *cantus firmus*.[46] Obviously it differs from both Power's and Pseudo-Chilston's own description of the sights of discant, in which the sound is above the sight. Here it is plainly
below, and there is no ambiguity about the advice to set the
sight even with the plainsong and the voice a fifth below it. As
Trowell interprets this passage, the faburden is visualized either
at a third above the tenor or in unison with it; hence by transposition it sounds a third or fifth below. In practice, the treble
remains uniformly above the tenor at a fourth, but the fabur-
dener starts a fifth below the tenor, then proceeds to the third
below, and during the course of the piece he may freely alternate
the third with the fifth below the *cantus firmus* (making sixths
and octaves with the treble), providing that there are no consecutive fifths.[47]

Two important points emerge from this concise description
of faburden. One, as Trowell shows most persuasively, has to
do with the meaning of the word itself. It does not refer to the
interval of a fourth (*Fa*) between any two voices, but rather to
the crucial fourth notes, C, F, and B flat, in the three hexa-
chords. Since the faburden singer is always transposing down a
perfect fifth there is never a B natural involved. The fifth below
F will always be B flat, or *Fa* of the soft hexachord, and never
B natural, or *Mi* of the hard hexachord. Trowell also points out
that the technique of transposing to the lower fifth explains the
strong emphasis on the subdominant in English music of the
fourteenth and fifteenth centuries.[48] The second important point

45. Meech, "Three Musical Treatises," p. 263.
46. Trowell, "Faburden and Fauxbourdon," p. 50.
47. Ibid., p. 52.
48. Ibid., p. 53.

is that the resulting faburden line does not actually duplicate the shape of the original chant melody as it would if it were strictly parallel.[49] Sixteenth-century faburden pieces, such as John Redford's *O lux on the faburden* in the Mulliner Book, are written on the faburdens to the plainsong and not on the original chant, and the faburden of *O lux* does not resemble the original chant very closely since it could alternate the third or fifth below it.

Since the treble always remains a fourth above the *cantus firmus,* the faburden is either a sixth or an octave below the treble. In this form it appears as the most likely model for Binchois' pieces, and, as Trowell points out, Binchois is far more likely than Dufay to have discovered English techniques early in the fifteenth century.[50] Dufay's fauxbourdon, and the type most often encountered in Continental manuscripts, has the *cantus firmus* in the top voice, and the tenor written out as well. Trowell believes that even this form may have had a precedent in English compositions and that Monachus was describing both faburden and fauxbourdon as English practices, faburden in the chapter "De modis anglicorum" and fauxbourdon in the "Regule Contrapuncti anglicorum."[51] Monachus was writing in the last third of the fifteenth century, however, when the two types had ceased to be so distinct. But the earlier English practice, as described in Pseudo-Chilston's treatise, is clearly different from fauxbourdon and shows faburden as an improvisatory technique which is based on the sights theory. It could well have been of popular origin, and was probably used in connection with folk music or other forms less sophisticated than the composed Masses and motets of the Old Hall manuscript. While it makes use of the sights which Power discusses in his treatise on discant, faburden itself is quite distinct from discant proper, and Power, in fact, does not even mention it.

After discussing the sights, Lyonel Power continues along the lines established by earlier writers with regard to the teaching of discant. He goes very systematically through all the consonant intervals, showing first all the ways of discanting by starting with

49. See Frank Ll. Harrison, *Music in Medieval Britain,* pp. 411–12, Example 216.
50. Trowell, "Faburden and Fauxbourdon," pp. 76–77.
51. Ibid., pp. 65–67.

a third and alternating it with a fifth, then with a sixth, then
with an octave. Then he takes up the fifth, which may alternate
with a sixth, an octave, a tenth, or a twelfth; then the sixth,
which alternates with a third, fifth, octave, tenth, or twelfth;
then the octave alternating with a tenth or twelfth, and so on,
up through the fifteenth. Power was very thorough, and he left
nothing unsaid, even at the expense of being repetitious. This
penchant for detailing every possibility was a hallmark of medieval theoretical writing, and Power's explicit presentation shows
how deeply he was imbued with the traditional methods of
teaching discant theory. His first musical example, which has
been the source of much confusion regarding English discant,
must be interpreted with this in mind. Some scholars have taken
the first three examples of Power's treatise to mean three-voiced
composition, with the upper two voices progressing in parallel
motion. This meaning is not implicit in Power's examples or
in the text. He begins by saying: "Ferst for thirde & fyfte, thou
shalt haue thi pleyng-song: re, vt, my, re, ffa, my, sol, ffa, la sol.
Vnto the same playng thu mayst discant a 6te with a 8te, a 10e
with a 12e, a 13e with a 15e." [52] The example follows, showing
how the third-fifth and the sixth-octave are visualized on the
staff at the treble sight. In the manuscript, the scribe has erroneously written 8-10 instead of 6-8. This is clearly a mistake,
which Georgiades has corrected in accordance with Power's own
prefatory remarks.[53] (See Example 2.) Charles Burney, and many

EXAMPLE 2

others after him, have interpreted this like the figured bass of
two centuries later. They have assumed that the two voices discant simultaneously, one going from the third to the fifth, and
the other from the octave to the tenth, or, with the correction,
from the sixth to the octave. There is no real justification for
this assumption. Georgiades has pointed out that if one is to read
this as though it were a figured bass, one would have to read in

52. Meech, "Three Musical Treatises," p. 248.
53. Georgiades, *Englische Diskanttraktate*, p. 15. See also p. 15, n. 3.

the same fashion the example given for discanting a twelfth with a fifth or sixth.[54] (See Example 3.) If the same principle were

EXAMPLE 3

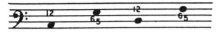

followed here, the result would be an interval of a second between the fifth and sixth, and such a dissonance was strictly forbidden. In this latter example Power has plainly stated that these are alternative, and not simultaneous, ways of discanting a given tenor, for he introduces the example by saying: "[F]or a twelfe with a 5te *or* a 6te" (italics are this author's).[55] The conjunction "or" is missing from Power's first example, probably because it was not considered necessary; it is only in the light of subsequent musical theory that the possibility of simultaneous performance even arises. This first example is really a short cut. Since the same tenor—re, ut, mi, re, fa, mi, etc.—can be discanted in different ways, he gave illustrations of both ways at the same time. (The possibilities he mentions actually represent only two different ways of discanting, since the tenth-twelfth and thirteenth-fifteenth are simply an octave higher than the third-fifth and sixth-octave.) The practice of listing several possibilities at once was not foreign to discant theory treatises. Anonymous XIII gives the same example as Power but supplies the missing conjunction, "or," when he introduces it by saying that on a given tenor "on doilt dire tierces, quintes ou sixte double." [56] In the treatise of Pseudo-Tunstede the same tenor line is found, with instructions to discant it in exactly the manner Power has described. There is no suggestion in Pseudo-Tunstede's treatise that the various ways of discanting are to be employed simultaneously, for they are widely separated in context.

Georgiades recognized the two-fold function of these examples and was careful to point out the error in previous discus-

54. Ibid., p. 21. See Also p. 35, n. 15.
55. Meech, "Three Musical Treatises," p. 256.
56. *CS, 3,* 497b.

sions of this passage, even though he did not altogether dismiss
the possibility of successive sixth chords. Such voice-leading in
sixth chords, he stated, might indeed be possible if more than
two voices were involved, but it could only be regarded as a
secondary result of the theory and should not be taken as the
prime purpose.[57] It is questionable, however, whether such
voice-leading could be considered even a secondary result of
discant theory. There is no explicit direction with regard to
performing these two discants together in any of the treatises,
and there is not sufficient justification for assuming that Power
was advocating such a procedure. Treatises on discant had always dealt with just one voice at a time against the tenor, and
if Power had been intent upon advancing a theory of three-
voiced composition he would surely have made a point of it
instead of adopting unquestioningly an older formula for presenting examples.

It has been necessary to dwell at some length on these first
three examples of Power's treatise because this is the part of the
document that has given rise to the belief that English discant
treatises advocated unlimited parallelism. Any extended parallelism can be inferred from these examples only on the assumption
of simultaneous performance. Between any discanting voice and
the tenor, parallel motion was strictly limited. Power expressly
forbids more than three consecutive thirds or sixths:

> Also ther is a rwle that descanteris may sette & syng 3 jmper-
> fite a-cordis to-gedir, & it is treu, bothe of one keende & of
> diuerse kendis. Exemplum: Of one keende, as 3ᵉ 3dis, 3ᵉ
> 6tis, 3ᵉ 1ois, 3 13is. Exemplum: Of diuerse keendis, aas a
> jmperfite of one keende with a jmperfite of of [sic] a-nothir
> keende, as a 3de with a 6te. So we may sette & syng in
> diuerse keendis 6 jmperfitis in one keende as 3 jmperfitis
> and no more.[58]

Power's rule cannot be dismissed as a mere gesture, even though
it appears rather haphazardly halfway through the treatise.
It is quite apparent from the whole treatise that Power did not
intend that any more than three consecutive imperfect intervals

---

57. Georgiades, *Englische Diskanttraktate*, p. 35.
58. Meech, "Three Musical Treatises," p. 252.

should be written, for he illustrates painstakingly how one, two, or three imperfect intervals in succession may progress to a perfect interval, but never more than three.

Other treatises vary as to the number of consecutive imperfect intervals permitted. Torkesey allows only two.[59] Cutell, who was writing in the fourteenth century, allows as many as five: "And of all imperfite acordis it is leveful to take 3, 4 or 5 of a kynd and the pleynsong ascend or descend." [60] Pseudo-Chilston and the author of the Cambridge Ms. Corpus Christi 410 II allow five,[61] while the anonymous writer of the B.M. Add. Ms. 21455, No. 9, implies that even four is a good many.[62] Georgiades has made a table showing the number of consecutive imperfect intervals allowed by the theorists.[63] The fact that the number is almost invariably prescribed indicates that a limitless succession of thirds or sixths was out of the question. Parallel motion was never admitted without some restriction in any of the treatises on discant.

Richard Crocker has made an interesting point in suggesting that chains of parallel thirds or sixths in the fourteenth century were analogous to nonharmonic tones of functional harmony. The manner in which they are discussed in the treatises does indeed justify this interpretation:

> At this time the progressions major sixth to octave, major third to fifth, and minor third to unison take on more and more importance as the building blocks of counterpoint. These progressions acquire the force of necessity: their conclusion becomes obligatory . . . Viewed from this angle, a succession of consecutive sixths or thirds is the interruption of expected resolution—of "function," if you will . . . The parallelism allowed here is less significant than the resolution required.[64]

Similar motion, also, had been permitted under certain restricted conditions. It was pointed out above that this type of

59. Bukofzer, *Geschichte*, p. 136.
60. Ibid., p. 142.
61. Meech, "Three Musical Treatises," p. 260; Bukofzer, *Geschichte*, p. 146.
62. Bukofzer, *Geschichte*, p. 139.
63. Georgiades, *Englishe Diskanttraktate*, p. 52.
64. Crocker, "Discant, Counterpoint, and Harmony," pp. 11–12.

progression was sanctioned even by the earliest writers, and particularly when it was from an imperfect to a perfect interval. In view of these possibilities it should not be assumed that English writers were referring to unlimited parallel motion when they wrote such passages as this: "And with these acordis of descaunt euery descanter may ryse in voyse & falle with the plain-song, excepte out of one perfite in-to a-nother bothe of one kynde, as it is a-for rehersid." [65] What is probably meant by this is a judicious mixture of perfect and imperfect consonances. Another of the English treatises, No. 10 in the B.M. Add. Ms. 21455, contains the sentence: "Sed non debes ascendere nec descendere cum plano cantu in concordanciis perfectis, sed in concordanciis imperfectis potes bene ascendere vel descendere ad libitum tuum." [66] This surely cannot mean that one may literally write unlimited consecutive thirds or sixths, for the author has already stipulated that only two or three imperfect concords may be written in succession, and that they must be followed by a perfect interval. The author of another treatise from the same manuscript (No. 9) provides an explanation, almost identical with that of Anonymous VIII, of how the discanter may ascend or descend congruently with the tenor provided that the interval is greater or smaller than that by which the tenor moves: "If the *cantus firmus* ascends a fourth or a fifth the discant may ascend a second or third. And the same is true of descending. If the *cantus firmus* ascends a second or a third the discant may ascend a fourth or fifth. And the same is true of descending." [67] The examples of this type of similar motion include both consecutive perfect intervals of different kinds, such as fifths and octaves, and alternate perfect and imperfect intervals, such as the sixth and fifth. In Lyonel Power's treatise, too, there are examples of similar motion, specifically in discanting an octave with a tenth and a twelfth with a tenth.[68] (Cf. Example 4.)

It can be seen from this survey that the rules of discant given in the fifteenth-century English treatises fall into two general categories—those dealing with parallel motion, and those dealing with similar motion. Parallel motion was forbidden between

65. Meech, "Three Musical Treatises," p. 258.
66. Bukofzer, *Geschichte*, p. 141.
67. Ibid., p. 140.
68. Meech, "Three Musical Treatises," pp. 253 and 257.

perfect consonances and limited to a maximum of five between
imperfect consonances. Similar motion was sometimes allowed
between unlike perfect intervals but freely admitted between imperfect and perfect. Certainly these treatises advocated strongly
the frequent use of thirds and sixths. ("And it es to wite that
the mo inperfite tones that a man synges in the trebull, the
meriere it es.") [69] But nowhere do they advance a theory of unlimited successions of imperfect consonances or of the simultaneous use of thirds and sixths to produce what was later to
be called a 6/3 chord. Even Pseudo-Chilston, who says that "it
is fayre & meri singing many jnperfite cordis to-gedir," [70] permits one to be merry only to the extent of singing five thirds
or sixths together. Then gravity must be restored by the fifth or
octave. As we have seen, Pseudo-Chilston was more lenient in
this respect than Power, whose sterner disposition did not allow
indulgence in more than three. There can be no doubt that the
use of successive thirds and sixths was a privilege to be exercised
with care. It was adapted to the theory of discant without fundamentally altering one of the basic premises of that theory, i.e.
contrary motion.

EXAMPLE 4

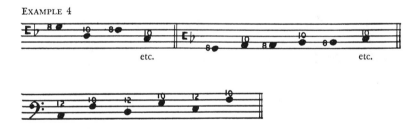

The rules for discanting conform in nearly every respect to
those of the earlier Continental writers, even down to the order
of presentation. The English theorists were obviously familiar
with the traditional meaning of "discant," and their treatises
reflect no desire to institute a radical change in that concept.
There is, in these writings, none of the self-consciousness that
generally characterizes revolutionary theories. Neither is there
the indifference to or ignorance of earlier teaching that would

69. Georgiades, *Englische Diskanttraktate*, p. 28.
70. Meech, "Three Musical Treatises," p. 260.

indicate an entirely different purpose in these fifteenth-century English treatises. They adhered too closely to both form and content of the *Ars Nova* theoretical writings to permit the interpretation that they were directed only toward popular or folk usage.

The term "discant" undoubtedly retained the essential elements of its original meaning throughout the fifteenth century. It continued to refer to the style of rhythmically equal voices in contrast to that in which a melodically florid upper voice is combined with a slowly moving tenor part. But the treatises on discant, from the end of the thirteenth century on, do differ in one important respect from those dealing with organum. That is in the use of thirds and sixths, which were not permitted at all in the twelfth-century organum, but which formed an essential part of all discant theory from the time of the *Ars Nova* on. Discant style, according to the note-against-note principles given by Power, would be inconceivable without the extensive use of imperfect consonances, whether they occurred consecutively or in alternation with perfect intervals. Long two-part sections in discant style had been possible in organum because of a fundamentally different concept of rhythm.

In organum, the theory of consonance and dissonance was dependent upon a system of modal rhythm. Because it was only the first interval of the rhythmic foot that was required to be consonant, the intervals in between enjoyed unlimited freedom. The second or third notes of a foot were actually unessential tones, in the tenor as well as the discant part. The movement between perfect consonances was thus relieved by imperfect consonances and even by dissonances. The two voices, furthermore, could move in consecutive perfect intervals from one to the other of these intermediate notes, or even away from and approaching the essential intervals. This is amply demonstrated by such examples as the Versus *Tamquam sponsus* from the *Magnus Liber* of Leonin.[71] There could, for that matter, be consecutive fifths from the beginning of one foot to the beginning of another because the intervening intervals obscured the sheer parallelism.[72]

It was only in the second half of the thirteenth century, when

71. Waite, *The Rhythm of Twelfth-Century Polyphony*, Transcription, p. 7.
72. Ibid., Transcription, p. 6. See especially the passage "de celis."

modal rhythm began to disappear and each note acquired an autonomous rhythmic value, that it became necessary to treat every note in the tenor as an essential tone. And it was only at this point that it was deemed necessary to place a theoretical restriction on consecutive perfect intervals in discant style. Parallelism in itself had never been regarded as a desirable element in composition. It had been tolerated in improvisatory practices, as in the earliest organum, but it was never really accepted in theory. Hence, consecutive perfect fifths and octaves were banned as soon as the rhythmic innovations made it possible for them to be used in too glaring a fashion.

It was in the early fourteenth century, when the principles of mensural notation became firmly established, that expressions such as "nota contra notam" and "punctus contra punctum" appeared, and the elliptical term "contra-punctus" emerged as a synonym for "discant." The new terminology has an obvious relationship to the new understanding of rhythm, for it expresses quite concisely the notion that now every note was important—not just every second, third, or fourth note. In discant style now every vertical interval had to be consonant—not just the first one of every foot. It was manifestly impossible, therefore, for discant style to develop any further unless the third and sixth were released from their earlier restrictions. The only alternative, with the ban placed on consecutive perfect intervals, would have been a rather barren succession of alternate fifths and octaves.

Continental composers were, in a sense, in a dilemma, for they continued to regard the third and sixth as imperfect intervals which should not be used at essential melodic points. They solved the problem by abandoning discant style for the most part and developing instead the organal style with reference to the *cantus firmus.* The tenor, though rhythmically organized now, moved in relatively slow notes, while the discant maintained a relationship of perfect consonances with every change of the tenor, but in the interim was allowed elaborate melismata consisting of unessential notes, or, in modern times, nonharmonic tones. This was the style known as *cantus fractibile,* or *floratura,* or *figurativa,* in which dissonances were permitted on the smaller note values. It was not regarded as strict discant.

English composers, on the other hand, had clung to the ideal of discant. It remained a live tradition in England, while on the Continent it was overshadowed by the advances made in pure, unfettered melodic writing. The English did not merely adhere slavishly to conductus style, as many authors put it. They were rather more imaginative. They retained the discant style of early organum, but adapted it to the new requirements of mensural notation by broadening the concept of consonance—that is by admitting the free use of imperfect consonances.

At first there were severe restrictions placed on the use of these imperfect consonances. They had to be preceded and followed by perfect intervals. Cutell, who was writing in the fourteenth century, describes this as an older technique when he writes:

> Also the old techyng was that a man shal never take none imperfite acord bot if he hade a perfite after him, as after a 3 a 5 and after an 8 [10?] a 12 and after a 13 a 15. bot now it is levyd the techers of descant that after a 3 a man take a 6 or after a 6 a man may take a 10.[73]

By Cutell's time, as he says, there was considerably more freedom in the use of imperfect intervals. He himself, in fact, allowed not only alternate, but even consecutive imperfect intervals. Discant theory, then, even by the fourteenth century, had come to admit both imperfect consonances and a limited amount of parallelism. There is nothing radical about Power's rule permitting three consecutive thirds or sixths. Compared to Cutell, who allowed five, he was conservative. The comparison is significant, however, for it shows that the real innovations in discant theory came not with the fifteenth century, but with the *Ars Nova,* as a result of the development of measured rhythm. Furthermore, the novelties appear in both Continental and English manuscripts, as Georgiades has pointed out.[74]

73. Bukofzer, *Geschichte*, p. 142.

74. *Englische Diskanttraktate*, chap. 4. See especially pp. 57–58, 65–66. Georgiades was mistaken, however, in saying that the number of consecutive thirds and sixths was unlimited in the treatise of Anon. XIII (p. 59). The passage he cites, though rather ambiguous, seems to refer rather to the type of similar motion described by other theorists—i.e. when one voice leaps a fourth or more the other may move in the same direction, but stepwise. Further on in the treatise Anon. XIII says specifically: "Et ne doilt on faire que II ou III tierces ou sixtes l'une après l'autre sans moyen" (*CS, 3,* 497a).

There is abundant evidence in English music from the thirteenth century on of the direct application of discant theory.
For one thing, the English continued much longer than their
European contemporaries to cultivate forms which had traditionally been composed in discant style; the conductus, for example, did not disappear from English repertory until late in
the fourteenth century when the votive antiphon took over its
favored position.[75] The Worcester fragments and the index to
the lost collection at Reading reveal a predominance of motets,
conductus, and ritual tropes at a time when French composers
were evolving the cantilena style of the chanson. Because the
English retained many of the forms which were characterized
by equally active sung parts and simultaneous text-declamation
they also retained the score form of notation instead of choir
book format. Ernst Apfel divides his study of fourteenth- and
fifteenth-century English music into two chapters, one devoted
to those pieces which were notated in parts and one for those
in score. He makes the point that the conductus, because all
voices declaimed the text simultaneously, was still written in
score form, while the motet and rondellus were written in
parts.[76] (Many of the motets, however, are written in discant
style.) In addition to the conductus, most of the earlier polyphonic forms involved pieces with a single text which was sung
simultaneously by all parts, and these survive in Worcester,
notated in score form—i.e. an Organum, an Alleluia, sequences,
hymns, and movements from the Mass Ordinary.[77]

In utilizing discant style, the English had begun to regard the
third and sixth in a tolerant fashion even as early as the end of
the twelfth century. The conductus in honor of the accession
of Richard the Lion-hearted in 1189, *Redit aetas aurea,* is the
earliest example.[78] One from the late thirteenth century, *Jesu
Cristes milde moder,*[79] is a perfect illustration of what Cutell

75. Frank Ll. Harrison, "English Church Music in the Fourteenth Century,"
New Oxford History of Music, 3 (London, 1960), 82.

76. *Studien, 1,* 34.

77. Ibid., p. 57.

78. Alfred Einstein, *A Short History of Music* (New York, 1947), p. 260. See
Gustave Reese's discussion of this type of composition in *Music in the Middle
Ages* (New York, 1940), chap. 14.

79. Reese, *Music in the Middle Ages,* p. 389.

called "the old techyng," i.e. the constant alternation of thirds
with perfect intervals. There are also innumerable examples of
English music from the late thirteenth century on in which a
few consecutive thirds and sixths appear within passages in
contrary or conjunct motion. Probably the most charming piece
in all of Medieval English music is the thirteenth-century two-
part song, *Edi beo thu hevene quene.*[80] It has a lilting melody
in modal rhythm, and it sounds as if there were an almost continuous succession of parallel thirds between the parts, with
occasional fifths and unisons sprinkled in. In reality the parts
are written in such a way that there are only nine points where
the voices move in a parallel progression, and only twice is there
a succession of as many as three parallel thirds. The sound of
parallelism is achieved by voice crossing, as when one voice
holds an A while the other leaps from F below it to C above it.
By any standards the song is a small masterpiece, but it makes
one a trifle suspicious of English craftiness. It seems as though
the composer, while scrupulously observing the letter of the
law, quite deliberately violated the spirit. Whatever the motives
prompting the composition of *Edi beo,* English predilection for
the soft sound of the imperfect consonances appeared early in
discant writing and by the fifteenth century had become a dom-
inant feature.

It was pointed out at the beginning of this chapter that discant
was, in principle, for two voices only. The extent to which discant theory dominated English musical thinking can be seen
by the almost continuous English cultivation of two-part writing
from the thirteenth century through the fifteenth. Ernst Apfel
mentions the series of two-voiced motets in the Bodleian Ms.
Lyell 72, which appear in the Montpellier Ms. with three
parts.[81] William de Wicumbe, whose name appears in the index
of a lost collection of polyphony at Reading (in the same manuscript as *Sumer is icumen in*) is known to have written a roll of
two-part music during the four years he spent at Leominster.[82]
By the late fourteenth and fifteenth centuries, the carols, the

80. *New Oxford History of Music, 2* (London, 1954), 342.
81. *Studien, 1,* 38.
82. Harrison, *Music in Medieval Britain,* p. 135. See also Bertram Schofield,
"The Provenance and Date of 'Sumer is Icumen in'," *Music Review, 9* (1948), 84.

repertory of the Pepys Ms. 1236, the Ashmole Ms. 191, and the Ritson Ms. (B.M. Add. Ms. 5665) all reveal a preoccupation with the technique of two-part composition in a style that was singularly free of the ornamental figurations of *cantus fractibile* or *floratura*. Bukofzer called attention to the importance of this duet style when he wrote:

> The reflection of such highly consonant duets can be found not only in the works of Dufay, but also those of Binchois. This is important for the as yet unwritten history of the duet style (or what Besseler calls "motettisches Duo") and the origin of flowing rhythm ("Stromrythmus"), both of which were developed apparently with the active participation of English composers.[83]

It seems now as though England was a singularly important "participant" in this evolution. Duet style and flowing rhythm, as well as the new method of handling consonances, can be traced directly to the theory of discant that was taught and practised more extensively in England than anywhere else. They are, in a sense, all mutually dependent within that theory.

The importance for the Netherlands school of this duet style, with its harmonic and rhythmic connotations, should not be underestimated. It played a significant role in the large works, such as Masses and motets, of Ockeghem, Obrecht, and particularly Josquin. And it was the basis of the discant-tenor chanson. The discant-tenor chanson shows perhaps most strikingly the evolution of a new style on the Continent, for the chanson was the first category to abandon the essentially monophonic style of accompanied melody for a style in which the basic structure is polyphonic, i.e. a duet.[84] The basic duet of the chanson, to which a free contratenor was added, had a clear precedent in English music (i.e. the carols) and in English theory as well.

Although the English theorists were primarily concerned with the counterpoint of one discanting voice against the tenor, a third voice is specified by Pseudo-Chilston and some of the

---

83. Manfred F. Bukofzer, "Fauxbourdon Revisited," *MQ, 38* (1952), 40.

84. Ernst Apfel stresses the importance of this duet-basis in his article "Der klangliche Satz und der freie Diskantsatz im 15. Jahrhundert," *AMW, 12* (1955), 304.

anonymous writers as the counter, or countertenor. This third voice also belongs to discant. Pseudo-Chilston, for example, writes that "it is conuenient to declare the 9 acordis of the counter-tenor sight longyng to descant," [85] and the fragment (No. 8) from the B.M. Add. Ms. 21455 starts with: "It is to wyte that ther are 3 degres of discant. Out of all this togeder is gadered a contratenor." [86] The countertenor is simply a voice which, according to some theorists, was derived from the mene sight, and according to others, from all three sights of discant. In range, it appears generally to have been close to that of the mene sight voice, but with the difference that it might cross the tenor to go below it. A discanting voice below the tenor was not a novelty of the fifteenth century. Pseudo-Tunstede too, after giving the rules for discanting above the tenor, has a chapter entitled "Quomodo sub plano cantu discantandum est," in which he merely states that the same rules are to be followed as for discanting above.[87]

Pseudo-Chilston gives the clearest description of the function of this countertenor voice:

> Also a man that hathe a low voyce may syng a countertenor in-stede of a mene, ffor when the tenor is hye the countertenor may be low, and whan the tenor is low than the countertenor may be the mene. And alwey sette thi voce (*sic*) yn the same note & in the same twne that the plain-song is in, and alwey be-gynne & ende thi countertenor in a 5te and thi countergemel begynne & ende in vnisoun.[88]

Thus the tenor and countertenor form a gymel which begins and ends in unison, though read as a fifth when the mene sight is used. This description suggests that the countertenor was an improvised voice, since it visualizes its part by the sights. Yet it seems to have more freedom than an improvising faburden voice, for its rules are much the same as those for any other discanting part:

> Also, whan the plain-song ascendit, the cou[n]ter may shape his sight a-boue the plainsong to descende dounward to

85. Meech, "Three Musical Treatises," p. 260.
86. Bukofzer, *Geschichte*, p. 137.
87. *CS, 4,* 294.
88. Meech, "Three Musical Treatises," p. 261.

close with the plain-song in a 8te, with a 6te, nexte afor or a 5te. And if the plain-song descende, it is conuenient the cou[n]ter to ascende & close with the plain-song in a vnisoun, with a 3de next a-fore.[89]

Thus the countertenor, like any discanting part, should ascend when the tenor descends, and vice versa; it should observe the primary rule of discant, that of contrary motion.

The style of the Old Hall manuscript, from the first half of the fifteenth century, illustrates many of the points which emerge from the treatises on discant. Almost all the Old Hall Mass settings and motets for three voices are composed for a tenor, a countertenor, and a higher discant part. The discant parts are generally notated in the manuscripts with a clef a fifth higher than that of the tenor. This corresponds to the mene sight transposition of improvisation—i.e. a voice visualized at unison with the *cantus firmus* would sound a fifth higher. The contratenor, on the other hand, usually has a slightly lower clef, though sometimes the same one as the tenor. The tenor and contratenor frequently have a key signature of one or more flats, while the discant has one less flat.

The contratenor was the one voice which maintained a range roughly equivalent with that of the tenor until quite late in the fifteenth century. Earlier in the century, the other voices had begun to break away from the restrictions imposed by the tenor range. Georgiades makes the point that the theory of sights was actually an attempt to interpret this novelty in terms of older discant practice in which the various voices were all written in approximately the same range.[90] Now a voice could still be visualized within the range of the tenor but would sound a fifth or octave higher. The earlier Continental treatises on discant had seldom dealt with intervals larger than a tenth, whereas the fifteenth-century English treatises discuss intervals up to two octaves. By means of transposition of mene, treble, and quadreble sights these larger intervals could all be reduced to within one octave, that octave prescribed by the range of the tenor. During the fourteenth century, compositions written in discant style are characterized by a great deal of crossing of parts because the voices occupy very similar ranges and can generally be notated

89. Ibid., p. 263.
90. Georgiades, *Englische Diskanttraktate*, p. 87.

with the same clef. This is seen in the Mass sections from the Apt and Ivrea manuscripts and certainly in the Worcester pieces. But with the early fifteenth century, the discanting voices are released from the tenor; the range of the whole ensemble is expanded, and each voice acquires a degree of independence which it had not had before. This was an innovation within the tradition of discant itself.

Bukofzer has classified all the pieces in the Old Hall manuscript by identifying them with specific styles which, for the most part, had been characteristic of particular categories known in the Continental repertory. Thus, the first group is made up of "conductus-like" pieces (Mass movements, Marian antiphons, hymns, and sequences); the second group is called "caccia-like;" the third "free-treble," or "ballade style;" the fourth characterized by contrast of voice-grouping (all three groups comprise Mass fragments); the last two groups include isorhythmic Mass movements and motets. He felt that while the last five groups showed Continental influence, the first, "conductus-like" pieces which were notated in score, showed a decided English stamp.[91] Ernst Apfel has regrouped the Old Hall pieces into four categories: (1) conductus-like Mass fragments and antiphons without *cantus firmus,* in a note-against-note style, and written in score form (2) conductus-like Mass fragments and antiphons with *cantus firmus* (3) free Mass fragments without *cantus firmus,* including canonic and imitative pieces and those characterized by contrasting voice-grouping and (4) isorhythmic or isoperiodic motets and Mass movements with the tenor in long notevalues.[92]

It seems as though the compositions that both Bukofzer and Apfel describe as "conductus-like" could be better described as being in pure discant style instead of being identified with a specific category of music, the conductus, which was traditionally written in discant style. Bukofzer deliberately avoided the narrower term "ballade style" in favor of the more descriptive "free-treble" and would undoubtedly have rejected the term "conductus-like" for the same reasons had it not been for a misunderstanding of discant. The definition of discant, which was established in the organum and prevailed still in the fif-

91. *Studies,* pp. 53–58.
92. *Studien, 1,* 85–90.

teenth century, is based primarily on rhythmic considerations in the sense that the parts are rhythmically equal. Curiously enough, Tinctoris still defines it in his *Diffinitorium Musicae* (before 1476) in terms of the very precise rhythmic character of the clausulae sections: "Discantus est cantus ex diversis vocibus et notis certi valoris editus." [93] Thus while the term "conductus" implies simultaneous rhythmic motion with text declamation, most of the pieces grouped under the heading of "conductus-style" are more properly called "discant pieces," for they show the style of rhythmically equal voices in contrary motion in a predominantly consonant relationship.

Ernst Apfel makes a series of distinctions within discant and other English styles on the basis of the use of the interval of a fourth between voices. What he calls "freie Diskantsatz" is comparable to the Continental chanson, and has no fourths between discant and tenor; "klangliche Satz," like the Continental four-voiced motet in which tenor and contratenor together form a "bass," has fourths between the upper voices, even including the tenor when the contratenor is below it; "klangliche-freie Diskantsatz" is, as one might expect, a cross between the two, in that there are occasional fourths above the lowest part, tenor, but they are usually ornamental in function, and probably come from the chanson style. Apfel then postulates a fourth category based on voice functions; in this group the tenor is differentiated in long notes, while the contratenor makes a duet with the discant, thus taking over the role of the tenor in the "freie Diskantsatz." [94] With regard to the mixtures of style, Apfel rejects the idea that there was influence from the chanson to the Mass or motet on the grounds that the chanson had no *cantus firmus* and therefore had nothing to do with sacred pieces composed on a *cantus prius factus*. That is a strictly Continental point of view, however, for, as Harrison points out, the English had a habit "of fusing categories and techniques of composition which had normally been distinct in Continental practice, such as plainsong with the chanson, isorhythm with the polyphonic Mass, and the chanson with the isorhythmic motet." [95]

Attempts to explain medieval English music by means of a

93. *CS, 4,* 182.
94. *Studien, 1,* 90.
95. *Music in Medieval Britain*, p. 247.

comparison with Continental customs inevitably leads to some confusion, for the English were without doubt individual in their handling of both form and style. But underlying all the peculiarities of English musical behavior is the principle of discant. It accounts for the prevalence of genuinely contrapuntal writing in England throughout the fourteenth century and for the great predilection for consonances which characterized discant writing.

Part IV: The Musical Style

CHAPTER 6

The Masses of Frye

THE MASSES OF Walter Frye are composed in accordance with the principles of discant. Between tenor and discant there is not a sharp distinction, although the discant is a little more ornate. The tenor often starts in larger note values but seldom continues in that fashion for long. It invariably becomes more animated toward the ends of phrases and frequently quite soon after the beginning. The melodic lines are rhythmically simple and free of the elaborate, florid melismas which characterized the upper voices of early fifteenth-century Continental compositions. Nonharmonic tones are rare, for nearly every note in the discant part bears a harmonically essential relationship to the tenor. Dissonances do appear occasionally, however, and the most common form, that of the suspension, is generally handled consistently and in a manner compatible with the rules drawn up by Tinctoris and further refined by sixteenth-century theorists. In many instances, however, the use of dissonance appears haphazard and uncontrolled. Theoretical lack of interest in dissonance is matched by the apparent indifference of almost all English composers of Frye's generation to the practical application of the problem. Thus, dissonant passages, when they do occur in the works of Frye, are far more freely treated than they were to be in the sixteenth century.

While the three Masses are stylistically alike, the *Missa Flos regalis* stands somewhat apart from the other two, *Nobilis et pulchra* and *Summe Trinitati*. *Flos regalis* is, first of all, for four voices, while the other two Masses are for only three. The *cantus firmus* of *Flos regalis*, moreover, appears to be drawn from a unique source, while those of the other two appear in all the well-known Sarum books. All three of the Masses omit parts of

the CREDO text, but the two three-voiced Masses conclude with
the "non erit finis," while the *Missa Flos regalis* includes the
final "Et vitam venturi saeculi." Another small point differ-
entiating the *Missa Flos regalis* can be seen in the AGNUS DEI,
which starts directly with the polyphonic setting, while in the
other two Masses the first words are chanted.

The two three-voiced Masses illustrate the technique of two
discanting voices written against the tenor. One of these voices
is called the "contratenor," and in general this voice occupies
about the same range as the tenor, in the manner prescribed by
Pseudo-Chilston for the counter-tenor. In the *Missa Nobilis
et pulchra,* the tenor and contratenor cross one another continually. The contratenor of *Summe Trinitati* lies below the tenor
for the most part, but nevertheless does rise above it quite frequently. Tenor and discant cross only very rarely. Thus the two
voices, tenor and contratenor, may be said to form a gymel. The
gymel-like substructure of the *cantus firmus* compositions in the
Old Hall manuscript similarly represents the direct application
of the practice of countering, by means of which a gymel is
formed between the two lower voices. Bukofzer has pointed out
this characteristic in Masses and motets in which the borrowed
melody is in the middle voice. "Thus," he writes, "the repertory
of OH emphatically underlines the important position of the
gymel in English polyphony." [1] That it was an integral part of
English discant is seen by the use of the term "gemel" in connection with the discussions of the Countertenor.

Although the contratenor shares the range of the tenor, it is
linked more closely with the discant part in respect to rhythm.
The fact that any part should be more rhythmically active than
the tenor seems at first to contradict the basic assumption that
discant style depends upon a note-against-note relationship to
the tenor. Yet discant style does not imply simply simultaneous
motion from chord to chord. In the earliest form of discant
there was:

> an exact correspondence of both parts in that each contains
> the same number of notes in an ordo or the equivalent of
> the same number of notes, as when the sixth mode is placed

1. *Studies,* p. 49.

against the first or second mode so that there are two breves in one part against a longa in the other.[2]

In other words, within an ordo, or two longae, there might be several notes in one part against one in the other. In theory there could be as many as three, although in practice the fifth mode was seldom set against the sixth. It was, furthermore, typical of the duplum to have a more active part than the tenor, at least from about 1250 on. This same principle holds for the English discant of the fifteenth century. It does not imply chordal progression. All that really follows from the fifteenth-century theory of discant is that if there are to be more notes in the discant than in the tenor they must still be consonant with the plainsong. Discant style precludes a really melismatic upper voice simply because there are a limited number of consonant intervals over any given note in the tenor. By drawing upon all of these intervals, the composer might embellish the melodic line to some extent. The tenor note might be held for one or two breves, for example, while the discanting voice moves from a third above it to a fifth, then to a sixth and an octave. Thus the uppermost part, even within discant style, can be more florid than the tenor, as long as it adheres to a consonant relationship with the tenor. This is generally true, in fact, of the compositions in the Old Hall manuscript. But it is important to note that the contratenor, too, becomes more rhythmically animated than the tenor.

The similarity between discant and contratenor parts in English works is easily understandable from the point of view of the theory. The theoretical descriptions of the countertenor show that the English attitude toward this voice was quite different from the Continental. To the English, the contratenor was another discanting voice, for the "countir" was "contriuid out of the syght of the mene degre of descant & triuyd vpsodoun" (is contrived out of the mene degree of discant and turned upside down).[3] Hence in *cantus firmus* pieces, the contratenor partakes of the character of the discant rather than of the tenor. Among Continental composers, the contratenor shared the role

2. Waite, *The Rhythm of Twelfth-Century Polyphony*, p. 111.

3. Pseudo-Chilston. See Sanford B. Meech, "Three Musical Treatises," *Speculum, 10* (1935), 261.

of the tenor. In early fifteenth-century Continental compositions in which treble-dominated style prevailed, the tenor and contratenor formed a harmonic supporting bass together, upon which a rather florid melodic line rested. But in English theory and music, the "countering" voice did not function as another tenor. It was derived from the various sights of discant and was handled in the same fashion as a discanting voice. It is probably for this reason that in many of the Old Hall pieces, such as Roy Henry's GLORIA, the contratenor is rhythmically more animated than the tenor.[4] It is not always a melodic voice, to be sure, but it has a rhythmic vitality which enables it to function more flexibly than the tenor.

In one important respect, the contratenor differs also from the other discanting voice. The discant was ordinarily restricted to one sight, while the contratenor was allowed to change sights and to rise above or descend below the tenor. Hence the contratenor may be interpreted as a voice which, although following the same general rules as the other discanting voices, had a rather more comprehensive function to fulfill. It was apparently a voice which was composed after the tenor and discant and made to conform to them.

The countering voice is characterized by two different techniques. The more typical of these is illustrated by numerous passages from the Frye Masses wherein the contratenor acts as a harmonic supporting voice, filling in the triad. It has a rather angular melodic line because it is obliged to take whichever note is not supplied by the other two voices. This can be seen in the two three-voiced Masses of Frye, particularly in such examples as the following: *Missa Summe Trinitati,* GLORIA, mm. 20–30, ibid., mm. 156 ff., CREDO, mm. 130–50; *Missa Nobilis et pulchra,* GLORIA, mm. 85 ff., CREDO, mm. 25–40, AGNUS DEI, mm. 1–15.[5] It should be noted that in the last passage cited, from the *Missa Nobilis et pulchra,* the contratenor has a range of an octave and a fourth within the space of two measures. This wide range was one of the characteristic features of the contratenor in contrast to the other voices. According to Pseudo-

4. *The Old Hall Manuscript,* ed. A. Ramsbotham, H. B. Collins, and A. Hughes (Burnham, 1933–38), *1*, 34.

5. Walter Frye, *Collected Works,* ed. Sylvia W. Kenney, Nos. 10 and 11.

Chilston, the contertenor has nine "accords," four below and four above in addition to the unison with the plainsong.[6] Only five "accords," those falling within an octave, belong to each of the three regular sights of discant.[7] The discant parts of Frye's three-voiced Masses exceed an octave range by only one note, and that very rarely. (It is frequently in connection with the cadence forms, when the discant descends to the leading tone before the tonic.) The discant of the four-voiced *Missa Flos regalis* extends to a tenth, but in general the range stays within an octave.

The contratenor of the Frye three-voiced Masses also functions occasionally as a more melodic voice, like the discant. In general, the relationship of contratenor and tenor is one of contrary motion. But sometimes the contratenor moves in parallel motion with the discant, while the tenor remains relatively static. (See, for example, the *Missa Nobilis et pulchra,* GLORIA, mm. 212–13, CREDO, mm. 110–13, "Osanna I," mm. 95–98, and "Osanna II," mm. 198–99.) In passages of this type, the harmonic progression is severely restricted, and it is invariably the same progression which results from such voice-leading. The tenor lies in the middle, and the parallelism is in tenths between the two outer voices, the discant ranging from the sixth to the fifth and third above the tenor, and the contratenor moving from a fifth to a sixth and octave below the tenor (Example 5).

EXAMPLE 5

Nobilis et pulchra, SANCTUS, mm. 95 ff.

6. Meech, "Three Musical Treatises," pp. 260–61.
7. Ibid., p. 259.

Passages similar to this occurred with great frequency in English works of the mid-fifteenth century and came to have a considerable influence upon the style of the Netherlands composers. They will be discussed in more detail in connection with the chanson technique.

In Frye's four-voiced Mass, *Flos regalis,* the two primary functions of the contratenor are assigned more or less exclusively to two voices—the bassus on one hand and the voice, which is still called "contratenor," on the other hand. The bass voice, except when it is engaged in a duet, usually retains the bass function of the contratenor, moving for the most part in leaps of fourths, fifths, and octaves. The contratenor has more the character of a real discanting voice. This division of labor is not invariably maintained. The contratenor too acts sometimes simply as a filling voice, taking whatever note is essential to the harmony. But in general this voice has a more melodic character than has the bassus.

The melodic style of discant is necessarily somewhat restricted because of the mutual dependence of the voices. Purely ornamental melodic figures are totally absent, and each voice maintains an even rhythmic flow with comparatively little variation in time values. Out of these restrictions imposed by the note-against-note relationship to the tenor emerge certain clearly defined characteristics. The individual melodic line is given to repetition which is sometimes perfectly literal, as in Example 6. More often, the phrase is varied in some fashion. In Example 7, the contratenor phrase is repeated exactly, but the effect of repetition is obscured by the unessential melodic and rhythmic variations in the tenor part. This type of device is characteristic of the style as a whole. The most frequent form of all is the

EXAMPLE 6

Summe Trinitati, SANCTUS, mm. 53–54

Ibid., mm. 133–36

line in which there is no exact sequence or melodic repetition, but the melody revolves constantly around one high note, or one interval, which recurs again and again within a very short period (Example 8).

EXAMPLE 7

Nobilis et pulchra, GLORIA, mm. 153ff.

EXAMPLE 8

Flos regalis, GLORIA, mm. 16ff.

Ibid., CREDO, mm. 70ff.

Ibid., AGNUS, mm. 60ff.

Frye's sequence technique follows much the same procedure. Sometimes it is exact and literal, as in both voices of Example 9. Sometimes it is melodically exact, but rhythmically displaced in such a way that the tactus falls at a different point each time (Example 10). But more typical is the sequence which is not melodically exact. In both excerpts of Example 11, the first presentation of the figure differs in one interval from the sec-

EXAMPLE 9

Flos regalis, AGNUS, mm. 57ff.

EXAMPLE 10

Summe Trinitati, AGNUS, mm. 98ff.

EXAMPLE 11

a) *Nobilis et pulchra,* KYRIE, mm. 44ff.

b) *Flos regalis,* SANCTUS, mm. 20ff.

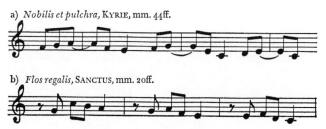

ond and third. In Example 12 the melodic line deviates even further, although the rhythmic formulation of the first presentation is retained. The purely rhythmic sequence is the most characteristic of all (Example 13). In the next excerpt (Example 14) this sequence technique is applied to four-voiced writing, in which three of the voices have rhythmic sequences. The tenor and bass have the same pattern, in what might be called a rhythmic canon, while the discant has an entirely different figure. Only the contratenor is free.

EXAMPLE 12

Nobilis et pulchra, KYRIE, mm. 64ff.

EXAMPLE 13

Summe Trinitati, SANCTUS, mm. 113ff.

EXAMPLE 14

Flos regalis, GLORIA, mm. 59ff.

This is the form in which the very limitations of discant style are placed to greatest advantage, for it is the setting of all voices against one another in conflicting rhythmic schemes that intensifies the musical effect. Similarly, passages in which the two lines are intertwined depend largely on the rhythmic cross-accents for effect (Example 15). The harmony is static and the melody is repetitive to the point of being monotonous, but there is an intriguing effect achieved by such crossing and recrossing of parts and the avoidance of any simultaneous cadencing. Even the ostinato, which is a form of pure repetition characteristic of the style, is utilized in such a way that the implied regularity is never apparent. In Example 16 the contratenor has an ostinato figure; above it, the discant has a melody which is set entirely at cross-purposes with the phrasing of the contratenor figure.

EXAMPLE 15

Nobilis et pulchra, CREDO, mm. 43ff.

EXAMPLE 16

Summe Trinitati, AGNUS, mm. 71ff.

As a general rule, the range of all voices but the contratenor in the Frye Masses is limited to about an octave, or one sight in theory. For the most part, the voices pursue a rather noncommittal course in the middle, but occasionally Frye gives evidence of breaking away toward real amplitude of line. There are several places where the melody rises or descends directly for one note over an octave. But such passages are relatively rare, and generally the shift to a higher range is achieved by the use of an octave leap, after which the melodic line turns back within the octave. The octave leap, which is almost a cliché in Frye's works, appears almost invariably in the same context, entering on an offbeat after a rest of one minim (Example 17).

The triadic form of many English melodies has been discussed too often to warrant much consideration here. Frye's works abound in such phrases as these (Example 18), the last

EXAMPLE 17

a) *Flos regalis,* GLORIA, mm. 6ff.

b) *Summe Trinitati,* SANCTUS, mm. 25ff.

c) *Nobilis et pulchra,* CREDO, mm. 45ff.

EXAMPLE 18

a) *Flos regalis,* AGNUS, mm. 8off.

b) Ibid., mm. 114ff.

c) *Flos regalis,* GLORIA, mm. 1-3.

of which is the motto beginning for all four movements of the *Missa Flos regalis*. Melodic formulas of this type result almost inevitably from the practice of discant, since the discanting voice, by using the various notes of the triad, can maintain a continuously consonant relationship with the tenor even though it is more rhythmically active.

Frye's Masses are all constructed in cyclic form. The movements of the Ordinary are closely unified not only through the tenor *cantus firmus* but also by means of melodic formulas which recur in the discant parts. All three Masses have motto beginnings which include the lower voices as well as the discant. Two of the Masses, *Flos regalis* and *Summe Trinitati,* open with introductory duos, of which the first two or three measures comprise the motto. In the *Missa Nobilis et pulchra* all three voices enter immediately with a two-measure phrase which recurs in all four of the succeeding movements. Strict adherence to a motto beginning is not particularly characteristic of English Masses of the fifteenth century. In the *Missa Alma redemptoris* of Leonel Power, for example, the motto does not appear at all in the AGNUS DEI, and it is varied considerably in the other movements. Similarly, in the Mass on *Fuit homo missus,*[8] which is presumably of English origin, the motto deviates widely from the first presentation.

However consistent Frye may have been in the use of mottos, he employed a different rhythmical scheme for each of the three Masses. The *Missa Summe Trinitati* is written entirely in tempus imperfectum. The other two Masses are characterized by alternation of duple and triple time. Each movement of *Nobilis et pulchra* begins with tempus perfectum, changes to imperfectum for the middle section, and then has a short, and generally more rhythmically animated, closing section in tempus perfectum. The *Missa Flos regalis* has a bipartite division for each movement, opening with tempus perfectum and closing with imperfectum.

In all three Masses the liturgical chant which serves as a *cantus firmus* appears uncolored in the first movement and remains melodically unchanged throughout the succeeding move-

8. *Documenta Polyphoniae Liturgicae Sanctae Ecclesiae Romanae,* Serie I, No. 9 (Rome, 1950).

ments. It has been pointed out in connection with the two English cyclic Masses, *Alma redemptoris* and *Rex saeculorum,* that both the rigid and free handling of the *cantus firmus* go back to the very earliest beginnings, and that both forms continued to be used throughout the period of *cantus firmus* Mass composition.[9] Frye, although he colored the tenor melody freely in his motet *Sospitati dedit,* seems to have preferred the unornamented form for Mass composition.

In the *Missa Nobilis et pulchra* the tenor is dropped from the musical texture for one section of each movement. This was a common procedure. But there are, in addition, some sections in which the tenor continues but abandons the melody of the chant. Two such sections interrupt the course of the tenor melody at exactly the same points in all five movements, with the exception of the AGNUS DEI, which has only one interpolation. In the first movement they occur at the beginning of the "Christe" and the beginning of the "Kyrie II"; in the GLORIA, at "Domine Deus, Agnus Dei" and "Qui sedes"; in the CREDO, at "Et incarnatus est" and "Et ascendit"; in the SANCTUS, at "Gloria tua" and "Benedictus"; and in the AGNUS DEI, at "Miserere nobis." All of these sections consist of duos of tenor and contratenor, with the exception of the "Benedictus," which is a duo for tenor and discant. They function rather like musical tropes.

One of the striking features of Frye's *Missa Nobilis et pulchra* is the length of the KYRIE. This movement, in which the basic structure for the following movements is established, is the longest of all of them. The KYRIE is 232 measures long; the GLORIA, 230; the CREDO, 220; the SANCTUS, 215; and the AGNUS DEI, 163. (The omission of the second chant-free interpolation accounts for the brevity of the AGNUS DEI.) In the Masses of Netherlands composers, the KYRIE was generally much shorter than the GLORIA or CREDO, and usually shorter than the SANCTUS as well. The long KYRIES were characteristic of English Mass settings because of the troped texts. In the *Missa Fuit homo missus,* for example, the KYRIE, GLORIA, and CREDO are exactly the same length—67 measures. Frequently the KYRIE was not set polyphonically at all by English composers, but when it was

9. Oliver Strunk, review of *Documenta Polyphoniae Liturgicae,* p. 108.

included, it was almost always troped. The Cockx *Missa Sine nomine* of BR 5557, which has the KYRIE trope *Deus creator,* and the Pseudo-Binchois Mass using the trope *Omnipotens pater* both have relatively long KYRIES.

From the point of view of structure, the KYRIE is the most interesting movement of Frye's *Missa Nobilis et pulchra.* It can be seen from an analysis of this movement that the various structural devices which are at the disposal of the musician are carefully set against one another in such a way that none of them coincide. A perfectly clear formal outline is provided by the tripartite KYRIE text. The trope, *Deus creator,* which appears in this Mass is a long one, having a complete four-line stanza for each exclamation of "Kyrie Eleyson" and "Christe Eleyson." Thus the text is subdivided into nine stanzas; three for "Kyrie I," three for the "Christe," and three for "Kyrie II." Frye has set this text, with its clear and unequivocal divisions, in such a way that the lines of demarcation are all obscured. He has imposed upon it a tripartite rhythmic scheme (tempus perfectum—imperfectum—perfectum) which never coincides with the major text divisions. Tempus imperfectum is introduced at the fifth stanza, i.e. for the second "Christe." The return to tempus perfectum comes only at the ninth and final stanza, the last "Kyrie" of "Kyrie II."

Frye has also divided the plainsong into three sections, but immediately clouded the issue by inserting musical tropes, thereby turning it into a fundamentally five-part melody. Stanzas 1 and 2 of the text have the first part of the chant; stanza 3 has no tenor; stanza 4 has the first musical trope; stanzas 5 and 6 have the second fragment of the chant; stanza 7 includes the second musical trope, and stanzas 8 and 9 the third fragment of the chant.

Even the voice grouping is handled in such a way as to minimize the text divisions of "Kyrie—Christe—Kyrie." The first "Kyrie" closes with a duet of discant and contratenor, and the "Christe" begins with a duo of contratenor and tenor. There is a full cadence between the "Kyrie I" and the "Christe," but between "Christe" and "Kyrie II" there is not even this concession to formal clarity, for the "Christe" ends with a duo of discant and tenor, and the ensuing duet of tenor and contratenor is merely spun out of the first duo. The contratenor enters to displace the discant and the tenor begins the new text even before the discant has concluded the final longa on the last syllable of "Eleyson." In neither case are all the resources of the choral group martialed at the close of a major text section.

The text itself is an elaborate one, and has deviated so far from the original purpose of troping that the words "Kyrie" and "Christe" are even omitted from the beginnings of stanzas. Only the words "Eleyson" at the end of each stanza serve to delineate the formal structure of this movement of the Ordinary.

To sum up, this KYRIE is governed by a text which is troped and a *cantus firmus* which is musically troped, but the tripartite plan of the movement is thoroughly obscured by the handling of the chant, the cadences, the rhythmic scheme, and the voice grouping. The conflicting relationship of these various elements can be seen in a diagram of the voice parts (D. = Discant; CT. = Contratenor; T. = Tenor). Tempus perfectum is indicated by O, tempus imperfectum by C. In the tenor part, the *cantus firmus* is represented by a solid line, and the free interpolations by a dotted line. The perpendicular lines mark final cadences.

Kyrie Kyrie Kyrie Christe Christe Christe Kyrie Kyrie Kyrie

O C O

D.
CT.
T.

For the most part, the pattern established in the KYRIE is maintained in the other four movements of the Mass. The free duets of tenor and contratenor occur at corresponding points. It is curious, however, that the AGNUS DEI, which is tripartite like the KYRIE, deviates more from the original scheme than do the other movements. In the first movement, the tenor was omitted only from one stanza of "Kyrie I," while in the last movement, the tenor is lacking from the entire second "Agnus." Tempus imperfectum is introduced only with the third "Agnus Dei," and the return to tempus perfectum occurs at the final "Dona nobis pacem."

The apparently disorderly way of changing from triple to

duple time has been observed in other English Masses of this period. Oliver Strunk, in his review of Power's *Missa Alma redemptoris,* found it striking that such a change should take place in the middle of the "Agnus Dei II." [10] In the *Missa Rex saeculorum,* the "Agnus III" starts in tempus imperfectum and returns to perfectum at "Dona nobis," just as in the AGNUS DEI of Frye's Mass. The Mass of Ricquardus Cockx in BR 5557 shows a correspondingly erratic disposition of tempus changes in both KYRIE and AGNUS DEI. It is all the more curious in this Mass because every movement except the AGNUS DEI concludes with at least a short section in tempus perfectum. But in the final movement, Cockx has introduced tempus imperfectum at the third "Agnus," and never reverted to triple time for the close of the Mass.

The plainsong Responsory which serves as the *cantus firmus* for Frye's *Missa Nobilis et pulchra* is uncolored melodically, although the rhythmical organization of the tenor in the polyphonic Mass, which is entirely arbitrary, reflects none of the original phrasing of the chant. There was, of course, no reason to observe phrasing which was determined by the text, since the text of *Nobilis et pulchra* was not meant to be sung even by the tenor in the Mass setting. Frye's tenor is given the text of the Ordinary either in full, when it is engaged in a duet, or by phrase incipits. Frye's disregard for the original phrasing of the chant melody is particularly noticeable in the placing of the free interpolations. One of these occurs at the beginning of a melisma which was written over the last syllable of the word "gaudia" in the Responsory text. This interpolation constitutes the entire tenor part for the first stanza of "Kyrie II." With the second stanza, the plainsong reappears in the tenor voice, at exactly the point where the interruption had occurred, and the melisma continues, concluding with the word "mundi." This melisma provides the *cantus firmus* for the whole second stanza of "Kyrie II," and the free interpolation thus seems like a substitute melisma.

A technique similar to this has been demonstrated by the three *Caput* Masses of Dufay, Ockeghem, and Obrecht. Otto Gombosi has pointed out that even though these composers re-

10. Ibid., p. 109.

tained the melodic line uncolored, they frequently distorted it by using the first tone of one phrase as the concluding tone of the preceding phrase and separating the two phrases by rests. Gombosi posed the question of whether such devices as these were originated by Dufay or whether he had observed them among English works, and said:

> It remains the task of future investigators to establish whether similar form devices, similar metric life, were known in English music of the time, and whether one or the other of the English composers under consideration could be singled out as the one to whom such procedures could be attributed.[11]

Judging by Frye's works, these devices were known in English music of the time. Probably there was no single composer to whom all such practices can be attributed. But there is no doubt that Frye's handling of formal elements identifies him with that group of English composers to whom Dufay and the later Netherlands composers were profoundly indebted. Frye's penchant for obscuring formal outlines by setting rhythmic and formal aspects against one another has been demonstrated by a detailed analysis of the KYRIE from his *Missa Nobilis et pulchra*. It has been shown that even when the opportunity of erecting a symmetrical structure between KYRIE and AGNUS DEI presented itself, Frye scrupulously avoided it. In these respects Frye reveals a wholly different attitude from that governing the musical aesthetic of early fifteenth-century Continental music. The symmetrical phrasing, balanced and periodic structure, and frequent cadencing of early fifteenth-century music are all abandoned in favor of a style in which every effort is made to conceal the structural framework.

Many of the structural and stylistic features discussed in connection with Frye's *Missa Nobilis et pulchra* are equally characteristic of his other two Masses and need not be described in detail for each one. But there are some aspects peculiar to each of the Masses which warrant special consideration.

The *Missa Summe Trinitati* is distinguished primarily for the

11. Otto Gombosi, review of Bukofzer, *Studies in Medieval and Renaissance Music*, JAMS, 4 (1951), 146–47.

handling of the *cantus firmus* material. Since there is no KYRIE, the arrangement of the chant is first formulated in the GLORIA. Both GLORIA and CREDO have the entire *cantus firmus* once, completely uncolored, and with the same rhythmical organization in both movements. In neither the SANCTUS nor the AGNUS DEI does the melody appear in its entirety, but those parts which are omitted from one do appear in the other. Thus, with some duplication, the entire *cantus firmus* is presented by the two movements together. In the SANCTUS, the tenor is tacet during the "Pleni sunt" and the "Benedictus," and the portions of the tenor melody which would have followed at these points are omitted. In the last movement, the tenor is dropped for the entire second "Agnus," and the corresponding portion of the chant is lacking. The sections of the chant which are omitted from the "Pleni sunt" and the "Benedictus" are supplied by the first and third "Agnus," while that deleted from the "Agnus II" appears in the "Osanna" of the SANCTUS.

This technique of allotting different fragments of the *cantus firmus* to the different movements seems, on the face of things, to be directly opposed to the ideal of unifying the whole Mass by the use of the same tenor. If the tenor melody were simply apportioned out, the relationship of the four movements would indeed be rather tenuous. But in this Mass of Frye's, the movements are even more tightly drawn together by dividing the melody among them, because the last two movements are mutually dependent for the complete presentation of the *cantus firmus,* which links them with the first two movements.

The tenor of the *Missa Summe Trinitati,* unlike that of *Nobilis et pulchra,* has no free sections. It is always bound to the *cantus firmus* material. Prolonged rests occur only in the tenor part of this Mass, and hence there are scarcely any duets involving the tenor. In this respect too, the *Missa Summe Trinitati* differs from the other three-voiced Mass in which the tenor is tacet only occasionally.

The *cantus firmus* of the *Missa Summe Trinitati,* because it is identical with that of the anonymous motet *Salve Virgo mater* (Trent 240), raises the question of the relationship between Masses and motets. Bukofzer, who made the identification, pointed out that the motet also shared the motto beginnings of

the four Mass movements.[12] Whether or not the Mass and motet
fall into the modern definition of "parody," the identical
rhythmic formulation of the melody and the use of the same
motto beginning indicate a close connection between them.
Another Mass in the Trent codex, Le Rouge's *Missa Soyez
aprantiz,* (Nos. 1031–35) shares its *cantus firmus* with two motets.
The Mass was apparently written on the tenor of Frye's chanson
So ys emprentid, but that chanson appears in Trent as a contrafactum, *Sancta Maria succurre* (Nos. 990 and 1029), and in addition there is the motet *Stella coeli extirpavit* which has the same
tenor. These are all Marian motets, and, as was mentioned in
Chapter 2, English composers of polyphonic Marian antiphons
frequently used *cantus firmi* belonging to texts other than those
they were setting. Possibly it was not a random selection, however. Daily Marian rites certainly impinged on all other ritual
celebrations, and since it is the Marian motets that show what
appears to be an erratic choice of *cantus firmi,* an explanation
may lie in their connection with particular Masses. It is conceivable that motets and Masses which shared the same *cantus
firmus* were intended for the same specific service. The English
may have had a stronger sense of liturgical propriety than has
been supposed. Frank Harrison's discovery that the *Benedicamus
Domino* was frequently drawn from a melisma in a specific chant
suggests that the music of the English liturgy was quite closely
unified,[13] and the choice of *cantus firmi* for Marian motets may
have been motivated by the same ideal.

The two Masses, *Nobilis et pulchra* and *Summe Trinitati* are
what Bukofzer calls "isorhythmic," i.e. the rhythmic formulation
of the chant in the first movement remains unchanged in the
others. In this respect the *Missa Flos regalis* stands apart, for the
rhythmic organization varies from movement to movement.
The first section of the tenor is given basically the same design
in the SANCTUS and "Agnus Dei I," but apart from this similarity
the handling of the chant is quite free. The phrases are broken
at different points, and the rhythmic figures are displaced. Here,
as in the other two Masses of Frye, the melody is apparently un-

---

12. Bukofzer, "English Church Music of the Fifteenth Century," *New Oxford
History of Music, 3* (London, 1960), 212.
13. *Music in Medieval Britain,* pp. 74–76.

colored. Since the original chant is unknown, it is impossible to be sure that the melody has not been ornamented, but the tenor of the Mass has the appearance of a liturgical chant without coloration, and it recurs with no melodic alteration in all four movements.

The *cantus firmus* is complete in the GLORIA and CREDO of *Flos regalis,* but one section of it is omitted from both the SANCTUS and the AGNUS DEI. In this Mass it is the same fragment which is lacking from the last two movements, when the tenor is tacet (during the "Pleni sunt" and the "Agnus II"). The section left out consists of seventeen measures in modern transcription, and while it is not accounted for anywhere in the last two movements, the lack is not a serious one artistically because there are so many recurrent motives in the chant that this section is very similar to other parts of it. The first four measures, for example, are a repetition, except for two notes, of the phrase immediately preceding them in the chant melody.

There is a great deal of thematic similarity in the discant part from one movement to another of the *Missa Flos regalis.* The reiteration of melodic material in the uppermost voice is particularly interesting in those sections from which the *cantus firmus* is lacking. In the "Pleni sunt," for example, there are several passages in the discant which appear also in the SANCTUS and "Agnus Dei I." In addition, one phrase from the "Pleni sunt" reappears, treated sequentially, in the "Agnus Dei II," from which the tenor is also missing. Thus, these two sections are linked together not by the *cantus firmus,* but by the melodic material of the discant. (Compare the "Pleni sunt," mm. 51–54 with the SANCTUS, mm. 14–17 and AGNUS DEI, mm. 14–16; also the "Pleni sunt" mm. 59–60 with the AGNUS DEI, mm. 55–57.)

In voice grouping, Frye employs constant variation. In two of the Masses, *Summe Trinitati* and *Flos regalis,* there are introductory duos for all movements. Some entire sections, such as the "Benedictus" and "Agnus Dei II," are set for only two voices. But beyond this rather perfunctory use of duos, Frye frequently reduces the musical texture to two parts. In the *Missa Summe Trinitati* this is done almost always by dropping the tenor, although there is an eight-measure duet of discant and tenor toward the beginning of the GLORIA. What is most characteristic of Frye's Mass technique is the unschematic alternation of duos formed by various combinations. In the *Missa Nobilis et pulchra,* for example, duos of discant and contratenor give way to contratenor and tenor, or discant and tenor are replaced by discant and contratenor.

In the four-voiced *Missa Flos regalis* there is, of course, a much wider range of possibilities for voice grouping. And yet there is only one three-voiced passage in the entire Mass. For the most part, the contrast is between duos of various combinations and the full four-voiced choir. When the tenor is tacet, the other three voices alternate to form a succession of duets. All four movements open with introductory duos of discant and contratenor, followed by discant and bass. In the GLORIA, the duet of discant and bass at "Qui tollis" is superseded by contratenor and bass, which, in turn, are followed by a combination of discant and contratenor.

It is seldom that a striking contrast is intended by the shift of range effected through this alternation of voices. More often than not, the second pair of voices emerges almost imperceptibly from the first. There is always one voice common to both duets, for the tenor of the *Missa Flos regalis* does not take part in the duos. There is seldom a sharp break in the rhythmic flow, and frequently the change is effected by the anticipatory entrance of a third voice to replace one of the preceding parts just before it stops. This can be seen, for example, in the "Et incarnatus" of the CREDO, in which the bass joins the discant and contratenor for two breves, and then the discant drops out while contratenor and bass continue. This same technique is seen in the opening of the SANCTUS. The "Pleni sunt" is composed almost entirely for a duet of discant and bass. Only the last thirteen measures include the contratenor to make up the one three-voiced section of the whole Mass.

This four-voiced Mass of Walter Frye emphasizes above all the importance of the bicinium technique for the English composers around the middle of the century. In the three-voiced Masses, the omission of the tenor, or of any one voice, results automatically in a duet. But when the tenor is withdrawn from the four-voiced texture, there remains a trio—a trio which is almost never used as such but is deliberately broken down into a succession of duos.

This duet style seems to be related to the practice of discant.

Discant was taught in terms of two-part writing, of one voice set against another, and while it can be applied to any number of parts, the style lends itself most successfully to two-voiced composition. It was pointed out earlier that Frye's melodic writing was based on an understanding of consonance implicit in discant theory. The rather aimless melodic lines, the sequential technique, the preoccupation with one or two notes within a phrase, and the gymel-like relationship of tenor and contratenor are all characteristic of a style which results from the note-against-note relationship of the discanting voices to the tenor. The cultivation of duet style, even within a four-voiced Mass such as *Flos regalis,* is an equally significant index of the extent to which the ideal of discant had begun to find expression in one of the greatest musical forms of the fifteenth century.

CHAPTER 7

The Chansons of Frye

THE CHANGE of style which took place around 1450 is illustrated more clearly by the chanson than by any of the other musical forms. As the leading category during the first half of the century, the chanson was identified with one specific style and one particular function. The motet underwent various changes in the course of the century, both in style and function. The large ceremonial motets, frequently polytextual and isorhythmic, gave way in the latter half of the century to a purely liturgical form, with one Latin text and usually with a *cantus firmus*. During the transitional period, many experimental forms emerged—sometimes with the *cantus firmus* elaborated in the discant, sometimes with no *cantus firmus*, sometimes in caccia style and sometimes in what has been called "conductus style," i.e. discant style. The chanson motet may or may not have been an independent category apart from the practice of making contrafacta, but the mere fact that motets were formed out of secular songs is indicative of the changing status of the motet as a musical category.

The Mass provides even less of a standard to be applied throughout the fifteenth century, since it was only around 1450 that the major form of the cyclic Mass was developed. The individual and paired Mass movements of the first half of the century, like the motets, had borrowed stylistically from secular literature.

The chanson alone borrowed its style from no other category. Moreover, its function did not change during the course of the century. It was a highly refined genre which served to enhance the secular festivities of the court, and it remained, until the very end of the century, a small form in which were compressed all the most essential elements of style.

During the middle years of the fifteenth century, the ballade form was discarded in favor of the rondeau, and the virelai was superseded by the bergerette. Finally, at around 1500, the "formes fixes" were rejected altogether in favor of a free and more elaborate polyphonic setting. But during the fifteenth century there was no fundamental change of a formal nature in the structure of the chanson. The ascendancy of the rondeau had very little to do with the musical form in which chansons were written since rondeau, virelai, and ballade were all composed basically of two major musical sections. The whole form was determined ultimately by the manner in which the text was apportioned to these two sections, and was, then, primarily a literary consideration. The ballade alone had one distinguishing musical feature, the rhyme between endings of the two sections, but there was no essential difference among these secular forms from the point of view of style and function.

The chanson, then, provides the standard by which the stylistic change of 1450 may be measured most easily. On the Continent during the first half of the century, the predominant chanson style was that of the accompanied melody with a rather ornate vocal line, set against two voices which were rhythmically less active, the tenor and contratenor. This technique of the accompanied solo song was so inextricably identified with the chanson literature that the term "ballade style," derived from the foremost category of that time, has been used by scholars to describe any composition written in this style.[1] The transition from this style to one in which discant and tenor are coupled against a harmonic contratenor took place around the middle of the century.

The chansons of Walter Frye are early examples of the discant-tenor style. Because of this relatively advanced technique, they have heretofore been dated much too late. Arthur Vogel assigns a date of 1480 to *So ys emprentid*.[2] Catharine Keyes Miller, however, feels that a comparison of the Frye chansons with

1. Handschin has objected to the use of the term "ballade style" for various reasons. See Jacques Handschin, "Les études sur le XVe siècle musical de Ch. Van den Borren," *RB, 1* (1946–47), 94.
2. "The English Part Song around 1500," abstract in *BAMS*, 4 (1940), 10.

Plate 1. Ely Cathedral: Exterior of the West Tower and the South West Transept.

Plate 2. Ely Cathedral: Exterior, South View.

Plate 3. Ely Cathedral: Choir, showing 14th-century stalls moved from the Octagon to their present posit in the 19th century.

e 4. Madonna and Child with SS. Catherine and Barbara, detail of Angel with Music Scroll. Attributed to the Master of the Embroidered Foliage. Chiesa Madre, Polizzi Generosa, Sicily.

Plate 5. Madonna and Child with Six Angel Musicians (Frontispiece), detail of Angel at left of the Mado
Paris, Féral Collection.

6. *Mary, Queen of Heaven*. Master of the St. Lucy Legend. National Gallery of Art, Washington, D.C., Samuel H. Kress Collection.

Plate 7. Mary, Queen of Heaven (Plate 6), detail of Singing Angel at left of Mary.

Plate 8. Mary, Queen of Heaven (Plate 6), detail of Singing Angel at right of Mary.

Plate 9. Mary, Queen of Heaven (Plate 6), detail of Singing Angel kneeling at left of the Trinity, above M

works in the B section of the Ritson manuscript makes a slightly earlier date more probable. She concludes that 1470 or shortly thereafter would be the latest acceptable date.[3] Mrs. Miller, perhaps out of excessive caution, was still far too late in her estimate. She was perhaps influenced by Bukofzer, whose estimate of 1470 is based on the assumption that the Mellon chansons represented original copies.[4] We now know that at least with respect to the Frye chansons the Mellon repertory is decidedly retrospective. If Frye's *Alas, alas* could have been copied by Schedel in the early 'sixties, after it had already been changed into a Latin motet and the cadences altered, it must have been composed about or before 1460. *So ys emprentid* and *Myn hertis lust* are stylistically even a little earlier than *Alas, alas* and can therefore be dated before 1460, probably in the middle 'fifties at the latest. Possibly they were even considerably earlier.

The dating of the Frye chansons is significant, for it shows a real discant-tenor style to have been in evidence in English works by about 1455 at least. *The Princesse of Youth,* which seems in some respects to be earlier than the Frye chansons, is nevertheless constructed in the same fashion, with tenor and discant accompanied by a harmonic contratenor. It has generally been assumed that these chansons represent an adaptation of the Burgundian duet style. This is an inevitable conclusion if they are dated even as early as 1470, when the style was well established. But a comparison of the Frye chansons with Continental works of the 'fifties and 'sixties makes this attribution of priority questionable. Two of Frye's chansons, *Myn hertis lust* and *So ys emprentid,* belong in the group which Helen Hewitt classifies as "Late Burgundian," and the other two, *Tout a par moy* and *Alas, alas,* exhibit the slightly more advanced style which Hewitt calls "Early Netherlands." [5]

In the first two of the Frye chansons, there is no imitation, but the tenor and discant are both written in cantabile vocal lines, while the contratenor moves in a more angular fashion. The contratenor has a rhythmic as well as a harmonic function to

3. "A Fifteenth-Century Record of English Choir Repertory: B.M. Add. Ms. 5665," unpublished Ph.D. dissertation, Yale University, 1948, pp. 76–77.

4. "An Unknown Chansonnier," p. 31.

5. Helen Hewitt and Isabel Pope, eds., *Harmonices musices Odhecaton A,* pp. 61–62.

fulfill, for it is often this voice which keeps the motion going after the cadence. (See m. 41 of *So ys emprentid,* and m. 40 of *Myn hertis lust.*) [6] The contratenor is probably an instrumental part, while both discant and tenor are meant to be sung. This is apparent not only from stylistic considerations, but also from the way in which they are copied into the Mellon manuscript. Complete texts are given only to the discant, but the *secunda pars* of each of these compositions gives text incipits for the tenor voice, while the contratenor has only the inscription "Contra." This is also true of Bedingham's *Gentil madonna,* which is sandwiched between the two Frye compositions, and in which the text incipit of the tenor part includes the entire first line. Such a long incipit would not be necessary merely for identification of the part. Hence, it must be assumed that the whole text is to be sung by the tenor. Certainly both discant and tenor of Frye's *Ave Regina* must have been sung, since both the paintings showing it portray singers reading the tenor part (Plates 4 and 5). In these chansons of Frye, as well as in the *Ave Regina* and *Trinitatis dies,* the essential notes of the cadence are found in tenor and discant parts, one having tonic—leading tone—tonic, and the other, mediant—supertonic—tonic.

The ballade texts are set phrase by phrase, according to the divisions of text lines. Each line begins syllabically, with fairly long note values, and then becomes more rhythmically animated, particularly on the final syllable of the text. This is exactly the style of the two "late Burgundian" chansons in the Odhecaton: *Ales regres* (No. 57) of Hayne van Ghizeghem and *Les grans regres* (No. 71).

The other two compositions of Frye are a little more advanced in style. In both *Alas, alas* and *Tout a par moy,* as well as in the anonymous *The Princesse of Youth,* there is rudimentary imitation at the beginnings of phrases between discant and tenor. The imitation in these works is not yet utilized as an important structural element, and there are no rests in the contratenor part to emphasize the imitative entries. This rather tentative type of imitation is handled in an almost identical fashion by Vincenet in *Fortuna per ta crudelte (Odhecaton,* No. 60) and Compère in *Mais que ce fust (Odhecaton,* No. 87).

6. References for the Frye chansons are to Walter Frye, *Collected Works,* ed. Sylvia W. Kenney.

Of the Continental composers whose works show a real kin-
ship with those of Frye, there is not much biographical information at hand. Hayne van Ghizeghem may have had contact
with Frye through the chapel of the Count of Charolais (see
Chapter 3). Nothing is known about Vincenet, but Compère is
commonly supposed to have been born about 1450. This seems
a little late, but in any case he must have been considerably
younger than Frye. Thus Frye's secular song cannot be explained
through the influence of these composers. If anything, Hayne,
Vincenet, and Compère must have been indebted to Frye or to
other English composers of his generation.

It was pointed out in Chapter 4 that at least two of Frye's
chansons must have been composed in England, and not after
he had gone to the Continent where he might have been subjected to the influence of Continental composers. This assumption was based on the relationship of the Frye chansons to the
works in the Ashmole manuscript 191 (published in *Early
Bodleian Music, 2,* 66–73). The similarity in style between the
Frye chansons and those of the Ashmole manuscript has important implications because all but one of the Ashmole songs
are for two voices only. Frye's compositions, while having three
voices in the Continental chansonniers, are composed basically
as duets with accompanying contratenor. This style implies a
sure and facile technique of two-part writing which is very much
like that of the Ashmole songs. In all of Frye's songs, and in
those in Ashmole, the two voices of the bicinium are written in
very nearly equal rhythmic values, with a consonant relationship
between them. They are, in fact, in pure discant style.

There are five consecutive thirds or sixths, at the most, between tenor and discant, but for the most part the two voices
move in contrary motion. While extended parallelism occurs
infrequently between these two voices, alternate imperfect consonances occur with great regularity. The sixth follows the third
in exactly the fashion prescribed by Power. (See m. 8 of *So ys
emprentid,* and m. 2 of *O kendly creature* in the Ashmole Ms.)
Similarly, the third follows the sixth, as in mm. 6–7 of *Alas, alas.*
At the beginning of *Alas, alas* there are actually seven consecutive thirds between tenor and discant. Usually, however, the
voices are syncopated in such a way that the parallelism is obscured, as in the opening measures of the *Ave Regina* and

measures 17–20 of *So ys emprentid.* In this last example, the
interval between tenor and discant is essentially a sixth throughout, and yet the syncopation, use of suspensions, and the insertion of one essential fifth, even though for only a minim,
allays the softness of the constant intervallic relationship. It is
interesting, too, that this is the only one of Frye's ballades in
which this particular section, the ending of the *prima pars,* is
not repeated literally at the end of the *secunda pars.* When this
passage recurs in the *secunda pars,* the lower parts are varied,
and the tenor no longer adheres to the sixth relationship with
the discant. Frye perhaps felt that the limits of parallel motion
had already been exceeded, and did not want to repeat the
passage.

There is no doubt that while pure consecutive imperfect
intervals of one kind were frowned upon, the effect achieved
by constant use of imperfect intervals was highly valued. "And
it is to wite that the mo (re) imperfit tones that a man synges in
the trebyll the merrier it is," [7] and "also it is fair singing merry
for to sing many imperfite acordes togeder." [8] It is instructive to
study the way in which this "merry" effect was achieved without
infringing the rule about consecutive thirds or sixths. The
syncopation discussed above was one method. Another is seen in
the use of voice-crossing. In measures 43–47 of *Alas, alas* the
discant and tenor maintain a constant relationship of a third,
but first the discant has the upper line, and then the tenor. This
type of device is accounted for even by the theorists, since
Power's example of three sixths followed by three tenths produces essentially the same result, and it was freely used even in
the thirteenth century (see the discussion of "Edi beo" in
Chapter 5).

It should be noted, too, that implied parallelism, as in *Ave
Regina* and *Alas, alas,* is conspicuously counteracted by the
contrary motion of the contratenor. Real parallel motion among
all three parts appears only occasionally at the cadences. The
songs in the Ashmole manuscript show less of this artful use of
consecutive thirds and sixths, but there are occasional examples
in such passages as mm. 26–29 of *O kendly creature.*

7. B.M. Add. Ms. 21455, No. 8, published in Bukofzer, *Geschichte,* p. 138.
8. Cambridge, Corpus Christi Ms. 410, II, published in Bukofzer, *Geschichte,*
p. 146.

This comparison of the two repertories (the English songs in Mellon and those of Ashmole 191) suggests that the relationship between them was simply one of chronology—i.e. that the three-voiced compositions of Frye are a logical sequence to the style of two-part writing seen in the Ashmole songs. This would be an acceptable interpretation were it not for the fact that *So ys emprentid,* albeit just a fragment, actually appears in the same manuscript with this series of two-part compositions. This implies that it, too, existed at least for a short time as a two-voiced composition. *So ys emprentid* would, indeed, be quite satisfactory simply as a duo of discant and tenor, without the contratenor of the Mellon chansonnier. All of Frye's chansons and chanson-motets, in fact, seem to have been conceived originally as bicinia in the tradition represented by these songs of the Ashmole manuscript. There is a delightful account by Tinctoris of a performance of Frye's *Tout a par moy* with only discant and tenor parts, a report made less in the interest of style than in a feat of vocal ventriloquism of some sort. Tinctoris describes hearing a miraculous performance by his fellow-countryman, Gerard of Brabant, who rendered all by himself simultaneously, and to perfection, these two parts of the rondeau: "supremam partem simul cum tenore, non voces alternando." [9]

There is further evidence provided by the Frye manuscripts on this matter. The two-voiced textless ballade in the Prague Strahov codex is one example. The two parts fill the verso folio entirely and there is no room for a contratenor part to be copied in.[10] The same is true of the painting of the Madonna (from the Féral Collection, Paris), which shows a music book containing the discant and tenor of Frye's *Ave Regina* (Plate 5). The instrumentalist angels may have been playing a contratenor part, but there is no music for it. The music book which served as the painter's model is no longer extant, but there must have been at that time such a book presenting the piece as complete with only two voices.

A rather striking coincidence with regard to pictorial repre-

9. K. Weinemann, *Johannes Tinctoris und sein unbekannter Traktat "De inventione et usu musicae"* (Regensburg, 1917), p. 34. See also Dragan Plamenac, "Browsing through a Little-Known Manuscript," p. 106.

10. See Plamenac, "Browsing through a Little-Known Manuscript," Plate I.

sentations of music is revealed by another painting of a Madonna surrounded by angels singing an *Ave Regina* from written music. This is the "Mary, Queen of Heaven" by the Master of the St. Lucy Legend (ca. 1485) in the National Gallery of Art (Samuel H. Kress Collection) in Washington [11] (Plates 6–9). The musical notation is perfectly legible in the tenor and discant parts, which are labeled, provided with text, and portrayed as being sung (Plates 7 and 8). A third part, also being sung, looks as though it were a pure fabrication of the artist (Plate 9). It is not readable, the note forms are not authentic, and the entire aspect of this part is totally at variance with the clarity of tenor and discant parts. (There is also a fourth part, sung from a book by a group of angels, but the music is not visible to the spectator). The discant and tenor parts are copied onto single sheets, while the third and fourth parts are in choir books of moderate size. The duet sung by the two angels in the foreground is a quite respectable one—though not inspired—and has some features in common with Frye's *Ave Regina.* It uses the same text, that is the shorter, rhymed antiphon and not the older liturgical text, and it has, like Frye's, a fermata at the end of the first phrase, after "Ave." The coincidence of text, of phrasing, and of the use of only two real voices suggests a certain tradition in the portrayal of music in fifteenth-century paintings.

What the instrumentalist angels in these paintings were supposed to have played is difficult to judge. Possibly they simply doubled the singers. Possibly a third part was added or "countered" in the fashion described by Pseudo-Chilston, which could have been improvised. It seems unlikely that a dozen angels scattered around various corners of the canvas should have been wholly in accord on the matter of improvisation, but this was perhaps a matter of indifference to the painter, and it does not preclude the possibility of a third "countered" voice.

One of the songs in the Ashmole manuscript, *Go hert, hurt with adversite,* does have this counter voice included. In the others, one could surely have been improvised, but it could not have been improvised in a perfunctory method of parallelism. The two existing voices are written basically in a style of con-

11. This painting was called to my attention by Noah Greenberg.

trary motion, and the added part would have to be adapted to the consonances of the original duet. This is the nature of the Frye contratenor, which functions sometimes as a harmonic bass, sometimes as a middle filling voice between tenor and discant. The rather ill-defined character of the contratenor was equally typical of the Continental discant-tenor chanson. It was obviously a voice whose function was to add to an already complete duet.

This duet style was the first indication of the new trend in fifteenth-century music. On the Continent during the fourteenth —and even to some extent the thirteenth—centuries, the uppermost part had been the leading melodic voice, the vehicle of the text. The tenor and contratenor provided the framework on which that single melody rested. In the early years of the fifteenth century, those two lower parts were sometimes consolidated into a "solus tenor" which may have supported two upper voices. The discant-tenor chanson represents a complete reversal of function, for a new kind of duet is formed by discant and tenor, and this duet is supported by a single accompanying part, the contratenor. There were forms in fourteenth-century French music which resembled the discant-tenor structure superficially—the chasse and the double discant chanson. But in these compositions, the tenor retained its position as a cornerstone of the structure and the duet was comprised of two discants. The duet, then, did not include the tenor but was erected over the basic line provided by the tenor.

The tenor *cantus firmus* tradition of the French and English composers was a strong one, and the tenor voice, in spite of its melodically subordinate role, retained always a position of great importance, whether it was a *cantus prius factus* or not. Tinctoris defines the tenor as the foundation of the piece, with no qualifications as to category. The contratenor, by definition, had always been a voice which was written against the tenor and shared its function. Hence, in the fifteenth-century "ballade style" the tenor and contratenor were paired in a supporting role to form the polyphonic accompaniment to the melody. In the discant-tenor chanson, the tenor and contratenor are separated. The contratenor has been deserted, as it were, by the tenor, which now casts its lot with the discant.

Because the tenor had always been the fundamental voice for French composers, its relationship with any of the others was always a rather strict one. Hence the correct intervallic relationship between tenor and discant was not new for the northern composers. What was new was the rhythmic equivalence of these two voices and the increased use of thirds and sixths. It has been demonstrated already that these two aspects go hand in hand. The tenor, in becoming the melodic equal of the discant, did not relinquish its traditional function. As the two voices drew closer together stylistically, the discant sacrificed its elaborate melismata, but the tenor abandoned none of its primary characteristics. It merely became more melodic, while retaining its role as the governing voice.

In the older ballade style, the contrast between the melodic discant and the slower tenor was specifically emphasized, whereas after 1450 this difference was minimized. The question of whether melodies borrowed from chansons of the second half of the century are tenors or discants is problematic, simply because they are no longer distinguishable one from the other. The famous *L'homme armé* melody, which was presumably a simple monophonic chanson, achieved its most enduring fame as a tenor in Netherlands Masses and polyphonic chansons.[12] Monophonic chansons in general came to be widely used as either discants or tenors of polyphonic compositions during the last part of the fifteenth century. The two monophonic chansonniers from the end of the century, Paris, Bibl. nat., f. fr. Mss. 12744 and 9346 (the Bayeux Ms.), contain fifty-four melodies which were used in polyphonic settings as discants or tenors. The Tournai chansonnier is made up almost entirely of tenor parts.[13] There is also a collection of seventeen tenors, bound together with polyphonic chansons in the Paris Ms. n.a., f. fr. 4379.[14] This idea of combining the functions of superius and tenor within one style was one of the major innovations of the fifteenth-century Netherlands composers. It was undoubtedly prompted by a model in which duos of melodically equivalent voices played an important role.

12. Gustave Reese, *Music in the Renaissance*, pp. 73, 149–50.
13. Ibid. See also Gustave Reese and Theodore Karp, "Monophony in a Group of Renaissance Chansonniers," *JAMS*, 5 (1952), 4–15.
14. Reese, *Music in the Renaissance*, p. 206, n. 103a.

It is apparent from the repertory of early fifteenth-century England that two-part writing in discant style enjoyed a favor there that it did not have on the Continent. This is seen not only by the Frye chansons and the Ashmole manuscript but also by the Bodleian manuscript, Douce 381, which contains five English two-part songs, one French two-part song, and one French three-part song.[15] Certainly the carol literature provides abundant evidence of the high regard in which duet forms were held in England. It is, furthermore, implicit in the theoretical treatises that the duet resulting from the addition of one discanting voice to the tenor was intended to provide a perfectly satisfactory composition by itself. The mere fact that none of the theorists discuss at all the problem of three-voiced texture is evidence that they thought primarily in terms of a basic duet, to which, of course, the contratenor could be added. The assumption that English discant refers to three-part improvisation has obscured this aspect of English music.

Continental composers never adopted a two-voiced style to the same extent that the English did. The French chanson contined to be a three-voiced category. But the relationship of the three voices to one another changed, and the self-sufficient duo of tenor and discant became fundamental to the structure. Early evidence of this change is provided by accounts of the performance in two parts of a work which has survived in chansonniers only in the three-voiced versions. The chronicle of Mathieu d'Escouchy, giving the details of the famous Banquet du Voeu at Lille in 1454, proves that *Je ne vis oncques la pareille* was sung in this fashion:

> Apprez que l'eglise et le pasté eurent chascun quatre fois joué, sy entra ung cherf merveilleusement grant et bel . . . Et par dessus . . . estoit monté ung josne filz de eage de XII ans . . . Et à l'entrée de la salle commencha ledit enfant le dessus d'une chansson moult hault et cler, et ledit cherf lui tenoit la teneur sans avoir autre personne, sy non l'enfant et l'artiffice du cherf, et nommoit on la chanchon qu'ilz disoient: *Je ne vis oncques la pareille.*[16]

15. Published in facsimile in John Stainer, ed., *Early Bodleian Music, 1*, Plates XX-XXV.

16. Jeanne Marix, *Histoire de la musique*, p. 39.

This description proves that only discant and tenor were sung. But the reiteration of the fact that there were only two ("sans avoir autre personne, sy non l'enfant et l'artiffice du cherf") suggests that it was something of a novelty at that time. The fact that both parts were vocal is also striking, for this kind of performance would not have been at all appropriate to the earlier French chanson in "ballade style." [17] This composition, which is attributed to Dufay in most sources containing three-voiced versions, is indeed composed as a discant-tenor chanson and is characterized by frequent use of thirds and sixths between those two voices.

The tradition of two-part writing did not flourish in England alone. It was mentioned in Chapter 1 that some scholars, notably Stephan and Besseler, have traced the origins of the Burgundian duet style to Italy, rather than to England. More recently Kurt von Fischer has emphasized certain Italian elements. While it is true that Italian composers cultivated duet forms extensively during the fourteenth and early fifteenth centuries, they did not actually produce a contrapuntal style which could be said to account for the new direction which Continental music took around the middle of the century.

In Italy, just as in France, the style of fourteenth-century music is characterized by the "organal" relationship of the tenor to the other voices, rather than by discant style. Following Pierre de la Croix, the Italians had developed a style of rhythm which, by its very nature, tended to preclude a real note-against-note style, for the basis was the division of the breve into from two to twelve smaller values with no regard for the intermediate divisions. Thus, the melodic line was composed of groups of notes, of almost any number, which were sung within the time limits of one breve. Apel compares this florid melodic style with that of the coloraturas of seventeenth-century arias.[18] Italian music during the fourteenth century was, in fact, primarily a soloistic art and quite incompatible with the ideal of discant.

By the beginning of the fifteenth century, Italian music had been influenced by the French and had succumbed to the di-

---

17. Olivier de la Marche used the word "chanta" rather than "tenoit." See Marix, *Histoire de la musique*, p. 39, n. 4.

18. Willi Apel, *The Notation of Polyphonic Music*, p. 89.

visions of mensural notation by means of modus, tempus, and prolatio. The rhythmic activity became more evenly divided among the parts, and the duet style was indeed characterized by two equally important parts. But certain features of the florid style remained. The two-voiced compositions from this period frequently exhibit a style of rhythmic alternation, in which one voice has an active figure over a sustained note in the other part, after which the situation is reversed, and the second voice has the moving part. Jacobus de Bononia's *Uselletto selvaggio* illustrates this type of alternation (Example 19). This type of writing

EXAMPLE 19

From *Uselletto selvaggio*, Jacobus de Bononia

After J. Wolf, *Geschichte der Mensural-Notation, 3,* 99

represents an orderly and schematic division of labor between the two voices. There are not simultaneous melodies, but only one, which alternates between the two voices. There is no continuous flow and interweaving of the two parts, but rather a

continuous effect of one sustained voice with one melismatic
one. This type of writing was typical of early fifteenth-century
Italian music and is seen also in works of Ciconia, such as his
O virum—O lux—O beate Nicholae (Example 20). Kurt von

EXAMPLE 20

From *O virum—O lux—O beate Nicholae,* J. Ciconia

After H. Besseler, *Die Musik des Mittelalters
und der Renaissance,* p. 204.

Fischer also makes the point that a great deal of parallelism in
Italian trecento polyphony indicates the importance of monophony in Italy until as late as 1350. "Indeed," he writes, "one
occasionally receives the impression that this many-voiced writing grew more or less directly out of monophony." [19]

The hocquet is also used in Italian music to achieve equal
voice movement, as can be seen by the examples from *Amor
amaro* (Example 21). In the second of these examples, the
tendency to evolve one melodic line out of the two voices in
alternation is particularly clear. Imitation in early fifteenth-
century Italian music is also handled in this fashion. It is primarily related to the technique of repetition seen frequently in

19. Kurt von Fischer, "On the Technique, Origin, and Evolution of Italian
Trecento Music," *MQ, 47* (1961), 41 and 50.

the single melodic line. An excerpt from *Mercè mercè, O morte* (Example 22) shows a melodic phrase which is literally repeated in the superius. In Ciconia's *Una panthera* (Example 23) we see the same repetitive technique, but this time distributed between two voices instead of just in one. This style, then, like the ballade style of France, is essentially based on the ideal of one sustained voice and one melodic voice, even though the melody may alternate between two voices.

Heinrich Besseler's belief in the importance of Italian music for the Netherlands style is not based solely on the evidence of

EXAMPLE 21

a) From *Amor amaro,* anon.

b)

After F. Ghisi, "Italian Ars Nova Music,"
JRBM, 2 (1947), Suppl. pp. 19, 20.

EXAMPLE 22

From *Mercè, Mercè,* anon.

After F. Ghisi, "Italian Ars Nova Music,"
JRBM, 2 (1947), Suppl. 17

a predilection for two-voiced writing. In his *Bourdon und
Fauxbourdon* Besseler advances the theory that Dufay's works
of the 1430s are profoundly indebted to the Italian motet of

EXAMPLE 23

From *Una panthera*, J. Ciconia

After F. Ghisi, "Italian Ars Nova Music,"
JRBM, 2 (1947), Suppl. 7

around 1400, which in turn was based on the fourteenth-
century caccia.[20] The caccia is indeed a form which resembles
the discant-tenor structure superficially in that there are two
melodic voices accompanied by one harmonic part. It consisted
of a canon (usually strict) between the upper two voices, and a
free tenor which served as a harmonic foundation. It is this free
tenor which Besseler regards as the prototype for Dufay's harmonic "bourdon" contratenor.

There are several reasons why this explanation is unsatisfactory. In the first place, the French had their own equivalent of
the caccia, the chasse, and there is no reason why they should
have turned to Italy for this particular tradition. Furthermore,
while the equating of the Netherlands contratenor with the
Italian tenor is easily accomplished in retrospect, it is not so
likely to have been done by fifteenth-century composers for
whom the concept of the "tenor" implied a quite specific role.

Besseler, in his preoccupation with the contratenor-bass line,
tends to regard this voice with its changing function as the most
significant one. He points out chansons of Dufay dating from
the 1430s in which the contratenor plays a strictly harmonic role,

20. *Bourdon und Fauxbourdon,* p. 79.

like that of the tenor in the caccia. But in these compositions, such as *Helas ma dame* and *Je languis en piteux martire,* the tenor too plays a rather more harmonic than melodic role. It is still not a melodic voice and it cannot be said to form a real bicinium with the discant in the sense of the discant-tenor chanson. These compositions, then, must have been composed in the older tradition, as solos with two accompanying voices, rather than as bicinia with a third voice added.

For Besseler it is actually the role of the contratenor which determined the new style. In order to graft the Italian tenor technique onto the Netherlands *cantus firmus* composition, he says, Dufay extended the contratenor range downward so that it acquired the position of a real bass.[21] It seems inconsistent with French musical traditions, however, that a subsidiary voice such as the contratenor should have determined the new style. It was the tenor which was conceived first and which provided the foundation of the work. The contratenor was adapted to it, whether in "ballade style" or discant-tenor style. Although for a short time the Dufay contratenor did function, like the Italian tenor, as a bass voice, it returned, around 1440, to its original place in the middle of the composition. The contratenor-bass, then, was not an invention that had enduring results at that time. Furthermore, it was not long before the contratenor became a more cantabile voice, like the discant and tenor. The very fact that the contratenor kept fluctuating is significant, for it suggests that this voice, far from being a determining factor in the development of the style, was the part which had to be adapted to the changes which took place in the relationship between tenor and discant.

Even assuming that the Netherlands contratenor was modeled on the caccia tenor, it is impossible to equate the discant-tenor duet of the new Netherlands chanson with the canonic upper voices of the caccia. There are several aspects of the caccia structure which are directly opposed to the ideal of the Netherlands chanson as it first emerged. The bicinium of the caccia, like that of the chasse, did not include the tenor, whereas the basic duet of the Netherlands chanson was comprised of tenor and discant. The inclusion of the tenor was a decisive factor, for it resulted in a duet which could be quite independent of the

21. Ibid., p. 89.

third voice. The canonic upper voices of the caccia are not really independent. The interval of the fourth appears frequently between these two voices at important points in the phrase, and a third voice is necessary to supply the lower fifth. This relationship is equally characteristic of the motets written in caccia style, such as Ciconia's *Venetiae mundi—Michael* [22] and *O virum—O lux—O beate Nicholae.*[23]

The question of fourths has been studied in some detail by Charles Warren Fox, who has compiled statistics to show that one of the characteristics of the Netherlands chanson was a nonquartal style, that is, one in which there are no essential fourths between any two voices.[24] Out of about a thousand chansons examined by Fox, a hundred and fifty prove to have no fourths. Any one of the three voices can, in effect, be omitted. Fifteen per cent is not a startling quorum, and, as Fox himself points out, no composer was governed exclusively by this nonquartal ideal.[25] Nevertheless, the research of Fox does emphasize the extreme care with which Netherlands composers in general handled that particular interval. It was regarded as a dissonance which could not be written over the tenor on an accented beat.

Certainly between tenor and discant of the Netherlands chanson the ban on fourths was strictly observed. Although only seven of the chansons in the Copenhagen chansonnier are written in a pure nonquartal style, Jeppesen has pointed out that all of them can be performed without the contratenor.[26] Thus, the bicinium formed by these two voices, unlike that of the caccia, is entirely independent of the accompanying third voice.

Whether or not the contratenor and discant can be performed alone is irrelevant, since the only indications of performance of two parts alone involve the discant and tenor, not the contratenor. It was the discant and tenor of *Tout a par moy* that were sung by Gerard of Brabant and of Dufay's *Je ne vis oncques*

22. Published in Charles Van den Borren, *Geschiedenis van de Muziek in de Nederlanden* (Antwerp, 1949), *1*, 78–79. See also Clercx, *Johannes Ciconia, 2,* 183.

23. Published in Besseler, *Die Musik des Mittelalters,* p. 204. See also Clercx, *Johannes Ciconia, 2,* 173.

24. "Non-Quartal Harmony in the Renaissance," *MQ, 31* (1945), 33.

25. Ibid., p. 38.

26. *Der Kopenhagener Chansonnier,* p. xlvii.

that were performed at Lille in 1454. And it is only the tenor and discant I of Dufay's *La belle se sied* that are preserved in the Bologna Ms. Univ. 2216.[27] Fox makes the point that the non-quartal style did not evolve from a desire to write in such a way that one of the voices could be omitted, since there are very few examples of "reduction." The process must be understood to work in the other direction, however. It was a question of adding a third voice, not of reducing to two. It is highly improbable that a three-voiced composition, once completed, would ever be performed without one of its parts. But we are concerned with the manner in which the composition was originally conceived, and the expendable contratenor is significant in this respect.

In examples of chansons which appear for only two voices in one manuscript and three in others, it is the earlier manuscripts, such as Strasbourg Ms. M.222.C.22, which have the two-voiced version.[28] There is no doubt, then, that the duo of discant and tenor was written first and was intended to be a quite self-sufficient composition. This concept of a completely independent bicinium, free of any dissonant fourths, could not have been derived from the canonic duo of the Italian caccia-influenced motet. There was a tradition of duets with expendable contratenors in the Italian trecento madrigal, but, as Kurt von Fischer points out, the contratenor which is omitted from some manuscripts does not assume the same function as the French contratenor. It is basically a vocal part, hence really a second superius part.[29]

Another characteristic which distinguishes the Italian motet forms from the early discant-tenor chanson is the imitative relationship of the two paired voices. The Italians had a strong predilection for canon and literal imitation. This heritage of the caccia is seen particularly in Ciconia's motets, such as *O virum—O lux—O beate Nicholae*,[30] *Ut te omnes—Ingens dummus Paduae,* and *O felix templum*.[31] While the northern composers

27. Charles Van den Borren, *Guillaume Dufay*, p. 268.
28. Ibid., p. 297.
29. Fischer, "On the Technique," pp. 44–45.
30. Published in Besseler, *Die Musik des Mittelalters*, p. 204.
31. Published in Charles Van den Borren, *Polyphonia Sacra* (Burnham, 1932), pp. 180 and 243.

placed the emphasis on intervallic relationships, the Italians regarded the imitation as of primary importance. Imitation is not a factor in the early discant-tenor chanson. Even though it appears in later works of Dufay, there is none in his *Je ne vis oncques*. The relationship of the tenor and discant in this composition is strictly one of counterpoint based on contrary motion. Among the late Burgundian chansons of the Odhecaton there is no imitation, even though tenor and discant form an autonomous duet.

Imitation penetrated the discant-tenor chanson in its second stage, and eventually became a leading factor in chanson composition. But it was not there at the outset. The first step was the equalization of the voices. It is almost inevitable that two melodic lines, equally important and yet mutually dependent, should come sooner or later to imitation in some fashion. And in the development of the fifteenth-century chanson it appears as just such a by-product of the bicinium technique, which was originally conceived quite apart from considerations of imitation. The absence of any imitation at all in many of Ockeghem's works is striking in view of his position in the Netherlands school. Ockeghem was concerned largely with the problem of combining two, three, four, or even five voices of equal melodic importance, and this ideal found expression quite apart from the technique of imitation. Ockeghem's style, like that of the discant-tenor duet in the chanson, was governed by the principle of contrary motion.

Besseler's study of fifteenth-century music clarifies many important points with regard to the new Netherlands style, but it overemphasizes the influence of Italy. We have seen that there were a great many aspects of Italian fifteenth-century music which were basically incompatible with the discant-tenor ideal. English musicians, on the other hand, had actively cultivated a tradition which can very well account for the new duet style. The works of Frye, presumably written in England some time before 1455, exhibit all the characteristics which Besseler attributes to the conjunction of French and Italian musical traditions and the consequent evolution of a contratenor-bass. In the Frye chansons, the contratenor is generally the lowest part and frequently functions as a harmonic support, even though it jumps above the tenor in the octave-leap cadences.

These chansons, moreover, have an autonomous duet of tenor and discant which provides the basic framework of the composition. Besseler maintains that the discant-tenor framework was evolved by Continental composers through fauxbourdon, in which the relationship of a sixth prevailed between the outer voices.[32] One of the points made by Fox, however, is that strict adherence to the principle of nonquartal harmony results not in parallel sixths between outer voices, but in parallel tenths. (Any middle voice would necessarily form a fourth with one of the outer voices if they were a sixth apart.[33]) While a completely nonquartal style cannot be taken as the criterion, it is nonetheless significant that in the majority of Burgundian and Netherlands chansons, it is *not* the tenor which accompanies the discant at a sixth below, but the contratenor which runs parallel with the discant at the interval of a tenth. The close of Ockeghem's chanson *Ma bouche rit* illustrates this relationship of the three voices.[34]

This technique has been discussed in connection with the Frye Masses. It is equally characteristic of his chansons. In *Alas, alas,* for example, the discant and contratenor maintain an almost constant relationship of a tenth for six measures (mm. 9–15). Between tenor and discant of the Frye chansons this sort of facile two-part writing in parallel motion is rare. The relationship is one primarily of contrary motion. But the contratenor, added to an already complete bicinium, served sometimes as a harmonic support and sometimes in the capacity of a parallel voice to either the discant or the tenor. Occasionally it accompanies the tenor in parallel motion, but at a third or sixth below.[35] It is not inconsistent with the role of the contratenor to pair it in this fashion with discant or tenor if it is understood to be a third and optional voice, whose function is merely to enrich.

Certainly in the chansons of Frye, as well as in the discant-tenor chansons of Continental composers, the contratenor is

32. *Bourdon und Fauxbourdon,* pp. 163 and 165.

33. Fox, "Non-Quartal Harmony," p. 33.

34. Hewitt and Pope, eds., *Odhecaton,* No. 54, mm. 69–70.

35. See Dufay's "Vostre Bruit" in *Guillaume Dufay: Zwölf Geistliche und weltliche Werke zu 3 Stimmen,* ed. Heinrich Besseler, vol. *19* of *Das Chorwerk* (Wolfenbüttel, 1932), No. 12.

expendable. It enriches, by accompanying the discant in tenths, but it is not essential to the musical structure, for the other two voices alone are written in perfect counterpoint. Since it was in England during the fifteenth century that counterpoint was conscientiously cultivated and taught, under the name of "discant," the new chanson style must be said to have derived much of its inspiration from English music, in which the ideals of discant found expression.

CHAPTER 8

The Motet and the Carol Literature of England

THE ONLY ONE of Frye's works which is clearly and indisputably a motet is his *Sospitati dedit,* preserved in the Pepys Ms. 1236. The *cantus firmus* of this composition is freely colored and wanders between tenor and discant. In one verse there are even traces of it in both parts simultaneously. The migrant *cantus firmus* technique, seen also in many of the Old Hall Masses, is commonly assumed to be of English origin and is probably related to the practice of discant. The particular rhythmic form in which the chant is cast for the polyphonic setting is equally appropriate to any one of the voices in discant style. It could not be so easily transferred from one voice to another if there were a decided contrast in the character of the voices, as in the Continental treble-dominated style. This motet of Frye's, more than any of his other works, reveals the pure note-against-note technique of discant, for there is no real distinction among the three voices. All are written exclusively in breves, semibreves, and minims, with occasional semiminims. The contratenor, though more angular in its melodic line, is nevertheless the rhythmic equal of tenor and discant.

Frye's *Sospitati dedit* is set in alternate two- and three-voiced sections. In this respect it is closely related to the secular song style of English composers such as Banastir [1] and also to the carols and Latin motets of the Egerton Ms. 3307, the Oxford Ms. Seldon B 26, and the Ritson manuscript (B.M., Add. 5665). The first four lines of Frye's motet are set for three voices, the fifth for two, the sixth for three, the seventh for two, and the

1. See Arthur Vogel, "The English Part Song around 1500," p. 100.

eighth for three. The final "Sospes regreditur, Deo gratias, Amen" concludes the work with a three-voiced setting. (It is the contratenor which drops out for the fifth and seventh lines.) Presumably alternate soloistic and choral performance is implied, as in the carols.

One may question the influence of such a semipopular form as the carol on the more sophisticated art forms such as the motet. But there are decisive links between the carols and the English motet and song style of the mid-fifteenth century. The carols were a genre peculiar to England alone. They are not easily classified, for they partake of both sacred and secular elements, and stylistically they are related to both motets and chansons. John Stevens, in his introduction to *Medieval Carols*, writes:

> The courtly French *virelai* and the Italian *ballata* are closely related to the carol from the formal point of view, while the Italian *lauda* resembles the carol in form and in spirit. It is clear that in the carol we have the English representative of this family, and its importance is substantiated by the survival of nearly 500 distinct vernacular lyrics in this form. . . . It was, indeed, an English forme fixe, comparable in some degree to *ballade, rondeau* and *virelai* on the Continent.[2]

In one sense, then, the carols must be regarded as the English equivalent of the chanson. There was not, in England, such a wealth of secular song literature as on the Continent during the early fifteenth century. The few English secular songs which survive are scattered among Masses, motets, and carols in various manuscripts such as Ashmole 191, Egerton 3307, Seldon B 26, B.M. Add. 5665, and Douce 381. The carols, on the other hand, appear in large numbers in manuscripts up to around 1450. Two of the important carol sources, B.M. Ms. Add. 5665 (Ritson) and the Cambridge Trinity College Roll, Ms. o.3.58, date from the first half of the century, while Seldon B 26 and Egerton 3307 are from about 1450.

The English carol did not exist in strict isolation from cere-

2. John Stevens, ed., *Medieval Carols*, vol. 4 of *Muisca Britannica* (London, 1952), p. xiii.

monial and liturgical forms. It is not surprising, after all, that the English form corresponding to the Continental chanson should be in the guise of religious music, for the English had cultivated sacred forms in the thirteenth and fourteenth centuries, long after the Continental composers had begun to concentrate on the development of secular genres. The widespread incorporation in the carols of texts from the Catholic liturgy bespeaks a strong indebtedness to the materials of the motet. The use of the *Ave regina coelorum* text in various parts of burdens and stanzas of carols has already been mentioned. The text in honor of St. Edmund, *Ave rex gentis,* was also used for this purpose, as were many other liturgical texts.[3]

The carols, moreover, were processional compositions, not necessarily used for religious ceremonies, but nonetheless connected with processional activities.[4] It has become apparent that much of the liturgical polyphony, from the earliest period on, is related to processional rites, and the practice of drawing *cantus firmi* from the Processional still prevailed in the fifteenth and sixteenth centuries. The Ritson manuscript is devoted, to a considerable extent, to these forms, and both Frye's motet, *Sospitati dedit,* and his *Missa Summe Trinitati* are based on processional chants.

The stylistic relationship of the carols to contemporary motet and Mass composition is seen partly in the use of alternate two- and three-voiced settings. This was not merely a technique analogous to that of the introductory duos of Continental Masses and motets, but rather the result of the development of the carol itself from a two-voiced to a three-voiced form. It is this aspect of the carols that is significant from the point of view of the evolution of Continental music in the fifteenth century.

It has been said that the early two-voiced carols were composed essentially as gymels.[5] The term "gymel" first appeared in the fifteenth century and referred in most instances simply to two-voiced compositions.[6] In late fifteenth- and early sixteenth-century choir books, it was frequently used to indicate solo

3. Greene, *The Early English Carols,* pp. lxxxiv–lxxxv.
4. Stevens, *Medieval Carols,* p. xiv.
5. Bukofzer, *Studies,* p. 168.
6. Bukofzer, "Popular Polyphony in the Middle Ages," *MQ,* 26 (1940), 36.

duets, and apparently in this case was simply a synonym for "duo," which also appeared frequently in the same circumstances.[7] The term "gymel," as we have seen, occurs in the theoretical literature in connection with the contratenor, which occupies the same range as the tenor. (See Chapter 5.) In any case, the term seems to have been used consistently to denote a duet composed of equally important voices. In the two-part carols, the absolute equivalence of the voices is obvious. There is no question of leading voice and counterpoint against it, for even the cadence lines are interchangeable, i.e. sometimes the upper voice has leading tone—tonic, and the lower voice supertonic—tonic, and sometimes vice versa.[8] (This inverted cadence form is to be found similarly in the Frye chansons.)

In the later carols, the ensemble was expanded to include three-voiced sections as well as duos, and these were frequently constructed merely by adding another voice to the already self-sufficient bicinium. Completely new second burdens, in fact, are relatively rare. More often than not the second burden, for three voices, is a variant of the two-voiced first burden. The third voice is usually placed in the middle (in the score form of notation), although it generally occupies about the same range as the lowest voice, thereby forming a gymel like that of the tenor and contratenor in English Masses. In the majority of the carols, the repetition of the original two voices does not last throughout the whole second burden. In *Princeps pacis,*[9] for example, it lasts only four measures. In *O clavis David,* however, it lasts for ten. In *Sing we to this merry company* the first six measures of the second burden present only minor deviations in the two outside voices from the original two-part burden. In *Nowell, Nowell, the boarës head* the first five measures include a literal repetition of the two voices of the first burden. In *Salve sancta parens* the two burdens are thirteen measures long, and the outside voices of the three-part version differ from those of the two-part form only in measures 5 and 6.

In four of the carols the entire second burden, usually from twelve to fifteen measures long, is constructed simply by the

7. Bukofzer, *Studies,* p. 188.
8. Ibid., p. 168.
9. All carols referred to are to be found in Stevens, *Medieval Carols.*

addition of a third voice to the first burden. These are: *Saint Thomas honor we, Illuminare Jerusalem, Verbum patris,* and *Have mercy of me.* In all four of these carols, the added voice, which is fitted against a duet in contrary motion, is characterized by leaps of fourths and fifths and triadic formulas. It is, in fact, exactly like the contratenor of the Frye chansons and the discant-tenor compositions of Continental composers.

The obvious relationship of this technique to that of the Burgundian discant-tenor chanson has been rather neglected. To be sure, the carols were an exclusively English category, and there is no evidence that they were known on the Continent. Bukofzer points out the parallel development between the carols and the Burgundian chanson, and says that it is "all the more surprising as there is no contact between the forms." [10] But the technique of discanting and of adding a third, "countering" voice in this fashion was certainly known to the English composers who went to the Continent. Undoubtedly Frye's chansons, which are the prototypes for the Burgundian discant-tenor chanson, are related to the same tradition as that which produced the carols.

There are, in fact, many stylistic similarities between the carols and the Burgundian chansons. Bukofzer refers several times to the "similarity in tone" between the two repertories, and points out specifically the opening of the carol *Princeps serenissime,* which is identical with the beginning of the famous *L'homme armé* melody.[11] There is also another carol, *Pray for us,* which begins in exactly the same fashion.

The identification of the *L'homme armé* melody with the carol literature suggests that the composer of the original chanson may have been the Englishman, Robert Morton, and not Antoine Busnois, as Aaron testified a hundred years later.[12] The rather square-cut and modally rhythmic character of the *L'homme armé* melody is much more characteristic of discant style than of any of the Continental styles of the early fifteenth century. Busnois was unquestionably influenced by English

10. Bukofzer, *Studies,* pp. 165–66.

11. Ibid., p. 160.

12. For a discussion of this point, see Oliver Strunk, "Origins of the *L'homme armé* Mass," *BAMS,* 2 (1937), 25.

music, and if there were no early setting of the text by an
English composer, Aaron's attribution might be acceptable
without qualification. But Morton's chanson appears in the
Mellon manuscript with those of Frye. It too may have been
composed at a considerably earlier date, and could have been
the model for all the Netherlands Masses on the *L'homme
armé* theme. At all events, the relationship of the carols to this
melody which was so popular among Netherlands composers is
a further indication of the importance of English technique in
the formulation of the new style on the Continent.

Another aspect of the Netherlands style which is related to
that of the carols is the tendency to break away from symmetrical, balanced phrasing and regularly spaced cadences. Avoidance of simultaneous cadencing in all voices is one of the
principal characteristics of Ockeghem's nebulous polyphonic
style. It is also typical of the late Burgundian chansons, in
which the tenor and discant cadence together, but the motion
is continued by the contratenor. The melodic lines of the English carols are anything but symmetrical, and the phrase lengths
are uneven. Within the normal scheme of mensuration there
are countless difficulties in transcription simply because the
carols do not maintain a regular rhythmic pulse according to
the principles of tempus and prolatio. Alternation of hemiola
with regular tempus imperfectum, prolatio maior, is very conspicuous in the carol literature, and it appears also in the type
of rhythmic displacement used so effectively in the late works
of Dufay and those of Obrecht and Josquin, for the purpose of
obscuring the regularity of the tactus. Hemiola was not a novelty
in itself, but with the rise of a style in which the avoidance of
regularity appears to be a prime factor, its use becomes highly
purposeful.

The melodic style of the carols, even before 1450, is smooth
and unadorned. The elaborate melismata of Italian music are
quite foreign to the English melodic lines, which, on the whole,
are simple, pliant, and often quite graceful. The tendency
toward simplification of the melodic line has long been recognized as one of the changes which took place in Continental
music around 1450. (See, for example, Chapter 8, "Der Neue
Stromrhythmus," in Besseler's *Bourdon und Fauxbourdon*.)

The carols, because they were a less sophisticated art form than the motets and Masses, are rather stereotyped. Many of the basic stylistic devices which characterize the works of such composers as Dunstable, Power, and Frye recur time and time again in their simplest form, almost as clichés, in the carols. Hence the carol literature provides a sort of dictionary of musical phrases and figures for the English musical style of the fifteenth century.

CHAPTER 9

The Influence of English Musical Style upon the Netherlands Composers

A. Dufay and Binchois

THE WORKS of Dufay exhibit an extraordinary variety of means. There are very few chansons which are alike, and while it is easy to see a change in style between his early works and those of his late years, it is not so easy to trace a logical and systematic line of development between the two. Dufay utilized almost every conceivable technique, even reverting in some instances to a form resembling the thirteenth-century motet. His *Je ne puis—Unde veniet*,[1] for example, has a Latin sacred text in the tenor and a French secular poem in discant and contratenor. Polytextuality is also seen in another of his chansons, *Resvelons nous*,[2] in which this text appears in the discant, while tenor and contratenor have a canon on an ostinato figure, with the words: "Alons ent bien tos avec moy." Dufay was undoubtedly influenced by the Italian caccia style in some of his compositions, such as *Ma belle dame souveraigne*.[3] His rondeau, *Par droit je puis*,[4] is constructed along the lines of the caccia, with two canonic upper voices accompanied by a contratenor. Similarly, his *Hé! Compaignons*[5] is written for two paired voices with two accompanying contratenors, one of which is optional. Van den Borren has pointed out that in these compositions, which appear to be modeled directly on Italian forms, Dufay aban-

1. J. F. R. and C. Stainer, eds., *Dufay and His Contemporaries* (London, 1898), p. 143.
2. Ibid., p. 132.
3. Published by Heinrich Besseler in *Bourdon und Fauxbourdon*, p. 262.
4. Stainer, *Dufay and His Contemporaries*, p. 115.
5. Ibid., p. 127.

doned the tenor *cantus firmus* tradition altogether.[6] In Dufay's mature works, however, the tenor reappears and plays a role of major importance.

These early Italian compositions of Dufay attest his genius in being able to write at will in styles completely foreign to his own tradition. Whether they can be said to have had a decisive influence upon his style as a whole, or upon the Netherlands style in general, is questionable. Dufay, like Mozart, was eclectic, and his experiments in styles other than French are numerous. This eclecticism, the wide scope of activity, and the facility of technique exhibited by Dufay's chansons make it hazardous to attribute too much importance to isolated ventures into one particular style. The second quarter of the fifteenth century was a period of experimenting and searching for a new style. Dufay's work is a reflection of this experimental attitude, and his turn toward Italian music during his youth shows no evidence of having been more than a temporary interest.

The versatility of Dufay is not seen to such a degree in the works of Gilles Binchois. While Binchois achieved considerable variety of expression, the techniques he employed were in general more uniform, and he shows a rather more consistent approach throughout his work than does Dufay. There is no indication of any Italian influence on his work;[7] his foreign connections were all with the English. Binchois served in the retinue of the Duke of Suffolk for a number of years during the 'twenties, and in this capacity undoubtedly had close contact with English musicians. Whether he actually went to England is not known, although there is some evidence that he made a short visit there before going, in 1430, to the Burgundian court, where he remained until his death in 1460.[8]

Stylistically, Binchois' works show a strong resemblance to those of his English contemporaries. Conflicting attributions for his motets are all to English composers (Sandley, Dunstable, and Power), and it is significant that the rondeau *Tout a par moy*, which is attributed to Frye in the Mellon Chansonnier, is

6. *Etudes sur le quinzième siècle musical*, p. 133.

7. Reese identifies Binchois' name with an Italian song, *Deducto se'* (*Music in the Renaissance*, p. 86), but Wolfgang Rehm does not include it in his collected edition, *Die Chansons von Gilles Binchois*.

8. Jeanne Marix, *Histoire de la musique*, p. 179.

ascribed to Binchois in another source. His having composed
as many as seven ballades may also be an indication of English
influence. One of these, *Deuil angoisseux,* provided the *cantus
firmus* for an English Mass preserved in Trent 90 (attributed
to Bedingham and Langensteiss). Binchois' chanson has exactly
the same structure as the Frye ballades, with a rhymed ending
of nine measures between *prima* and *secunda partes,* and a
"clos" ending which includes the "ouvert." And, like Frye's
ballades, Binchois' *Deuil angoisseux* also became a motet. (*Re-
rum conditor,* in Trent 88, No. 345.)

There are at least five aspects of Binchois' style which relate
his works to those of Dunstable and Frye and the carol repertory. These are: the melodic style, the general range, the euphonious relationship of tenor and discant, the character of the
tenor line, and the character of the contratenor part.

One melodic figure which appears in at least six of Dunstable's motets is characteristically English and is found in a great
many of the carols. It also appears conspicuously in the chansons of Binchois. With the exception of the first note, the second
phrases of Binchois' *De plus en plus,* Frye's *Tout a par moy,*
Dunstable's *Sancta Maria non est,* and the carol *Illuxit leticia*
are identical. (See Example 24.) A variant of this same phrase

EXAMPLE 24

a) *De plus en plus,* Binchois.

b) *Tout a par moy,* Frye

c) *Sancta Maria non est,* Dunstable

d) *Illuxit leticia,* Carol

can also be seen in Binchois' *Se j'eusse un seul peu d'esperance,* Dunstable's *Sancta Maria succurre,* and the carol *St. Thomas honor we* (Example 25). It is instructive to compare another

EXAMPLE 25

a) *Se j'eusse un seul peu d'esperance,* Binchois

b) *Sancta Maria succurre,* Dunstable

c) *St. Thomas honor we,* Carol

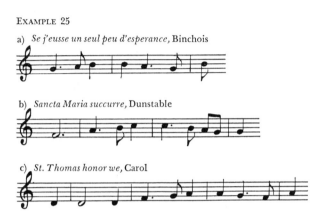

quite similar melodic line from Binchois' *Adieu, adieu, mon joyeux souvenir* with the opening of one of the songs in the Ashmole Ms. 191, *O kendly creature,* and with the carol *Princeps serenissime* (Example 26). The first two measures of the

EXAMPLE 26

a) *Adieu, adieu,* Binchois

b) *O kendly creature,* anon. (Ashmole Ms. 191)

c) *Princeps serenissime,* Carol

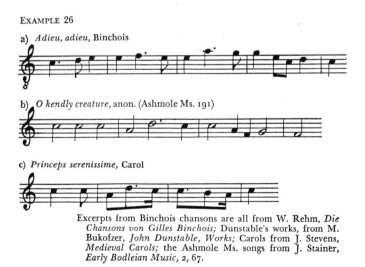

Excerpts from Binchois chansons are all from W. Rehm, *Die Chansons von Gilles Binchois;* Dunstable's works, from M. Bukofzer, *John Dunstable, Works;* Carols from J. Stevens, *Medieval Carols;* the Ashmole Ms. songs from J. Stainer, *Early Bodleian Music,* 2, 67.

carol and the Ashmole song are exactly the same, while the
second and third measures of the Ashmole song are identical
with the third and fourth measures of Binchois' chanson.

The last measure of the examples from *Adieu, adieu* and *O
kendly creature* is something of a motto which, at first appear-
ances, seems too ubiquitous to be significant. Jeppesen mentions
it as being typical of the chanson literature. He cites two examples by Binchois, one by Dunstable (*Puisqu'amour*), and one by
Caron, and he refers to one from Bedingham's (?) *Grant temps.*[9]
While the phrase is a very common one in the Burgundian
chansons, it is important to note that the earliest examples of
it are found in works by English composers, or those related to
them, and that it is an idiomatic figure in the carols. Other
examples by Binchois are to be found in *De plus en plus* and
Vostre alée me desplaist. This figure appears in the opening
line of the tenor part in Frye's *Ave Regina,* is quite conspicuous
in the discant part of *Myn hertis lust* (*Grant temps*), and occurs
in the minor form in *So ys emprentid* (Example 27). This particular motive is one of the triadic forms so commonly associated with English music and, as was pointed out in Chapter 7,
is to be related to the practice of discant. The frequent appear-

EXAMPLE 27

a) Binchois, *De plus en plus*   *Vostre alée*

b) Frye, *Ave Regina*

Myn hertis lust   *So ys emprentid*

c) Carols, *Make us merry*   *Spes mea*

9. *Der Kopenhagener Chansonnier,* p. xxi.

ance of triadic melodies in Binchois' chansons, apart from the specific form just cited, suggests in itself a rather general influence of discant style. The opening notes of *Deuil angoisseux,* for example, are those of the F major triad.[10]

The works of Binchois contain many other melodic traits which can be identified with those of his English contemporaries. His *Mon seul et souverain desir* begins with a figure which is almost exactly like the opening phrase of the discant in Frye's *Ave Regina* (Example 28). It was a phrase which was characteristic of Frye and Dunstable alike, and also appears extensively in the carols.[11] A final example, from the ending of Binchois' *Plains de plours et gemissemens,* when compared to the early two-voiced carol, *Alma redemptoris mater,* serves to show the similarity between Binchois' melodic style and that of the carols (Example 29).

Binchois' chansons are also related to the carols in respect to the range of the parts. Many of the carols are written in a range

EXAMPLE 28

a) Binchois, *Mon seul et souverain desir*

b) Frye, *Ave Regina*

EXAMPLE 29

a) Binchois, *Plains de plours*

b) Carol, *Alma redemptoris*

10. Rehm, *Die Chansons von Binchois,* p. 27.
11. See, for example, carols Nos. 103, 76, 88, and 89 in Stevens, *Medieval Carols.*

that suggests a performance of all male voices. And it is quite
common to find, among the Binchois chansons, examples which
are best transcribed into modern notation in three bass clefs,
such as *Ay douloureux, disant hélas, Adieu ma doulce,* and
Amours et qu'as tu enpensé.[12]

Another aspect of Binchois' style which shows evidence of
English influence is the relationship of the tenor to the discant,
specifically the almost constant use of imperfect intervals between these two voices. While there are some octaves between
them, open fifths are comparatively rare. The tenor and discant
of Binchois' *Mon seul et souverain desir* or *Adieu, adieu,*[13] if
compared with the carol *Parit virgo,* show at once how similar
was Binchois' technique in this respect to that of the carols.
It is interesting to compare these, in turn, with Dufay's *Bon
jour, bon mois,*[14] which shows very little of the third or sixth
relationship between the two essential voices. In Dufay's later
chansons, such as *Je ne vis oncques* and *Malheureux cueur*[15]
there is a great deal of this "Panconsonance." But among Binchois' chansons, there are hardly any which do not reveal a very
consonant relationship of discant and tenor.

The chansons of Binchois are generally described as being
in "ballade" or "treble-dominated" style. The discant is the
most active voice, and the tenor is rarely the equivalent, rhythmically, of either discant or contratenor. Many of the idiomatic
figures in Binchois' work, and in the carols, are to be related to
the somewhat static character of the tenor line. The frequent use
of triadic forms in the melody has already been mentioned as
a device which produces alternate perfect and imperfect intervals over the same tenor note. Another figure, which is almost
a cliché in the works of Frye and Binchois, shows a similar
technique employed for the more advanced style of alternating
imperfect intervals alone. This is the rising interval of a fourth
in the discant. There are countless examples of this melodic
leap of a fourth, and in almost all cases the tenor is stationary

12. Jeanne Marix, *Les musiciens de la cour de Bourgogne au XVe siècle* (Paris,
1937), Nos. 25, 19, and 23. Rehm does not use the bass clef for the uppermost voice
in his edition, but rather the treble clef sung an octave lower.

13. Rehm, *Die Chansons von Binchois,* pp. 27 and 1.

14. Stainer, *Dufay and His Contemporaries,* p. 134.

15. *Guillaume Dufay,* ed. Heinrich Besseler, Nos. 9 and 11.

(Example 30). The tenor is a third below the first note of the discant, and, consequently, a sixth below the second. Thus, the alternation of third and sixth is achieved without having to change the tenor note at all. Tinctoris suggests this technique in Book III of his *Liber de arte contrapuncti,* in which he sets forth eight general rules. The third chapter is entitled: "Concerning the third general rule, which allows many concords, not only imperfect but also perfect, to follow continuously one after another, the tenor remaining in the same place." [16]

It has frequently been maintained that Continental attempts to emulate the rich, consonant sounds of English music are seen principally in fauxbourdon. But the use of fauxbourdon was very limited with regard to both composers and repertory. This type of melodic device, on the other hand, was one which lent itself easily to the Continental tradition of a treble-dominated style, while strict fauxbourdon did not. There are quite a few of the Binchois chansons in which the voices are disparate and the upper part clearly has more rhythmic activity. The melodic rising fourth is conspicuous in all of these works.

One rather striking feature of both Binchois' music and the

EXAMPLE 30

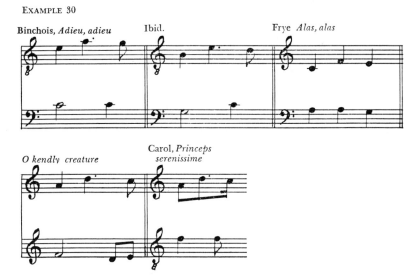

16. *Johannes Tinctoris, The Art of Counterpoint,* trans. and ed. by Albert Seay (American Institute of Musicology, 1961), p. 134.

carols is the fact that the tenor (or lowest voice of the carols) is
frequently written in a manner reminiscent of the regular
ordines of the organum, with a repetitive rhythmic scheme.
This can be seen especially in carols in which the lower voice
has what looks like a second or third mode rhythmic pattern to
which it adheres more or less closely. (See, for example, the
lower voice of *Verbum patris,* or that of the burden and chorus
of *Almyghty Jhesu.*) A melodic line cast in a basically modal
rhythm is also illustrated by the *L'homme armé* melody, of
which the prototype appears in the carol *Princeps serenissime.*
It is entirely logical that discant in England should have retained this link with the older practice. These rhythmic patterns
were, in fact, a heritage of the earliest discant style, in which
both voices in the discant sections were organized according to
the principles of modal rhythm. Kenneth Levy has pointed out
that English mensural notation developed independently of the
French and adhered much more closely to the older modal system.[17] Nevertheless, it is rather striking that this feature should
appear as late as the fifteenth century and even be taken over
by Continental composers who were subjected to the influence
of discant style from England. This technique is conspicuous
in the works of Binchois, especially in such chansons as *Se la
belle n'a le voloir, Vostre tres doulx regard, Amours et souvenir
de celle, Bien puis, Esclave puist yl,* and *Helas que poray je.*[18]

Still another feature of Binchois' style that shows him to have
been a disciple of the English composers is the active nature of
his contratenor parts. This can be seen, for example, in his
Kyrie Feriale.[19] In the majority of Binchois' chansons, the contratenor moves at a faster pace than the tenor and is linked
rather with the discant. In some of his earlier works it sometimes moves predominantly at an interval of a fourth below the
discant. But in his later works, the contratenor, like that of
Frye, often runs parallel to the discant in tenths. Equally indicative of the stylistic advance discernible in Binchois' works is
the use of the contratenor to keep the motion going after a

17. Kenneth Jay Levy, "New Material on the Early Motet in England," *JAMS, 4*
(1951), 227.
18. Rehm, *Die Chansons von Binchois,* pp. 42, 36, 7, 9, 13, and 14.
19. Marix, *Les musiciens de Bourgogne,* p. 158.

cadence, as in *Adieu, adieu* (m. 6), *De plus en plus* (m. 8), *Margarite, fleur de valeur* (mm. 4 and 8), *Plains de plours* (m. 17),[20] and many others. This device is particularly striking in *Vostre allée me desplait*,[21] where the contratenor initiates a figure which is then imitated by the other parts.

Like the Frye contratenor, that of Binchois usually has a less melodic character than the tenor and discant. In *Adieu, adieu* (m. 15), the contratenor descends in a series of thirds and fifths for over an octave and then continues in leaps of fourths and fifths. In *Adieu jusque je vous revoye* this voice moves in almost exactly the same angular fashion as the Frye contratenor, clearly as a harmonic voice, and sometimes fulfilling the function of continuing the rhythmic flow by means of a purely ornamental figure, such as a downward leap of a third or fourth and back (Example 31).

EXAMPLE 31

Frye, *Ave Regina*

Binchois, *Adieu jusque je vous revoye*

The importance of this duet style with a harmonic contratenor has been discussed in detail in Chapter 7. Its appearance in the works of Binchois is one indication of his close affiliation with English music. The treble-dominated aspect of Binchois' chansons is a little misleading, since it makes them resemble superficially the earlier Continental chansons. What is easily overlooked in these pieces is the significantly consonant relationship between tenor and discant and the role of the contratenor. The discant-tenor duet of many of Binchois' chansons is such that they can stand alone, like those of Frye or the two-voiced burdens of the carols. His *Adieu, mes tres belles amours*

20. Rehm, *Die Chansons von Binchois*, pp. 1, 10, 24, and 29.
21. Ibid., p. 41.

is preserved in one of the largest Binchois manuscripts with only two voices. The harmonic contratenor is quite unnecessary. This discant-tenor relationship in Binchois' chansons represents the first penetration of the elements of English discant style within the framework of the accompanied solo song.

Binchois was invariably mentioned by the theorists and poets, together with Dufay, as one of the important figures in the creation of the new style. And yet he is seldom given credit by modern historians for much beyond a gift for writing charming chansons. Too little emphasis has been placed upon Binchois' relationship with the English and the effect of English influence on his style, while too much emphasis has been directed towards Dufay's experiments with fauxbourdon. This imbalance is caused by the confusing of fauxbourdon with the English practice of discant. Historians who claim that Dufay's fauxbourdon was inspired by the English and that the English in turn were influenced by the Burgundian chanson are postulating a series of stylistic channel crossings that are quite superfluous. Even if fauxbourdon is recognized as an exclusively Continental phenomenon, the problem is unnecessarily confused as long as English music is not understood in the light of English theory.

Both Bukofzer and Besseler have believed that in his strict fauxbourdon Dufay was striving after the English full sonority of thirds and sixths, and that he was later able to utilize the same principles in a more flexible style.[22] But Bukofzer went even further in suggesting that it was this flexible style of Dufay's which came to influence English music. He described the compositions of the Egerton Ms. 3307, for example, as the first "to reflect the influence of fauxbourdon style, which appears here, however, characteristically transformed to stylized part writing." [23] Yet the style at which Dufay arrived in these free settings had been known and practiced by English composers at home and on the Continent. It was taught by English theorists. Dunstable's *Quam pulchra es* is an example of that style which was well-known on the Continent. So also was the setting of the same text by John Pyamour, who was at one time in France with the Duke of Bedford and who died as early as 1431.[24]

22. Bukofzer, *Studies*, p. 131; Besseler, *Bourdon und Fauxbourdon*, p. 118.
23. Bukofzer, *Studies*, pp. 130–31.
24. Ibid., p. 135.

Even in those works of Dunstable's which are in a more melismatic style, such as *Sancta Maria non est* and *Albanus roseo,* the discant maintains a constantly euphonious relationship with the tenor. This is the panconsonant style which characterized not only the works of Dunstable and Pyamour but also those of the younger English composers—Frye, Bedingham, Morton, Cockx, and their Continental colleague, Binchois.

Possibly it was necessary for Continental composers to experiment with fauxbourdon before arriving at a free consonant style. English composers, however, had done their experimenting earlier and in a different way, in the fourteenth century, and did not go through this particular phase of writing thirds and sixths. They had inherited a technique of handling imperfect consonances directly from the tradition of discanting. Thus the so-called "stylized part-writing" of the Egerton manuscript is understandable quite apart from Continental developments, within the framework of English theory and practice.

Fauxbourdon, then, may perhaps be understood as an attempt on the part of Continental composers to arrive at a certain facility in the handling of thirds and sixths in a style of rhythmically equal voices. It was an important step for Dufay. But it is significant that the rigid form of fauxbourdon plays a smaller role in the works of Binchois, whose contact with English composers was more direct and more lasting than Dufay's. The consonant, contrapuntal style of English music was assimilated more completely in the early works of Binchois, and it is in his music, rather than in Dufay's, that the importance of the English element in the formulation of the Netherlands style can best be understood and evaluated.

B. Busnois, Obrecht, and Josquin

The Netherlands composers at the end of the fifteenth century in whose works the influence of discant style is most apparent are Josquin, Isaac, Agricola, and particularly Busnois and Obrecht. They are, with the exception of Busnois, those composers who journeyed to Italy and whose style has heretofore been explained with reference to the Italian frottola. It can be seen now that many of the elements of style which have been laid to Italian influence can be explained through the works of

English composers of Walter Frye's generation. The fact that
Obrecht's first trip to Italy was not until 1474 has always been
a stumbling block. But his contact with the music of Frye was
undoubtedly earlier and hence provides a more logical explanation for the basis of his style.

A certain amount of importance may be attached to the fact
that three of these Netherlands composers borrowed literally
from Frye's works. Obrecht modeled a motet and a Mass on
Frye's *Ave Regina;* Agricola set the rondeau *Tout a par moy,*
retaining Frye's tenor; and Josquin wrote a Mass based on
Tout a par moy. Obrecht borrowed Frye's tenor as a *cantus
firmus* for his motet, uncolored, but transposed down a third
to the Dorian mode. He retained the ballade form of Frye's
Ave Regina, not only in the borrowed tenor but in the newly
composed voices as well. Hence, Obrecht's motet too has a
formal design of a b c b.

In Obrecht's Mass on *Ave Regina,* the tenor, still uncolored,
is restored to its original mode. The disposition of the *cantus
firmus* material is particularly interesting in the KYRIE, for
Obrecht used only the first phrase for the "Kyrie I," repeating
it once. The "Christe" then takes up the next phrase and continues with the Frye tenor up to the end of the *prima pars.* The
"Kyrie II" has the entire *secunda pars* of Frye's tenor. Thus,
the two identical sections of Frye's tenor, the endings of *prima*
and *secunda partes,* are found at the close of the "Christe" and
"Kyrie II" of Obrecht's Mass movement. This formulation of
the *cantus firmus* material, with the repetition of the first phrase,
is retained in the GLORIA and CREDO. Although the *cantus
firmus* is in the tenor part for the first four movements, it appears in the bass in the AGNUS DEI. In the three middle movements, the *cantus firmus* material is found also in other voices.
The introductory duos of GLORIA and CREDO, for example, are
comprised of mensuration canons on the tenor theme. And in
the SANCTUS, the contratenor has the theme in canon with the
tenor. The melody is never ornamented, but is altered by
rhythmical augmentation and diminution. Frye too seems to
have preferred the uncolored *cantus firmus* for Mass compositions, although he never subjected it to proportional alteration.

Josquin's use of material borrowed from Frye's work is seen
in his *Missa Faysant regretz,* of which the title is derived from

the *secunda pars* of the rondeau *Tout a par moy*.[25] Josquin apparently knew Agricola's setting of this text as well as Frye's. Agricola had used only Frye's tenor for a setting of the same text, but had written against it a contratenor ostinato figure. Josquin wrote an ostinato based on the same fragment, but placed it in the tenor. Moreover, he transposed it to all degrees of the scale, while Agricola's ostinato was limited to one pitch. Evidently Josquin was referring to Agricola's setting when he called his composition *Missa Faysant regretz* rather than *Tout a par moy*, but the entire discant of Frye's rondeau is quoted in the superius of Josquin's "Agnus III." This melody could not have been derived from Agricola, who did not use Frye's discant at all. Josquin must have known Frye's composition himself, then, instead of being dependent upon Agricola for the transmission of it.

The borrowing of material such as this does not in itself imply any real stylistic influence from one composer to another. But there are a great many features of Josquin's style, and certainly of Obrecht's, which are directly related to Frye's style. It is doubtful whether Obrecht had any direct contact with Frye, but a clear link between these two composers is provided by Antoine Busnois. It is well known that there was a close stylistic relationship between Obrecht and Busnois. Obrecht, moreover, followed Busnois' formulation of the tenor for his *L'homme armé* Mass.[26] They were both associated with churches at Bruges and may very well have been known to one another personally.

A close association between Frye and Busnois may also be assumed. There is no documentary evidence that Frye, like Busnois, served in the chapel of Charles, the Count of Charolais, but his music was certainly known there. A great many of Busnois' chansons are preserved, together with Frye's, in the Mellon manuscript, which is devoted largely to works by Burgundian composers. The Brussels manuscript 5557, which contains all three of Frye's Masses, also includes all but two of Busnois' motets as well as a Magnificat. We have seen that Frye's works formed the nucleus of this latter manuscript and must have antedated the works of Busnois. It has been suggested by Stephan and Sparks that the motets of Busnois were copied by

25. Josquin des Pres, *Werken*, ed. A. Smijers, *Missen, 3* (Amsterdam, 1950), p. 33.
26. Oliver Strunk, "Origins of the L'homme armé Mass," p. 25.

the composer himself, because of the extreme care exercised in clarifying the musical structure.[27] If Busnois did indeed copy his own works into this manuscript he must surely have been acquainted with the Masses in the earlier portions of the codex, since, as we have seen, his motets all occupy the position of "fillers" between gatherings. His *Anthoni usque limina* starts on the last verso of the gathering which contains Frye's *Missa Nobilis et pulchra*. Whether or not the theory advanced by Stephan and Sparks can be accepted, there is little doubt that Frye's works were known to the circles in which Busnois worked, and the influence of Frye's style is apparent in both secular and sacred works of Busnois.

Busnois is best known for his chansons. It is supposedly with Busnois, in fact, that the Burgundian chanson attained its classic type in the form of the imitative duet of discant and tenor coupled with a free, harmonic contratenor. This style, as we have already seen, was present in Frye's chansons of the 1450s. Only the imitation is lacking from the two earlier songs. But all of them are discant-tenor compositions, and since they were written as early as 1455 they must have preceded Busnois' formulation of the discant-tenor chanson. It was, then, from these English models, or possibly indirectly through Binchois, that Busnois derived the form of these compositions which have earned him such enduring fame.

There is also a strong stylistic similarity between the Frye and Busnois religious compositions in the Brussels manuscript. There is no evidence of the older treble-dominated style in the Busnois motets. All the voices move in much the same rythmic values, in a basically note-against-note relationship. Edgar Sparks, in his study of these compositions, writes:

> The motets exhibit many traits not entirely characteristic of the period. For instance, two of the works—*Noel, Noel* and *Verbum caro factum est*—are conspicuously harmonic in conception. The linear, horizontal aspect is subordinated to the vertical to a much greater degree than is customary . . . There is a predominance of complete triads, and the movement from chord to chord is generally clearly defined

27. Wolfgang Stephan, *Die burgundisch-niederländische Motette*, p. 89. See also Edgar H. Sparks, "The Motets of Antoine Busnois," *JAMS, 6* (1953), 217.

> . . . Busnois' harmony has a greater richness of sound than
> is characteristic of the earlier writers.[28]

These very aspects which Sparks sees as uncharacteristic are
closely related to the practice of discant as seen in the Masses
of Frye. Certainly, the almost chordal structure and the predominance of sixths and thirds in the complete triads strongly suggest English influence.

The melodic style too reveals the characteristic features associated with Frye's style. Sparks calls attention to certain peculiarities, pointing out that Busnois frequently abandons a
freely-flowing melodic line for one made up of repeated patterns, sometimes with both melodic and rhythmic repetition,
sometimes just rhythmic, and in combinations of voices.[29] An
example from his *Regina celi laetare I* shows this type of repetition (Example 32). The second example (Example 33), in
two parts, is obviously to be related to the excerpt from Frye's
Missa Flos regalis cited in Example 9 (Chapter 6), to illustrate

EXAMPLE 32

Busnois, *Regina celi* (BR 5557, fols. 87'–88⁰)

EXAMPLE 33

Busnois, *Anima mea liquefacta est* (BR 5557, fols. 83'–84⁰)

28. "The Motets of Antoine Busnois," 218.
29. Ibid., pp. 221–22.

imitative sequences. Busnois also displays a tendency to write
melodic lines which turn and return within a narrow framework, stressing always one high note, in the same fashion as
Frye (See Example 8). The excerpt from Busnois' Anthonius
motet (Example 34) shows a quite precise relationship to a passage from Frye's *Alas, alas,* with the constant touching on B flat
and then falling back. The typical octave leap of Frye's works
appears also in Busnois motets, used in precisely the same fashion, with the offbeat stress (Example 35).

The use of an ostinato figure, seen already in Frye's *Missa
Summe Trinitati* (Example 16), was also highly valued by Busnois. His motet *In hydraulis* contains a striking example of it.
In some respects Busnois' ostinato technique is related more
closely to Obrecht's than to Frye's. In one example (Example
36) of a fourfold ostinato figure, Busnois adds a few notes each
time. This is the technique that Obrecht used in the Benedictus
of his *Missa Fortuna desperata,* where a figure is repeated seven

EXAMPLE 34

a) Busnois, *Anthoni usque limina* (BR 5557, fols. 48ᵛ–49ᵒ)

b) Frye, *Alas, alas*

EXAMPLE 35

Busnois, *Anthoni usque limina* (BR 5557, fols. 48ᵛ–49ᵒ)

times in a descending sequence, becoming a little longer each
time.

Busnois' handling of the *cantus firmus* links him with Frye
on one hand and with Obrecht on the other. The Frye *cantus
firmus* is completely uncolored in the Masses, although it is
freely handled in the motet *Sospitati dedit*. Similarly, the melody
is colored in some of Busnois' motets, such as *Regina celi II*,
but in his Masses, *L'homme armé* and *O crux lignum*, it is given
in a perfectly straightforward, unadorned version. Busnois, like
Obrecht, went beyond Frye in subjecting the *cantus firmus* to

EXAMPLE 36

Busnois, *Anthoni usque limina* (BR 5557, fols. 49′–50°)

repetition with proportional diminution and augmentation.
This technique, as Sparks points out, was less characteristic of
Dufay, Regis, and Caron.[30]

The central theme of Sparks' article on the Busnois motets
is that there are many features of these works which clearly find
no precedent in the works of Ockeghem, but just as clearly point
to the achievements of the younger generation, especially of
Obrecht.[31] The precedent which is not to be found in Ockeghem's work is supplied by the English composers in general,
and by the work of Walter Frye in particular. Busnois handled
many of Frye's stylistic devices with rather more grace and with
a good deal more variety. But Frye's work reveals at a surpris-
ingly early date many of the elements which were utilized to

30. Ibid., p. 226.
31. Ibid., pp. 222, 226.

great artistic advantage first by Busnois, then by Obrecht and Josquin.

Obrecht's style is too well known to require much discussion. But certain features might well be pointed out in connection with Frye. In respect to *cantus firmus* technique, Obrecht stands close to the older English composer. Both employed ingenious and highly rational methods of arranging the *cantus firmus* material without coloring it. In one group of Masses, for example, Obrecht apportioned out the *cantus firmus* in such a way that each movement has only a part of it. In the *Missa Maria zart*, for example, a different fragment appears in each movement. Within each of the five movements, however, Obrecht repeated the assigned fragment several times, but always closed with a new one, which, in turn, served as the basis for the succeeding movement. In the *Missa Je ne demande,* the entire tenor is reiterated, in addition to the allotted fragment in the "Benedictus" and AGNUS DEI. The practice of dividing the *cantus firmus* and then ensuring the unity of the Mass by devices of this sort shows a certain relationship to Frye's handling of the *cantus firmus* in his *Missa Summe Trinitati,* in which, although neither the SANCTUS nor the AGNUS DEI has the complete *cantus firmus,* between them the entire melody is stated. Obrecht is even more methodical, but Frye's Masses already suggest this highly schematic disposition of uncolored *cantus firmus* material.

Bukofzer has given a good and comprehensive description of Obrecht's style when he mentions the telling use of the octave leap, the preoccupation with sequences, the spinning around within a framework of a fourth or fifth, and the motivic recurrences in extended passages in syncopation.[32] A comparison of a few passages from the works of Frye and Obrecht will serve to show how greatly indebted Obrecht was to the English composer.

The octave leap, which appeared in the same rhythmic context in almost every one of Frye's secular works and in Busnois' motets, was also used extensively by Obrecht, particularly in his secular songs. (See, for example, his *Tandernaaken,* in the *Odhecaton,* No. 67, mm. 42–43, 48–49, and 77–78.) Equally typical of both Obrecht and Frye is the very narrow framework within

32. *Studies,* pp. 292–96.

which a single voice will turn and return for several measures
(Example 37). The purely rhythmic sequence illustrated in Ex-
amples 13 and 14 in Chapter 6 also finds constant use in
Obrecht's work (Example 38). The ostinato appears everywhere
in Obrecht's Masses and motets and in some cases is carried to
extraordinary lengths. In the *Missa Malheur me bat,* it consists
of only two notes, E and F in the SANCTUS, and E and A in the
AGNUS DEI. This is very similar to the ostinato technique of
Busnois' *In hydraulis.* The ostinato has a clear precedent in the
Masses of Frye, however. It is striking that in the *Missa Ave
Regina,* which has Frye's tenor as a *cantus firmus,* Obrecht has
written a twelvefold ostinato figure (in the bass of the "Et
resurrexit") which is almost identical with that of Frye in the
Missa Summe Trinitati. (See Example 16.)

   The love of sequences of all types is everywhere apparent in
the works of Frye and Obrecht alike. But a very important feature of such forms as the sequence and ostinato was the fact that
they should be varied, rather than literal. This is expressly
stated by Tinctoris in his *Liber de Arte Contrapuncti:*

EXAMPLE 37

a) Obrecht, *Salve Regina* (a 3)

b) Obrecht, *Salve Regina* (a 6)

c) Frye, *Missa Flos regalis,* SANCTUS, mm. 31ff.

EXAMPLE 38

Obrecht, *Missa Maria zart,* GLORIA, mm. 51ff.

Hanc autem diversitatem optimi quisquo ingenii compositor aut concentor officit, si nunc per unam quantitatem, nunc per aliam, nunc per unam perfectionem, nunc per aliam, nunc per unam proportionem, nunc per aliam, nunc per unam conjunctionem, nunc per aliam, nunc cum syncopis, nunc sine syncopis, nunc cum fugis, nunc sine fugis, nunc cum pausis, nunc sine pausis, nunc diminutive, nunc plane, aut componat aut concinat.[33]

It was seldom that the Netherlands composers achieved the desired variation by embroidering the melodic line. In the first Osanna of Obrecht's *Missa Salve diva parens,* for example, the bass figure is varied simply by inversion and partially retrograde presentation of the same intervals (Example 39). In Frye's style, similarly, a literal sequence or ostinato is comparatively rare. Either the melody or the rhythm is varied, or else, as Tinctoris says, is "nunc cum syncopis, nunc sine syncopis."

Sequences, by their very nature, tend to clarify phrase structure, to make it more comprehensible and clearly defined. But the Netherlands composers, by their varied use of it, succeeded in obscuring phrase structure simply by staggering the sequential figure among the different voices in imitation, by inserting a ternary rhythmic sequence within a binary tactus, or by means of other related techniques. It is entirely consistent with the whole aesthetic of the new Netherlands school to strive for the

EXAMPLE 39

Obrecht, *Missa Salve diva parens,* "Osanna I," mm. 1ff.

Excerpts from Obrecht's works are from J. Wolf, *Werken van Jacob Obrecht*

33. *CS, 4,* 152. In Seay's translated edition, p. 139.

elimination of the symmetry and regularity which was so characteristic of the earlier music of the fifteenth century. This tendency to obliterate phrase divisions of any sort finds a parallel in Frye's deliberate obscuring of the Kyrie structure in his *Missa Nobilis et pulchra*. He was, then, a true precursor of the Netherlands school, in respect to form as well as style.

Certainly in the work of Josquin, devices such as these are made to serve the highest artistic purpose. The emphasis on one high note which recurs again and again within a melodic phrase, as seen in Example 8 (Chapter 6) is carried even further by Josquin (Example 40). Particularly striking in Josquin's melodic writing is the extraordinary variety achieved even within a line which is potentially monotonous. One example (Example 41), like many in Frye's works, revolves around a relatively small group of notes. The same figure enters in imitation in the altus, while tenor and bass enter consecutively with entirely different material. Even the melodically exact, but rhythmically displaced sequences, as in Example 42, find a precedent in the work of Frye (Example 10).

With Josquin, the technique of the bicinium is seen as the basis of the entire structure. Four- and five-voiced works are

EXAMPLE 40

Josquin, *Missa Pange lingua*, AGNUS II, mm. 56ff. (*Das Chorwerk*, 1)

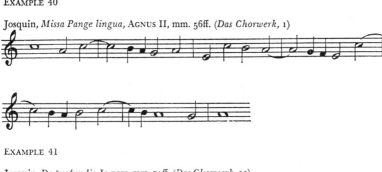

EXAMPLE 41

Josquin, *De profundis*, Ia pars, mm. 71ff. (*Das Chorwerk*, 33)

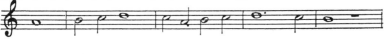

constantly broken up into successions of duos, in various voice combinations. This was the method employed by Frye in his only four-voiced Mass, *Flos regalis*. This development in Josquin's style serves to show how inextricably the Netherlands style was related to the practice of discant, in which the primary concern was with the art of writing one discanting voice over the tenor. In the secular literature of the late fifteenth century the technique of discanting has been shown to have been responsible for the evolution of the discant-tenor framework. In Mass and motet compositions, it resulted eventually in the utilization of the bicinium as a basic structural element. In compositions for three, four, and even five and six voices, then, the emergence of the duet form points unequivocally to the work of English composers during the fifteenth century.

EXAMPLE 42

Josquin, *Missa Pange lingua*, GLORIA, mm. 34ff. (*Das Chorwerk*, 1)

It has been shown in the preceding chapters that the major contribution of the English composers to the formation of the Netherlands style was the creation of a melodic line which maintained an almost continuously consonant relationship with the tenor. This type of melody has been seen to have evolved quite naturally out of the theory and practice of discant in England. In the hands of English and Netherlands composers alike, it resulted in a style which was fundamentally devoid of melodic ornamental notes or nonharmonic tones in general. But among the Netherlands composers, there was a tradition of two centuries during which melodic writing had been cultivated almost to the exclusion of contrapuntal art. Thus they were able to infuse into the note-against-note style of discant a lyrical quality that is lacking from any but the greatest of

English fifteenth-century music. Only Dunstable approached them in melodic fluency.

One of the most exquisite passages in Obrecht's works is the closing section of a four-voiced *Salve Regina* (Example 43). Such a passage cannot be explained by the theory of discant alone. The beauty of the melodic line, the graceful quality, and the purely lyrical effusion of such a melody as this are inconceivable within the theoretical limits of a strictly contrapuntal style. It appears to be much more closely related to the Continental tradition of the early fifteenth century, that of the ballade style, in which the melody predominated. But unlike the earlier melodies of Dufay, this one of Obrecht is composed almost entirely of tones which are consonant with those of the other voices— in sixths, thirds, or perfect intervals. And this new type of melodic line is unquestionably the result of the artistic credo brought to the Continent by English composers during the early and middle years of the fifteenth century.

This passage is perhaps not the most typical of the Netherlands style. Nevertheless it is one aspect of that style which was present from the beginning and which endured throughout the sixteenth century, particularly in the work of Palestrina. Even though melismatic, it cannot be identified with early fifteenth-century style, for it belongs unmistakably to the consonant idiom of the new musical era. It is, above all, an illustration of the artistic heights attained by the Netherlands composers through the conjunction of their own melodic heritage with the ideal of consonance which came to them from England.

EXAMPLE 43

Obrecht, *Sàlve Regina* (a 4)

After A. Smijers, *Van Ockeghem tet Sweelinck, 1, 3*

200

Bibliography

A. Music

Antiphonaire monastique, XIIIe siècle, codex F. 160 de la Bibliothèque de la Cathédrale de Worcester, Paléographie musicale vol. *12*, Tournai, 1922.

Antiphonale Sacrosanctae Romanae Ecclesiae pro diurnis horis, Rome, 1912.

Baxter, J. H., *An Old Saint Andrews Music Book* (cod. Helms. 628), facsimile ed., London, 1931

Besseler, Heinrich, *Altniederländische Motetten von Johannes Ockeghem, Loyset Compère und Josquin Des Prez*, Kassel, 1929.

Binchois, Gilles, *Die Chansons von Gilles Binchois*, ed. Wolfgang Rehm, Mainz, 1957.

Borren, Charles Van den, ed., *Pièces polyphoniques profanes de provenance Liégeoise (XVe siècle)*, Transcription and Commentary, Brussels, 1950.

————, *Polyphonia Sacra: A Continental Miscellany of the Fifteenth Century*, Burnham, 1932.

A Collection of Songs and Madrigals by English Composers of the Close of the Fifteenth Century, prepared for the members of the Plainsong and Medieval Music Society, London, 1891.

Collins, H. B., ed., *Missa "O Quam suavis,"* with introductions by H. B. Collins and Dom Anselm Hughes, Burnham, 1927.

Documenta Polyphoniae Liturgicae Sanctae Ecclesiae Romanae, Ordinarium Missae, Ser. I, no. 1, Guillaume Dufay, *Fragmentum Missae;* no. 2, Leonel Power, *Missa super Alma redemptoris mater;* Rome, 1947; no. 9, *Messa super Fuit homo missus*, Rome, 1950.

Droz, Eugénie, and Geneviève Thibault, eds., *Poètes et musiciens du XVe siècle*, Paris, 1924.

————, G. Thibault, and Y. Rokseth, eds., *Trois chansonniers français du XVe siècle*, Paris, 1927

Dufay, *Opera Omnia*, tomes 1–2, ed. Guillaume de Van, tome 3, ed. Heinrich Besseler, Rome, 1947–51.

————, Guillaume, *Sämtliche Hymnen zu 3 und 4 Stimmen*, ed. Rudolf Gerber, *Das Chorwerk*, vol. *49*, Wolfenbüttel, 1937.

————, *Zwölf Geistliche und weltliche Werke zu 3 Stimmen fur Singstimmen und Instrumente*, ed. Heinrich Besseler, *Das Chorwerk*, vol. *19*, Wolfenbüttel, 1932.

Dunstable, John, *Works*, ed. Manfred F. Bukofzer, *Musica Britannica*, vol. *8*, London, 1953.

Eitner, Robert, ed., "Das Buxheimer Orgelbuch im besitze der Kgl.

Hof- und Staatsbibliothek in München, Ms. 3725," *Monatshefte für Musikgeschichte, 19* (1887), Supplement 2, 1; and 20 (1888), Supplement 2, 41.

Frere, Walter Howard, ed., *Antiphonale Sarisburiense,* 3 vols. London, 1901–1925.

———, *Graduale Sarisburiense,* London, 1894.

Frye, Walter, *Collected Works,* ed. Sylvia W. Kenney, American Institute of Musicology, 196ᴄ

Gastoué, Amedée, ed., *Le Manuscrit de musique du trésor d'Apt. (XIVᵉ–XVᵉ siècle),* Paris, 1936

Ghisi, Federico, "Italian Ars Nova Music," *Journal of Renaissance and Baroque Music,* 2 (1947), Supplement 1.

Giesbert, F. J., ed., *Ein altes Spielbuch aus der Zeit um 1500. St. Gall. Stiftsbibliothek, Mss. Liber Fridolini Sichery,* Mainz, ca. 1936.

Graduale Sacrosanctae Romanae Ecclesiae de Tempore et de Sanctis, Tournai, 1948

Harrison, Frank Ll., ed., *The Eton Choirbook,* 3 vols. London, 1956–61.

Hewitt, Helen, and Isabel Pope, eds., *Harmonice musices Odhecaton A,* Cambridge, Mass., 1946.

Historical Anthology of Music, vol. *1, Oriental, Medieval and Renaissance Music,* eds. Archibald T. Davison and Willi Apel, Cambridge, Mass., 1947.

Hughes, Dom Anselm, ed., *Worcester Medieval Harmony of the Thirteenth and Fourteenth Centuries,* Burnham, 1928.

Hughes, Humphrey Vaughan, ed., *Early English Harmony,* vol. 2, London, 1913.

Isaac, Heinrich, *Missa Carminum,* ed. Reinhold Heyden, *Das Chorwerk,* vol. 7, Wolfenbüttel, 1930.

Jeppesen, Knud, ed., *Der Kopenhagener Chansonnier; das Manuskript Thott 291⁸ der Königlichen Bibliothek, Kopenhagen,* Leipzig, 1927.

Josquin des Pres, *De Profundis,* ed. Friedrich Blume, *Das Chorwerk* vol. *33,* Wolfenbüttel, 1935.

———, *Werken,* ed. Albert Smijers, Amsterdam, 1925–51.

Liber usualis. Missae et Officii pro dominicis et festis cum cantu Gregoriano, Tournai, 1934.

Locheimer Liederbuch und Fundamentum organisandi des Conrad Paumann, facsimile edition by Konrad Ameln, Berlin, 1925.

Madrigals by English Composers of the Close of the Fifteenth Century, prepared for the members of the Plainsong and Medieval Music Society, London, 1893.

Maldeghem, Robert Julian van, *Trésor musical, collection authentique de musique sacrée et profane des anciends maîtres belges,* 31 vols. Brussels, 1865–93.

Marix, Jeanne, ed., *Les musiciens de la cour de Bourgogne au XVᵉ siècle (1420–1467),* Paris, 1937.

Monumenta Polyphoniae Liturgicae Sanctae Ecclesiae Romanae, Ordinarium Missae, ser. I, tomus 2, 1, ed. Laurence Feininger, Rome, 1951.

Obrecht, Jacob, *Werken,* ed. Johannes Wolf, 4 Parts, Amsterdam, 1912–21.

Ockeghem, Johannes, *Sämtliche Werke,* ed. Dragan Plamenac, Leipzig, 1927; *Collected Works,* vol. 2, ed. Dragan Plamenac, New York, 1947.

———, *Missa Mi-Mi,* ed. Heinrich Bessler, *Das Chorwerk,* vol. *4,* Berlin, 1930.

Old Hall Manuscript, ed. A. Ramsbotham, completed by H. B. Collins and A. Hughes, 3 vols. Burnham, 1933–38.

Paris, Gaston, and Auguste Gevaert, *Chansons du XVᵉ siècle,* Paris, 1875.

Processionale Monasticum ad usum Congregationis Gallicae Ordinis sancti, Solesme, 1893 (réproduction photoméchanique, 1949).

Ringmann, Heribert and J. Klapper, eds., *Das Glogauer Liederbuch,* 2 vols. Kassel, 1936–37.

Sechs (i.e., *sieben) Trienter Codices, Denkmäler der Tonkunst in Österreich,* 7 (Bd. 14 & 15), eds. G. Adler and O. Koller, Vienna, 1900; *11* ¹ (Bd. 22), eds. Adler and Koller 1904; *19* ¹ (Bd. 38), eds. Koller and others, 1912; *27*¹ (Bd. 53), eds. R. Ficker and A. Orel, 1920; *31* (Bd. 61), ed. Ficker, 1924; *40* (Bd. 76), ed. Ficker, 1933.

Smijers, Albert, *Van Ockeghem tot Sweelinck,* 7 vols. Amsterdam, 1939–56.

Stainer, J. F. R., and C. Stainer, eds., *Dufay and His Contemporaries,* London, 1898.

Stainer, John, ed., *Early Bodleian Music, Sacred and Secular Songs,* vol. *1,* Facsimiles; vol. 2, transcriptions by J. F. R. and C. Stainer, London, 1901.

Stevens, John, ed., *Medieval Carols, Musica Britannica, 4,* London, 1952.

Tudor Church Music, vol. *3, John Taverner, Part II,* ed. C. P. Buck and others, London, 1924.

Willaert, Adrian, *Opera Omnia,* eds. H. Zenck and W. Gerstenberg, American Institute of Musicology, 1950–.

Wolf, Johannes, *Geschichte der Mensural Notation von 1250–1460,* vols. 2 and 3, Leipzig, 1904.

Wooldridge, Harry Ellis, *Early English Harmony,* vol. *1,* London, 1897.

B. BOOKS AND ARTICLES

Acta sanctorum, Junii, tomus 5, editio novissima, curante Jonne Carnandet, Paris, 1867.

Adler, Guido, ed., *Handbuch der Musikgeschichte,* 2 vols. 2d ed. Berlin, 1930.

———, "Über Textlegung in den Trienter Codices," *Riemann-Festschrift. Gesammelte Schriften . . . überreicht von Freunden und Schülern,* Leipzig, 1909.

Ambros, August Wilhelm, *Geschichte der Musik,* Leipzig, 1881–93.

Analecta Hymnica medii aevi, ed. G. M. Dreves in collaboration with C. Blume and H. M. Bannister, 55 vols. Leipzig, 1886–1922.

Anglès, Higini, "Un manuscrit inconnu avec polyphonie du XVe siècle, conservé à la Cathédrale de Ségovie," *Acta Musicologia, 8* (1936), 6.

Apel, Willi, *The Notation of Polyphonic Music, 900–1600,* Cambridge, Mass., 1945.

———, "Partial Signatures in the Sources up to 1450," *Acta Musicologica, 10* (1938), 1 and *11* (1939), 40.

Apfel, Ernst, "Der klangliche Satz und der freie Diskantsatz im 15. Jahrhundert," *Archiv für Musikwissenschaft, 12* (1955), 297.

———, *Studien zur Satztechnik der mittelalterlichen englischen Musik,* 2 vols. Heidelberg, 1959.

Aubry, Pierre, "Iter Hispanicum II," *Sammelbände der Internationalen Musikgesellschaft, 8* (1907), 517.

Auda, Antoine, *La musique et les musiciens de l'ancien pays de Liège,* Brussels, 1930.

Baillie, Hugh, "A London Guild of Musicians, 1460–1530," *Proceedings of the Royal Musical Association,* 83d Session, (1956–57), p. 20.

Barrois, J., *Bibliothèque protypographique, ou Librairies des fils du roi Jean, Charles V, Jean de Berri, Philippe de Bourgogne et les siens,* Paris, 1830.

Bartier, John, *Charles le Téméraire,* Brussels, 1944.

Bellerman, Heinrich, "Johannes Tinctoris Terminorum musicae diffinitorium," *Jahrbücher für musikalische Wissenschaft, 1* (1863), 55.

Bentham, James, *History and Antiquities of the Conventual Church of Ely Cathedral*, 2d ed. Norwich, 1812.

Besseler, Heinrich, *Bourdon und Fauxbourdon*, Leipzig, 1950.

———, *Die Musik des Mittelalters und der Renaissance*, Potsdam, 1931.

———, "Studien zur Musik des Mittelalters, I. Neue Quellen des 14. und Beginnenden 15. Jahrhunderts," *Archiv für Musikwissenschaft*, 7 (1925), 167.

———, "Von Dufay bis Josquin," *Zeitschrift für Musikwissenschaft*, *11* (1928), 1.

Bibliothecae Belgicae Manuscriptae, Insulis, apud Toussanum, n.d.

Birt, Raymond, *The Glories of Ely Cathedral*, London, n.d.

Blunt, J. H., ed., *The Myroure of Oure Ladye*, London, 1873.

Boer, Coenraad Lodewijk Walther, *Chansonvormen op het einde van de XVde eeuw*, Amsterdam, 1938.

———, *Het Anthonius-motet van Anthonius Busnois*, Amsterdam, 1940.

Bonenfant, Paul, *Philippe le Bon*, Brussels, 1944.

Borren, Charles Van den, "Actions et Réactions de la polyphonie néerlandaise et de la polyphonie italienne aux environs de 1500," *Revue belge d'archéologie et d'histoire de l'art, 6* (1936), 51.

———, "Considérations générales sur la conjonction de la polyphonie italienne et de la polyphonie du Nord pendant la première moitié du XVe siècle," *Bulletin de l'Institut historique belge de Rome, 19* (1938), 175.

———, "De quelques publications récentes relative à la musique italienne du moyen âge et de la Renaissance," *Bulletin de la Classe des Beaux-arts de l'Académie royale de Belgique*, 22 (1940), 164.

———, *Études sur le quinzième siècle musical*, Antwerp, 1941.

———, "The Genius of Dunstable," *Proceedings of the Musical Association, 47* (1920–21), 79.

———, *Geschiedenis van de Muziek in de Nederlanden*, 2 vols. Antwerp, 1949–51.

———, "Guillaume Dufay, centre de rayonnement de la polyphonie européene à la fin du moyen âge," *Bulletin de l'Institut historique belge de Rome, 20* (1939), 171.

———, *Guillaume Dufay, son importance dans l'évolution de la musique au XVe siècle*, Brussels, 1926.

———"Inventaire des manuscrits de musique polyphonique qui se trouve en Belgique," *Acta Musicologica, 5* (1933), 66, 120, 177, and *6* (1934), 23, 65, 116.

, "Le manuscript musical M. 222 C.22 de la Bibliothèque de Strasbourg (XV siècle)," Extract from *Annales de l'Académie Royale d'Archéologie de Belgique*. Antwerp, 1924.

—, *Les musiciens belges en Angleterre à l'époque de la Renaissance*, Brussels, 1913.

———, "Quelques réflexions à propos du style imitatif syntaxique," *Revue belge de musicologie, 1* (1946–47), 14.

———, review of Du Saar: *Het leven en de composities van Jacobus Barbireau, Revue belge de musicologie, 1* (1946–47), 135.

Brenet, Michel (pseud. Marie Bobillier), "L'Homme armé," *Monatshefte für Musikwissenschaft, 30* (1898), 124.

———, "Deux comptes de la chapelle-musique des rois de France," *Sammelbände der Internationalen Musikgesellschaft, 6* (1904), 1.

———, *Musique et musiciens de la vieille France*, Paris, 1911.

———, *Les musiciens de la Sainte-Chapelle du Palais*, Paris, 1910.

Brion, Marcel, *Charles de Téméraire, Grand Duc de l'Occident*, Paris, 1947.

Briquet, C. M., *Les Filigranes; Dictionnaire historique des marques du papier*, 4 vols. Geneva, 1907.

Brooks, Catherine, "Antoine Busnois, Chanson Composer," *Journal of the American Musicological Society, 6* (1953), 11.

Bruchet, Max, *Archives du Département du Nord. Répertoire numerique, Série B. (Chambre des comptes de Lillie)*, Lille, 1921.

Bukofzer, Manfred F., "The Beginnings of Polyphonic Choral Music," *Papers of the American Musicological Society for 1940* (Richmond, Virginia, 1946), p. 23.

———, "Caput Redivivum: A New Source for Dufay's Missa Caput," *Journal of the American Musicological Society, 4* (1951), 97.

———, "Fauxbourdon Revisited," *Musical Quarterly, 38* (1952), 22.

———, "The First English Chanson on the Continent," *Music and Letters, 19* (1938), 119.

———, "The First Motet with English Words," *Music and Letters, 17* (1936), 225.

———, *Geschichte des englishchen Diskants und des Fauxbourdons nach den theoretischen Quellen*, Strasbourg, 1936.

———, "The Gymel, the Earliest Form of English Polyphony," *Music and Letters, 16* (1935), 77.

———, "John Dunstable: A Quincentenary Report," *Musical Quarterly, 40* (1954), 29.

————, "Popular Polyphony in the Middle Ages," *Musical Quarterly, 26* (1940), 31.

————, review of John Stevens, ed., *Medieval Carols, Journal of the American Musicological Society, 7* (1954), 63.

————, *Studies in Medieval and Renaissance Music,* New York, 1950.

————, "Über Leben und Werke von Dunstable," *Acta Musicologica, 8* (1936), 102.

————, "An Unknown Chansonnier of the 15th Century," *Musical Quarterly, 28* (1942), 14.

Burney, Charles, *A General History of Music, from the Earliest Ages to the Present Period,* revised by Frank Mercer, New York, 1935.

Burbure, Leon de, "La musique à Anvers aux XIVᵉ, XVᵉ et XVIᵉ siècles," *Annales de l'Académie royale d'archéologie de Belgique, 58* (1906), 159.

Bush, Helen E., "The Laborde Chansonnier," *Papers of the American Musicological Society for 1940* (Richmond, Virginia, 1946), p. 56.

Butler, Alban, *The Lives of the Saints,* edited, revised, and copiously supplemented by Herbert Thurston, London, 1926–38.

Cartellieri, Otto, *La cour des ducs de Bourgogne,* Paris, 1946.

Caserba, Simon, *Hieronymus de Moravia O.P. Tractatus de Musica,* Regensburg, 1935.

Casteels, D. van de, *Maîtres de chant et organistes de Saint-Donatien et de Saint-Sauveur à Bruges,* Bruges, 1870.

Cauchie, Maurice, "Les véritables nom et prénom d'Ockeghem," *Revue de musicologie, 10* (1926), 9.

Chevalier, Ulysse, *Repertorium Hymnologicum,* 6 vols. Brussels, 1892–1921.

Clercx, Suzanne, ed., *Johannes Ciconia. Un musicien liègois et son temps,* 2 vols. Brussels (Académie Royale de Belgique, Classe des Beaux-Arts), 1960.

Cohen, Helen L., *The Ballade in French and English,* New York, 1915.

Coussemaker, Charles Edmond Henri de, *Notice sur les Collections musicales de la Bibliothèque de Cambrai,* Paris, 1843.

————, *Scriptorum de Musica medii aevi novam seriam a Gerbertina alteram collegit nuncque primum edidit,* 4 vols. Paris, 1864–76.

Cretin, Guillaume, *Déploration de Guillaume Cretin sur le trépas de Jean Ockeghem, musicien,* ed. E. Thoinan, Paris, 1864.

Crocker, Richard L., "Discant, Counterpoint, and Harmony," *Journal of the American Musicological Society, 15* (1962), 1.

Dart, Thurston, "Une contribution anglaise au manuscrit de Strasbourg?" *Revue belge de musicologie, 8* (1954), 122.

Davey, Henry, *History of English Music,* 2d ed. revised, London, 1921.

Devillers, Léopold, *Cartulaire des comtes de Hainaut,* vol. *5,* Brussels, 1892.

——, *Essai sur l'Histoire de la musique à Mons,* Mons, 1868.

Dèzes, Karl, "Der Mensuralcodex des Benediktinerklosters Sancti Emmerami zu Regensburg," *Zeitschrift für Musikwissenschaft, 10* (1927), 65.

Dix, Gregory, *The Shape of the Liturgy,* London, 1945.

Doorslaer, Georges van, "Aperçu sur la Pratique du chant à Malines au XVe siècle," *Annales du Congrès d'archéologie de Belgique en Anvers en 1930,* p. 465.

——, "La chapelle musicale de Philippe le Beau," *Revue belge d'archéologie et d'histoire de l'art, 4* (1934), 21 and 139.

——, "La fondation du chant à l'Eglise Notre Dame au dela de la Dyle à Malines," *Bulletin du Cercle archéologique, littéraire et artistique de Malines, 7* (1897).

——, "La maîtrise de St.-Rombaut à Malines jusqu'en 1580," *Musica Sacra,* Malines, 1936.

——, "Notes sur les jubes et les maîtrises des églises des SS. Pierre et Paul, de St.-John, de Notre Dame au dela de la Dyle et de St.-Rombaut," *Bulletin du cercle archéologique, littéraire et artistique de Malines, 16* (1906).

Droz, Eugénie and Geneviève Thibault, "Le chansonnier de la bibliothèque royale de Copenhague," *Revue de musicologie, 11* (1927), 12.

Einstein, Alfred, *A Short history of Music,* New York, 1947.

Eitner, Robert, "Das deutsche Lied des XV. und XVI. Jahrhunderts," *Monatshefte für Musikgeschichte, 8* (1876), Supplement, 1; *9* (1877), Supplement, 73; *10* (1878), Supplement, 145; *12* (1880), Supplement, 1; *13* (1881), Supplement, 93; *14* (1882), Supplement, 167; *15* (1883), Supplement, 243.

Ely Cathedral, *Custos Capellae rolls,* Dean and Chapter, Ely.

Evans, Seriol J. A., "Ely Almonry Boys and Choristers in the later Middle Ages," *Essays presented to Sir Hilary Jenkinson,* ed. J. Conway Davies, (London, 1957), p. 155.

Ficker, Rudolf von, "Epilog zum Faburden," *Acta Musicologica, 25* (1953), 127.

——, "Die Kolorierungstechnik der Trienter Messen," *Studien zur*

Musikwissenschaft (Beihefte der Denkmäler der Tonkunst in Österreich), 7 (1920), 5.

Fisher, Kurt von, "On the Technique, Origin, and Evolution of Italian Trecento Music," *Musical Quarterly,* 47 (1961), 41.

Flasdieck, Hermann M., "Franz. fauxbourdon und frühneuengl. faburden," *Acta Musicologica,* 25 (1953), 111.

Fortescue, Adrian, *The Mass. A Study of the Roman Liturgy,* 3d ed., revised, London, 1950.

Fox, Charles Warren, "Non-Quartal Harmony in the Renaissance," *Musical Quarterly, 31* (1945), 33.

Frere, Walter Howard, *Bibliotheca Musico-Liturgica,* London, 1901.

――――, *The Use of Sarum,* Cambridge, 1898–1901.

Friedrich, Carl J., *The Age of the Baroque,* New York, 1952.

Gábrici, Ettore, "Il Trittico di Polizzi," *Bollettino d'arte, 4* (1924–25), 158.

Gachard, L. P., ed., *Inventaire des Archives des Chambres des Comptes,* vol. 2, Brussels, 1845.

Georgiades, Thrasybulos, *Englische Diskanttraktate aus der ersten Hälfte des 15. Jahrhunderts,* Munich, 1937.

Gerbert, Martin, *Scriptores ecclesiatici de musica sacra potissimum,* 3 vols. Milan, 1931.

Ghisi, Federico, "Bruchstücke einer neuen Musikhandschrift der italienischen Ars Nova und zwei unveröffentlichte Caccien der zweiten Hälfte des 15. Jahrhunderts," *Archiv für Musikforschung,* 7 (1942), 17.

――――, "Italian Ars Nova Music; The Perugia and Pistoia Fragments of the Lucca Codex and Other Unpublished Early Fifteenth Century Sources," *Journal of Renaissance and Baroque Music, 1* (1946), 173, musical supplement to *Journal of Renaissance and Baroque Music,* vol. *1* (1947).

Gibbons, F. S. A., *Ely Episcopal Records: A Calendar and Concise View of the Episcopal Records Preserved in the Muniment Room of the Palace at Ely,* Lincoln, 1891.

Gombosi, Otto, "Bemerkungen zur l'Homme armé Frage," *Zeitschrift für Musikwissenschaft, 10* (1928), 609.

――――, "Ghizeghem und Compère. Zur Stilgeschichte der burgundischen Chanson," *Festschrift für Guido Adler* (Vienna, 1930), p. 100.

――――, *Jacob Obrecht: Eine stilkritische Studie,* Leipzig, 1925.

――――, review of Bukofzer, *Studies in Medieval and Renaissance Music* in *Journal of the American Musicological Society, 4* (1951), 139.

Greene, Richard L., *The Early English Carols*, Oxford, 1935.

———, "John Dunstable: A Quincentenary Supplement," *Musical Quarterly, 40* (1954), 360.

———, "Two Medieval Musical Manuscripts: Egerton 3307 and Some University of Chicago Fragments," *Journal of the American Musicological Society, 7* (1954), 1.

Grunzweig, A., "Notes sur la musique des Pays Bas au XVᵉ siècle," *Bulletin de l'Institut historique belge de Rome, 18* (1937), 73.

Haberl, Franz Xaver., *Bibliographischer und thematischer Musikkatalog des päpstlichen Kapellarchives im Vatikan zu Rom*, Leipzig, 1888.

———, "Wilhelm Dufay: Monographische Studie über dessen Leben und Werke," *Vierteljahrschrift für Musikwissenschaft, 1* (1885), 397.

Handschin, Jacques, "Les études sur le XVᵉ siècle de Ch. Van den Borren," *Revue belge de musicologie, 1* (1946–47), 93.

———, "The Sumer Canon and its Background, II," *Musica Disciplina, 5* (1951), 65.

———, "Zur Geschichte der Lehre vom Organum," *Zeitschrift für Musikwissenschaft, 8* (1926), 321.

Hannas, Ruth, "Concerning Deletions in the Polyphonic Mass Credo," *Journal of the American Musicological Society, 5* (1952), 155.

Harisse, Henry, *Grandeur et décadence de la Colombine*, 2d ed., revised, corrected, and augmented, Paris, 1885.

Harrison, Frank Ll., "An English Caput," *Music and Letters, 33* (1952), 203.

———, "The Eton Choirbook," *Annales Musicologiques, 1* (1953), 151.

———, "*Music in Medieval Britain*, London, 1958.

Harvey, John, *Gothic England: A Survey of National Culture*, London, 1947.

Henderson, W. G., ed., *Processionale ad usum insignis ac praeclarae Ecclesiae Sarum*, Leeds, 1882.

Houdoy, Jules, *Histoire artistique de la Cathédrale de Cambrai*, Paris, 1880.

Hughes, Dom Anselm, "Chant versus Polyphony for a Thousand Years: With Special Reference to England," *Musical Times, 87*, No. 1246 (December 1946), 362.

———, *Medieval Polyphony in the Bodleian Library*, Oxford, 1951.

———, "Sixteenth Century Service Music: The Tudor Church Music Series," *Music and Letters, 5* (1924), 145.

Huizinga, J., "L'État bourgignon, ses rapports avec la France et les origines d'une nationalité néerlandaise," *Le Moyen Age, 40* (1930–31), 171.

———, *The Waning of the Middle Ages,* Garden City, N.Y., 1954.

International Musicological Society, Report of the Eighth Congress, vol. 2, Reports, New York, 1962.

La Fage, J. A. L. de, *Essais de dipthérographie musicale,* 2 vols. Paris, 1864.

Le jardin de plaisance et fleur de rhetorique, vol. *1,* facsimile ed., Paris, 1910; vol. 2, Introduction and Notes, eds. E. Droz and A. Piaget, Paris, 1925.

Jeppesen, Knud, "Die 3 Gafurius-Kodices der Fabbrica del Duomo, Milano," *Acta Musicologia, 3* (1931), 14.

Julian, John, *A Dictionary of Hymnology,* London, 1908.

Jungmann, J. A., *The Mass of the Roman Rite: Its Origins and Development,* New York, 1951.

Juten, E. H., "Jacob Obrecht," *Annales de l'Académie royale d'archéologie de Belgique, 77* (1930), 441.

Kade, Otto, *Die älteren Passionskompositionen bis zum Jahre 1631,* Gutersich, 1893.

Kenney, Sylvia W., "Contrafacta in the Works of Walter Frye," *Journal of the American Musicological Society, 8* (1955), 182.

———, " 'English Discant' and Discant in England," *Musical Quarterly, 45* (1959), 26.

———, "Origins and Chronology of the Brussels Manuscript 5557 in the Bibliothèque Royale de Belgique," *Revue belge de musicologie, 6* (1952), 75.

Keuffer, Max, *Beschreibendes Verzeichnis der Handschriften der Stadtbibliothek zu Trier,* 4 vols. Trier, 1888–97.

Kirk, John Foster, *History of Charles the Bold,* 3 vols. Philadelphia, 1864.

Kornmüller, U., "Johann Hothby, eine Studie zur Geschichte der Musik im 15. Jahrhundert," *Kirchenmusikalisches Jahrbuch, 8* (1893), 1.

Korte, Werner, *Studie zur Geschichte der Musik in Italien im ersten Viertel des 15. Jahrhunderts,* Kassel, 1933.

———, *Die Harmonik des frühen XV. Jahrhunderts in ihrem Zusammenhang mit der Formtechnik,* Munster, 1929.

Krenek, Ernst, "A Discussion of the Treatment of Dissonances in Ockeghem's Masses, as Compared with the Contrapuntal Theory of Johannes Tinctoris," *Hamline Studies in Musicology, 2* (1947), 1.

Laborde, Count Léon de, *Les Ducs de Bourgogne. Études sur les* *lettres, les arts et l'industrie pendant le XVe siècle,* seconde partie, tome *1* (Preuves), Paris, 1849.

Lang, Paul Henry, "The So-called Netherlands School," *Musical Quarterly,* 25 (1939), 48.

Lederer, Victor, *Über Heimat und Ursprung der mehrstimmigen Tonkunst,* vol. *1,* Leipzig, 1906.

Levy, Kenneth Jay, "New Material on the Early Motet in England: A Report on the Princeton Ms. Garrett 119," *Journal of the American Musicological Society, 4* (1951), 220.

Linden, Albert Vander, "La musique dans les chroniques de Jean Molinet," *Mélanges Ernest Closson* (Brussels, 1948), p. 166.

Linden, Herman Vander, *Itinéraires de Philippe le Bon, Duc de Bourgogne (1419–1467) et de Charles, Comte de Charolais (1433–1467),* Brussels, 1940.

Lindenburg, Cornelius Willem Hendrinus, *Het leven en de werken van Johannes Regis,* Amsterdam, 1938.

Löpelmann, M., ed., *Die Liederhandschrift des Cardinals de Rohan,* Göttingen, 1923.

Lowinsky, Edward, "The Function of Conflicting Signatures in Early Polyphonic Music," *Musical Quarterly, 31* (1945), 227.

Ludwig, Friedrich, *Repertorium Organorum recentioris et motetorum vetustissimi stili,* 2 vols. Halle, 1910.

McFarlane, K. B., "England: The Lancastrian Kings, 1399–1461," *Cambridge Medieval History,* vol. *8,* Cambridge, 1936.

Maier, J. J., *Die Musikalischen Handschriften der k. Hof-und Staatsbibliothek in München,* Pt. I, Munich, 1879.

Marchal, J., *Catalogue des manuscrits de la Bibliothèque royale des ducs de Bourgogne,* 3 vols. Brussels, 1839–42.

Marix, Jeanne, "Hayne van Ghizeghem, Musician at the Court of the 15th Century Burgundian Dukes," *Musical Quarterly, 28* (1942), 276.

———, *Histoire de la musique et des musiciens de la cour de Bourgogne sous le règne de Philippe le Bon (1420–1467),* Strasbourg, 1939.

Mattfield, Jacquelyn A., "Some Relationships between Texts and Cantus Firmi in the Liturgical Motets of Josquin des Pres," *Journal of the American Musicological Society, 14* (1961), 159.

Meech, Sanford B., "Three Musical Treatises in English from a Fifteenth-Century Manuscript," *Speculum, 10* (1935), 235.

Meier, Bernhard, "Die Harmonik im cantus firmus-haltigen Satz des 15. Jahrhunderts," *Archiv für Musikwissenschaft, 9* (1952), 27.

Menner, Robert J., "Three Fragmentary English Ballades in the

Mellon Chansonnier," *Modern Language Quarterly, 6* (1945), 381.

Miesges, Peter, *Der Trierer Festkalender,* Trier, Lintz, 1915.

Miller, Catherine Keyes, "A Fifteenth-Century Record of English Choir Repertory: B.M. Add. Ms. 5665," unpublished Ph.D. dissertation, Yale University, 1948.

Mone, Franz J., *Hymni Latini medii aevi, 3* vols. Freiburg im Breisgau, 1854.

New Oxford History of Music, vol. *2,* ed. Dom Anselm Hughes, London, 1954; vol. *3,* eds. Dom Anselm Hughes and Gerald Abraham, London, 1960.

Orel, Alfred, "Die mehrstimmige geistliche (katholische) Musik von 1430–1600," *Handbuch der Musikgeschichte,* ed., Guido Adler (2 vols. Berlin, 1930), *1,* 295.

Orel, Dobroslav, "Stilarten der Mehrstimmigkeit des 15. und 16. Jahrhunderts in Böhmen," *Festschrift für Guido Adler* (Vienna, 1930), p. 87.

Osthoff, Helmuth, *Die Niederländer und das Deutsche Lied,* Berlin, 1938.

Padelford, Frederick M., "English Songs in Manuscript Seldon B 26," *Anglia, 36* (1912), 79.

Peignot, G., *Catalogue d'une partie des livres composant la bibliothèque des ducs de Bourgogne au XVᵉ siècle,* 2d ed. Dijon, 1841.

Pinchart, Alexandre, *Archives des Arts, Sciences et Lettres: Documents inédits,* Series 1, tome *1,* Ghent, 1860.

Pirenne, Henri, *Histoire de Belgique,* vol. *2, Du commencement du XIVᵉ siècle à la mort de Charles le Téméraire,* Brussels, 1908.

———, "The Low Countries," *Cambridge Medieval History,* vol. *8,* Cambridge, 1936.

Pirro, André, *Histoire de la musique de la fin du XIVᵉ siècle a la fin du XVIᵉ,* Paris, 1940.

———, *La musique à Paris sous le règne de Charles VI (1380–1422),* Strasbourg, 1930.

Plamenac, Dragan, "Autour d'Ockeghem," *Revue musicale, 9* (1928), 26.

———, "Browsing through a Little-Known Manuscript," *Journal of the American Musicological Society, 13* (1960), 102–09.

———, "A Post-script to the *Collected Works* of Johannes Ockeghem," *Journal of the American Musicological Society, 3* (1950), 33.

———, "A Reconstruction of the French Chansonnier in the Biblioteca Colombina, Seville," *Musical Quarterly, 37* (1951), 501; and *38* (1952), 82 and 245.

Ramos de Pareia, Bartolomeus, *Musica practica Bartolomei Rami de Pareia,* ed. Johannes Wolf, Leipzig, 1901.

Reese, Gustave, "The First Printed Collection of Part Music, The Odhecaton," *Musical Quarterly,* 20 (1934), 39.

———, *Music in the Middle Ages,* New York, 1940.

———, *Music in the Renaissance,* New York, 1954.

———, and Theodore Karp, "Monophony in a Group of Renaissance Chansonniers," *Journal of the American Musicological Society,* 5 (1952), 4.

Restori, Antonio, "Un codice musicale Pavese," *Zeitschrift für romanische Philologie, 18* (1894), 383.

Riemann, Hugo, *Handbuch der Musikgeschichte,* 2 vols. Leipzig, 1920-23.

———, "Das Kunstlied im 14.-15. Jahrhundert," *Sammelbände der Internationalen Musikgesellschaft,* 7 (1905-06), 529.

Rubsamen, Walter, "Some First Elaborations of Masses from Motets," *Bulletin of the American Musicological Society, 4* (1940), 6.

Saar, Johannes du, *Het Leven en de composities van Jacobus Barbireau,* Utrecht, 1946.

Samaran, Charles, "Cinquante Feuillets retrouvés des comptes de l'argenterie de Louis XI," *Bulletin philologique et historique du comité des travaux historiques et scientifiques 1928-29,* Paris, 1930.

Schering, Arnold, *Aufführungspraxis alter Musik,* Leipzig, 1931.

Schofield, Bertram, "The Provenance and Date of 'Sumer is Icumen in'," *Music Review, 9* (1948), 40.

———, and Manfred Bukofzer, "A Newly Discovered 15th-Century Manuscript of the English Chapel Royal," *Musical Quarterly, 32* (1946), 509; and *33* (1947), 38.

Schrade, Leo, "The Mass of Toulouse," *Revue belge de musicologie, 8* (1954), 84.

Schrevel, A. C. de, *Histoire du Séminaire de Bruges,* vol. *1,* Bruges, 1895.

Seay, Albert, ed., *Johannes Tinctoris, The Art of Counterpoint,* American Institute of Musicology, 1961.

———, "The Dialogus Johannis Ottobi Anglici in arte Musica," *Journal of the American Musicological Society, 8* (1955), 86.

Smijers, Albert, "De Illustre Lieve Vrouwe Broederschap te 's-Hertogenbosch," *Tijdschrift der Vereeniging voor Nederlandsche Muziekgeschiedenis, 13* (1932), 46, 181; and *14* (1935), 48.

———, "Vijftiende en zestiende Eeuwsche Muziekhandschriften in Italie met werken van Nederlandsche Componisten," *Tijdschrift der Vereeniging voor Nederlandsche Muziekgeschiedenis, 14* (1935), 165.

Sparks, Edgar, "The Motets of Antoine Busnois," *Journal of the American Musicological Society, 6* (1953), 217.

Squire, William Barclay, "Notes on an Undescribed Collection of Early English 15th Century Music," *Sammelbände der Internationalen Musikgesellschaft, 2* (1900-01), 356.

Stainer, Cecile, "Dunstable and the Various Settings of *O rosa bella,*" *Sammelbände der Internationalen Musikgesellschaft, 2* (1901), 1.

Stainer, John, "A Fifteenth-Century Manuscript Book of Vocal Music in the Bodleian Library, Oxford," *Proceedings of the Musical Association,* Session 22 (1925), p. 1.

Stauber, Richard, *Die Schedelsche Bibliothek,* Freiburg im Breisgau, 1908.

Steenmackers, Chan. Em., "L'école des choraux de l'Église Métropolitaine de Saint-Rombaut, à Malines," *Bulletin du Cercle archéologique, littéraire et artistique de Malines, 31* (1926), 53.

Stephan, Wolfgang, *Die Burgundisch-niederländische Motette zur Zeit Ockeghems,* Kassel, 1937.

Stevens, Denis, "A Recently Discovered English Source of the 14th Century," *Musical Quarterly, 41* (1955), 26.

Straeten, Edouard Van der, *La Musique aux Pays-Bas avant le XIXe siècle,* 8 vols. Brussels, 1867-88.

Striels, G., "De Zangkapel van de Kathedral van Antwerpen," *Musica Sacra* (Flemish ed.), *41* (1934), 35.

Strunk, Oliver, "Origins of the L'Homme Armé Mass," *Bulletin of the American Musicological Society, 2* (1937), 25.

————, review of *documenta Polyphoniae Liturgicae S. Ecclesiae Romanae,* Serie I, in *Journal of the American Musicological Society, 2* (1949), 107.

————, *Source Readings in Music History,* New York, 1950.

Swainson, C. A., *The Nicene and Apostles' Creeds,* London, 1875.

Sypher, Wylie, *Four Stages of Renaissance Style,* Garden City, N. Y., 1955.

Thoinan, Ernest (pseud., Antoine Ernest Poquet), *Les origines de la Chapelle-Musique des souverains de France,* Paris, 1864.

Tilley, Arthur A., "The Renaissance in Europe," *The Cambridge Medieval History,* vol. 8, Cambridge, 1936.

Tolhurst, John Basil Lowder, *The Monastic Breviary of Hyde Abbey,* vol. 6, the Henry Bradshaw Society vol. 80, London, 1942.

Trowell, Brian, "Faburden and Fauxbourdon," *Musica Disciplina, 13,* (1959), 43.

Trumble, Ernest, "Authentic and Spurious Fauxbourdon," *Revue belge de musicologie, 14* (1960), 3.

——, *Fauxbourdon, An Historical Survey,* Institute of Medieval Music, Musicological Studies, 3, Brooklyn, 1959.

Ursprung, Otto, *Die Katholische Kirchenmusik,* Potsdam, 1931-33.

Van, Guillaume De, "An Inventory of the Manuscript, Bologna Q. 15 (olim 37)," *Musica Disciplina, 2* (1948), 231.

——, "A Recently Discovered Source of Early Fifteenth Century Polyphonic Music, the Aosta Manuscript," *Musica Disciplina, 2* (1948), 5.

Vogel, Arthur, "The English Part Song around 1500," abstract in *Bulletin of the American Musicological Society, 4* (1940), 10.

Wagner, Peter, *Geschichte der Messe,* vol. *1, Bis 1600,* Leipzig, 1913.

Waite, William G., *The Rhythm of Twelfth-Century Polyphony,* New Haven, 1954.

Walker, Ernest, *A History of Music in England,* 2d ed. London, 1924.

Weinemann, K., *Johannes Tinctoris und sein unbekannter Traktat,* "De inventione et usu musicac," Regensburg, 1917.

Wilkins, Ernest Hatch, *Life of Petrarch,* Chicago, 1961.

Williams, George, "Ecclesiastical Vestments, etc., in King's College, Cambridge in the fifteenth Century—Part III," *The Ecclesiologist, 24* (1863), 99.

Wolf, Johannes, "Ein Beitrag zur Diskantlehre des. 14. Jahrhunderts," *Sammelbände der Internationalen Musikgesellschaft, 15* (1913–14), 504.

——, "Early English Musical Theorists," *Musical Quarterly, 25* (1939), 420.

——, *Geschichte der Mensuralnotation von 1250-1460,* 3 vols. Leipzig, 1904.

Wooldridge, Harry Ellis, *The Polyphonic Period,* vols. *1* and *2* of *The Oxford History of Music,* 2d ed., revised by Percy C. Buck, London, 1929–32.

Young, Karl, *The Drama of the Medieval Church,* Oxford, 1933.

Index